CREATING THE
SUSTAINABLE PUBLIC
LIBRARY

CREATING THE SUSTAINABLE PUBLIC LIBRARY

The Triple Bottom Line Approach

Gary L. Shaffer

 LIBRARIES
UNLIMITED™

An Imprint of ABC-CLIO, LLC

Santa Barbara, California • Denver, Colorado

Library of Congress Cataloging-in-Publication Data

Names: Shaffer, Gary L., 1963- author.
Title: Creating the sustainable public library : the triple bottom line approach / Gary L. Shaffer.
Description: Santa Barbara, California : Libraries Unlimited, an imprint of ABC-CLIO, LLC, [2018] | Includes bibliographical references and index.
Identifiers: LCCN 2018007763 (print) | LCCN 2017053414 (ebook) | ISBN 9781440857034 (ebook) | ISBN 9781440857027 (paperback : acid-free paper)
Subjects: LCSH: Public libraries—United States—Administration. | Public libraries—United States—Planning. | Public libraries—Administration. | Public libraries—Planning.
Classification: LCC Z678 (print) | LCC Z678 .S478 2018 (ebook) | DDC 025.1/974—dc23
LC record available at https://lccn.loc.gov/2018007763

ISBN: 978-1-4408-5702-7 (paperback)
        978-1-4408-5703-4 (ebook)

22 21 20 19 18   1 2 3 4 5

This book is also available as an eBook.

Libraries Unlimited
An Imprint of ABC-CLIO, LLC

ABC-CLIO, LLC
130 Cremona Drive, P.O. Box 1911
Santa Barbara, California 93116-1911
www.abc-clio.com

This book is printed on acid-free paper ∞

Manufactured in the United States of America

This book is dedicated to the memory of my mother, Sherrill Wieland Shaffer, and my grandmother, Laverne (Verna) Wieland. If brains are built and not handed out, these two women built mine.

Contents

Author's Note

This book uses terms such as *customer* and *community member* instead of *patron* and *citizen*. The former is used because, to the author, it better implies a sense of service; the latter, because not all individuals using public libraries are citizens. When coming across these words in the text, readers should substitute whatever words they feel most comfortable using. However, readers also know that words are important and that the use of different words implies different meanings. When one's existence or one's institution's existence may hinge on the use of a particular word such as *customer* versus *patron* or *user*, she or he will happily take up the word, whereas others, under less threat, may continue to remain less cautious.

Preface

I wrote this book out of a profound sense of love, respect, and wonder, which I hold for the institution that is the public library. I truly believe that beyond my parents and grandparents, the public library was my first teacher, my first window onto the world. As a child, every two weeks without fail, I and my two brothers were transported to our local public library. Although my parents instilled a love of reading, the library was where I got my profound need to read fulfilled. An early user of the card catalog, I would look up any manner of subject in which I was interested and be connected to a book on that topic. I was a voracious reader and the library satiated my hunger for knowledge. One of my happiest memories was the day I learned that I was not limited to just the books in the children's library, but could also check out books in the "grown-up" section of the library where my mother and older brother were browsing—though I was not yet age 11.

Today, I am proud of the way my fellow citizens across the country fund public libraries and often support them in the voting booth and when taking surveys. This said, as a former library system CEO of six years, I feel the institution is under threat. This threat comes from false beliefs about what is freely available on the Internet, as well as a lack of understanding of all the amazing services and lifelines that public libraries provide. I do not, however, lay the blame for this threat squarely at the feet of my fellow citizens, politicians, or their colleagues in city and county government. Rather, I feel it is up to those of us who work in public libraries and the public library sphere to better enlighten our community members about the value of the institution, just as we have done with the dispensing of knowledge throughout the decades.

This book is meant to provide those working in public libraries a way to ensure the sustainability of their institutions, using tools and frameworks that are prevalent in today's business world. This book could also be considered a public library management text that suggests a sustainability framework as the best means to run a public library. Although triple bottom line (TBL) sustainability was brought into being by work out of the United Nations and the business world, it is applicable to all types of organizations. In addition, even though this book is presented through the lens of TBL sustainability, the majority of the practices suggested were born in public libraries or are heavily used by many leading public libraries. Thus, it is a homegrown text. The goal of the book is to ensure the long-term sustainability of the institution of the public library: Not to have it limp along in something remotely resembling its present state, but rather to have it thrive in an adaptive way to help ensure the successful support of our collective communities' hopes, wishes, and dreams.

I am eternally grateful to the libraries and companies that participated in the research that informs this book. Without their open and honest sharing, as well as their gift of their valuable time, this book would not have been possible.

I hope you will enjoy reading this book as much as I have enjoyed assembling it for you. Additionally, after you have begun to incorporate the practices described within its cover, I know you will be well on your way to your sustainability journey and to a library that thrives, not just survives!

Warm regards,
Gary L. Shaffer, PhD

Acknowledgments

This book is my thank-you note to the thousands of public library administrators, librarians, and library workers who dedicate their lives to helping community members change their lives for the better. All of you and your communities deserve sustainable public libraries. I would also like to thank Susan Grode for her timely and thorough advice, as well as Jim Matarazzo, Toby Pearlstein, and Mónica Colón-Aguirre for their oversight of my dissertation, which greatly informed this book. To the company sustainability practitioners, public library directors, and deputy director who participated in my research (you know who you are) . . . from the bottom of my heart, thank you. Finally, I would like to acknowledge Blanche Woolls, Emma Bailey, and their colleagues at Libraries Unlimited for their tireless work in preparing this manuscript for publication.

1

What Is Triple Bottom Line (TBL)?

TBL covers the three aspects of sustainability. It moves the conversation of sustainability beyond just the environment to incorporate economic and social aspects as well. This could be for a single organization, a community, or a whole society. After all, if an organization is environmentally sustainable, ever-mindful of the planet and taking every possible precaution to not harm the environment, but instead enrich it, yet finds itself financially unable to sustain its operation, then the organization is not truly sustainable.

The same goes for an organization that operates in a vacuum within its community. Again, the organization may be diligent about minimizing its energy use or working hard to use only renewable energy such as wind, solar, or geothermal, but if it does not also support educational achievement in the local community from which it draws its workforce, again that organization would not truly be sustainable.

This last point in particular brings out the dual nature of the social sustainable aspect of TBL sustainability: the "people" part. Social sustainability covers not only the sustainability of the community or society in which an organization operates, but also the social sustainability inside the organization (which is typically considered the workforce). Thus, this book covers both external and internal dimensions of social sustainability.

WHERE DID TBL SUSTAINABILITY COME FROM?

The phrase "TBL sustainability" was first coined by John Elkington (1997), who defined the three domains as economic prosperity, environmental quality, and social justice. Elkington (1997) noted that TBL sustainability grew out of the environmental movement of the 1970s, in which he was heavily involved. The environmental movement did not, however, start with Elkington. Many contend that the movement grew out of the work of author Rachel Carson, whose book *Silent Spring* (1962) was one of the first works to connect detrimental environmental impacts to human activities: specifically, the heavy use of pesticides, particularly DDT.

But how did the world move from a sole focus on the environment to include these other aspects of TBL sustainability? Many global events took place, from man-made disasters to trouble in global markets. Two such events helped usher in TBL sustainability, one proactive, the other reactive. The first was spawned by the United Nations (UN) in the 1980s, when it convened the World Commission on Environment and Development (WCED, 1987). The WCED's first major report stated that "sustainable development is defined as development that meets the needs of the present without compromising the ability of future generations to meet their own needs." This report began to establish the TBL framework by connecting the environment, people, and economic development. The UN instructed the WCED to "raise the level of understanding and commitment to action on the part of individuals, voluntary organizations, businesses, institutes, and governments" (WCED, 1987, p. 347). In the years that followed, the term *sustainable development* became simply "sustainability," although the UN and other organizations that work in the developing world continue to use "sustainable development."

In the early 2000s, another pivotal event took place when global markets reacted to financial mishaps. Chief among them was the Enron scandal (Fox, 2003). Five years after America learned about the extent of this scandal, John Elkington (2006) asked, "What is business for? In whose interests should companies be run, and how? And what is the appropriate balance between shareholders and other stakeholders?" (p. 524). Elkington suggested that TBL, with its three aspects, implies that companies create value in many ways beyond just their bottom-line financials.

The work of the UN also continued, as the United Nations Environment Program (UNEP) division launched the Global Reporting Initiative (GRI). The GRI works to design and build acceptance of a common framework for reporting on the TBL of sustainability: that is, the economic, environmental, and social components for individual organizations. The sustainability reporting guidelines developed under the GRI are applicable to all types of organizations (UNEP, 2015).

Today, more than 7,500 organizations participate in the GRI. This initiative functions under the auspices of the GRI organization, which according to its website is (GRI, 2016):

An international independent organization that helps businesses, governments and other organizations understand and communicate the impact of business on critical sustainability issues such as climate change, human rights, corruption and many others. In 2002, the GRI was formally inaugurated at the UN as a new global institution and a collaborating center of the UNEP.

Please see Chapter 6 for further discussions of the GRI, as well as Appendix 4 for a copy of the various facets and requirements of a GRI report.

By 1997, Elkington had begun to apply TBL in the world of business for his client, Shell. As he did this, he began to use the term "the 3Ps" to signify the people, planet, and profit components of TBL sustainability. The 3Ps have been in use in the Netherlands (Elkington, 1997) and by groups as diverse as Sustainable Tulsa (2014) in the state of Oklahoma. While the terms *TBL sustainability* and the *3Ps* are more or less interchangeable, this book uses the term *TBL*.

WHY IS TBL IMPORTANT?

In a survey conducted by Quinn and Bates (2007) for the Center for Creative Leadership, 73 percent of leaders reported that TBL concepts were important to organizational success, while 87 percent reported that they would be important in the future. Nearly 70 percent of the leaders who responded to the survey represented the business sector.

Examples of sustainable practices from Fortune 100 companies include:

- A subsidiary of Johnson & Johnson (2012) that "provides healthcare facilities with a wider range of products which help reduce medical waste, save money, and maintain quality patient care."
- A program called Fuel Sense from FedEx (2014) that saved the company 59.8 million gallons of fuel, which equated to more than $200 million in savings in fiscal year 2013 alone.
- Employer-provided college tuition for Starbucks employees (Rooney, 2015).

Any organization can embrace these effective practices and other similar strategies. For some organizations, however, governmental regulation, increased awareness, and basic public demand have driven adoption of such TBL sustainability practices (Epstein, 2008). Soyka (2012) posited that there were two fundamental reasons why leaders should embrace sustainability. The first was obligation, because sustainability has public benefits; the second was the long-term financial growth of companies that embrace sustainability. According to Soyka (2012, p. 18), sustainable organizations are:

- Mission-driven
- Aware of and responsive to societal and stakeholder interests
- Responsible and ethical
- Dedicated to excellence
- Driven to meet or exceed customer/client expectations, and
- Disciplined, focused, and skillful

Why Should Public Libraries Embrace TBL?

The aforementioned characteristics seem as if they might describe most public libraries operating in the United States today, yet staff in public libraries have not readily embraced TBL sustainability. In research conducted by Kim and Yu (2011), when speaking to public library directors about sustainability, the directors equated sustainability with survivability. In other words, if the library can keep the doors open, it is acting in a sustainable manner. However, "keeping the doors open" can mean different things to different people when budget cuts loom. Half the libraries open in a system three evenings a week with a decimated book budget could mean surviving to some or sustaining to others. However, public libraries need to do more than just survive. In order to have resilient communities, public libraries must thrive!

This book proposes that a truly sustainable library is one that is open enough hours to meet the needs of the community it serves, has adequate and well-maintained facilities, and is taking advantage of the right mix of technology as well as staff. Additionally, it has adequate funding to achieve its goals and well-trained staff who are supported by the organization and the community. Due to proper needs assessment, community engagement, and outcomes measures, the library management and staff are confident that they are helping their community meet its collective goals. A sustainable library is also one that helps to sustain and even replenish the environment, not take away from it or harm it.

Nevertheless, with every new global technological advancement and national financial calamity, libraries' very existence are threatened, as are the jobs of librarians and their paraprofessional colleagues. Politicians and community stakeholders are quick to point out that "with everything on the Internet, we don't need libraries anymore." This statement not only misses the whole point of public libraries' reason for being, but is also naïve at best. However, it cannot be summarily dismissed by the profession. To do so could prove fatal. Librarians at their core are educators. If misinformation such as "We're not going to need libraries anymore" is out there, than librarians must dispel it. The very sustainability of libraries depends upon it.

This book is a practical, how-to-manual to show those working in public libraries how to ensure their institution's—therefore their profession's—sustainability. It illustrates time-tested TBL tools that leading companies and libraries have been using for many years to ensure their sustainability. These tools were extensively researched over a two-year time period from early 2014 to late 2015 by this author, who has successfully worked in upper management of public libraries for more than 10 years; six of those years were at a large library system as its CEO. He synthesized his research, checked it for practicality against his own experience and with his colleagues, and researched published TBL-sustainable companies' reports. Using his research, he then developed 12 research-based steps that one's library can follow to begin its sustainability journey; this includes a step that covers dispelling negative hearsay.

The good news is that many of the things happening in libraries are already or partially considered sustainable, such as incorporating LEED buildings, doing succession planning, and forming an independent library district or setting aside mandatory funding for the library within the municipality. Although library management may not be reporting on their success in a standardized TBL fashion to the community and stakeholders, they have already started on their sustainability journey.

However, if a library is to do more than survive, its management must report on its success financially, environmentally, and socially: that is, with regard to its workforce and in its community. For libraries that have not yet moved to report on their performance beyond output measures such as circulation, visits, program attendance, and reference interactions to outcome measures including the number of children prepared for kindergarten and number of customers who found jobs, the learning curve will be steeper but certainly not impossible. This text shows librarians how to do this.

The beauty of TBL is that it is integrated. If a library staff starts on its TBL journey incrementally and follows the steps outlined in this book, the library will be well on its way to doing more than just surviving: it will in fact be moving toward thriving.

A BRIEF INTRODUCTION TO THE TOOLS OF TBL

In the dual research study conducted by this author, sustainability practitioners at top-50 *Fortune* Most Admired Companies and leading library directors, and in one case a designee, were interviewed. The participating libraries were chosen in late 2015, because *Library Journal* had named them as a Library of the Year. Additionally, at all the libraries interviewed, the winning director was still in place, or the current director had previously been a member of the senior management team at the time the award was given. In the case of the companies, all of them publish their sustainability results in a transparent fashion. This provided an even more in-depth look at their sustainability practices. The findings of the first phase (the company phase) of the study were shared with the library directors and the one deputy director to see how the companies' sustainability practices resonated with them, and whether they engaged in similar practices. The library directors and deputy were then asked about their additional practices that aligned with TBL sustainability. Together all the results were synthesized into four sections—Economics, Environmental, Social (External), and Social (Internal)—with the following 12 steps for public libraries to begin their TBL sustainability journey emerging therefrom. The steps are listed here and then expanded upon in the following chapters of this book.

ECONOMIC

1. **Financial structure and monitoring**
   Form an independent library district or enact (via taxpayer vote or governing-body decision) a library-dedicated tax or portion of property tax. Consider using voter-approved operating funds for capital projects. Employ a rainy-day fund and a 501(c)(3) affiliated nonprofit foundation. Continuously look for revenue savings through productivity measures or revenue generators. Put fiscal guards in place. Monitor local, state, and national economic signals.

2. **Education message**
   Market the library as a branch of education for children, as well as lifelong learners, as this is the highest tax-funded sector in the United States. Align internal and external messaging appropriately.

3. **Continuously introduce new strategic initiatives**
   Continually expand offerings to better align with the parent jurisdiction's goals and maintain relevance. Sunset those initiatives that no longer serve the strategic direction.

ENVIRONMENTAL

4. **Leadership in Energy and Environmental Design (LEED) libraries**
   Begin or continue to add LEED buildings or LEED-equivalent library buildings to the cadre of library-owned/operated buildings. Include solar, wind, and geothermal power; harvest rainwater; and so on. Incorporate LEED technology and practices into existing buildings. Teach practices to interested customers via in-person and passive programs.

5. **Reduce fuel usage and greenhouse gasses (GhG)**
   Add alternative-energy fuel such as electric and natural gas to the vehicle fleet or insist that delivery vendors move to this model. Monitor and report out fuel reduction and greenhouse gasses (GhG) performance via actual reduction, as well as reductions brought about by more efficient operations.

6. **Recycle, reuse, track**
   Recycle all waste, including paper, plastic, aluminum, compost, and discarded books via sales or recyclers. Report out tons of waste diverted from landfills, including discarded materials sold, recycled, or donated.

SOCIAL (EXTERNAL)

7. **Align with community goals**
   Create the library's mission, vision, goals, and values (strategic plan) so that they align with those of the parent jurisdiction, community, and/or collective community leaders. Provide the

relevant programming (some via partners, others from all staff) to achieve the goals, and report achievements via outcome measures. Also mitigate risk and continually work to properly manage the library's reputation.

8. **Vendor compliance**
   Create and administer mandatory vendor surveys which provide assurance that all federal, state, and locally mandated labor and ethical sourcing standards are upheld.

9. **Employ excellent customer service**
   Have a customer service philosophy, utilize customer surveys and customer relationship management (CRM) systems, conduct a market segmentation study, employ a chief customer experience officer or advocate, and measure progress against previously mentioned outcomes. Ingratiate customers to the library.

SOCIAL (INTERNAL)

10. **Support the workforce**
    Start with good screening practices in the employee interview process. Provide robust onboarding and training including leadership development; cross-training; and federal, state, and locally mandated training; as well as safety training. Measure employee satisfaction, and uphold fair and equitable labor practices, including but not limited to hiring diverse individuals, veterans, and those on the lower end of the economic scale.

11. **Maintain open communications**
    Have an open-door policy and a pathway for employee feedback and input (not necessarily anonymous, the latter because many of the libraries participating in the study have moved away from anonymous feedback). Conduct performance reviews in a timely and thorough fashion. Create a learning organization.

12. **Recognize and interact with employees and teams often**
    Leadership teams should visit branches often, give out employee recognition awards, nurture employees, and encourage them to take on new challenges. Promote from within when possible/appropriate.

The following chapters take each facet of sustainability—economic, environmental, social (external), and social (internal)—and provide real-world examples of practices a public library team can implement to ensure their library's sustainability. Each chapter includes at least one *Sustainability Futurecast*. This *Futurecast* section is a challenge by the author for a library or the profession as a whole to consider exploring a sustainable proposal that as far as the author knows has not yet been successfully attempted in a public library, or at the very least is not a widespread practice in public libraries. Each chapter also includes a partial public library and company case study specific to that particular facet of TBL sustainability from the research, along with applicable questions for library staff to ponder. In Appendix 1, the reader will find eight complete case studies. These expand on the partial case studies presented throughout the book, should the reader wish to learn what other sustainable practices the featured library or company employed. Four company case studies and four library case studies are presented in their entirety. Library and company names are not used, in order to honor a commitment of anonymity to the research participants, which helped them to share more openly with the author. Chapter 6 follows the TBL sustainability facet chapters, and ties all the elements of TBL together. Last, sample sustainability reports and other related reports and guidelines are presented in the appendices. The author compliments the readers who, by reading this book, have expressed a desire to have a library that does more than survive, but instead presents its community with a library and thus a community that thrives!

REFERENCES

Carson, R. (1962). *Silent spring*. New York: Houghton Mifflin.

Elkington, J. (1997). *Cannibals with forks: The triple bottom line of 21st century business*. Stony Creek, CT: New Society Publishers.

Elkington, J. (2006). Governance for sustainability. *Corporate Governance: An International Review, 14*(6), 522–529.

Epstein, M. (2008). *Making sustainability work: Best practices in managing and measuring corporate social, environmental and economic impacts*. San Francisco: Berrett-Koehler.

FedEx. (2014). *Global connections: 2013 report on global citizenship*. Memphis, TN: Author.

Fox, L. (2003). *Enron: The rise and fall*. Hoboken, NJ: John Wiley & Sons.

Global Reporting Initiative. (2016). *G4 sustainability reporting guidelines*. Amsterdam, The Netherlands: Author.

Johnson & Johnson. (2012). *The growing importance of more sustainable product in the global healthcare industry*. New Brunswick, NJ: Author.

Kim, G., & Yu, S. Y. (2011). An exploratory study to develop an alternative model of public library management using the Institute of Museum and Library Services' public library statistics. *The Library Quarterly, 81,*(4), 359–382.

Quinn, L., & Bates J. (2007). *Leadership and the triple bottom line*. Greensboro, NC: Center for Creative Leadership.

Rooney, B. (2015, April 6). Starbucks to give workers a full ride for college. Retrieved from *CNN Money* at http://money.cnn.com/2015/04/06/pf/college/starbucks-college-tuition-arizona-state/

Soyka, P. (2012). *Creating a sustainable organization: Approaches for enhancing corporate value through sustainability*. Upper Saddle River, NJ: Pearson Education.

Sustainable Tulsa. (2014). *Bellmon awards program*. Tulsa, OK: Author.

United Nations Environment Program. (2015). *Raising the bar: Advancing environmental disclosure in sustainability reporting*. Nairobi, Kenya: United Nations Environment Program.

World Commission on Environment and Development. (1987). *Our common future*. Oxford, UK: Oxford University Press.

2

Economic Sustainability

As stated in the introduction, for a library to be truly sustainable it must also be financially sustainable. It must be able to operate within its means but still provide everything the community in which it operates expects or requests of it. This said, unlike a business which, when sales are booming, has additional revenue with which to attempt to meet demand, a library that is suddenly more heavily used than it had been in the recent past does not magically gain more funds for operation. However, a library that is heavily used by a broad spectrum of community members does have the ability to garner support to increase its funding. This chapter lays out some of the myriad steps public library staff can take to increase the library's economic sustainability.

I. FINANCIAL STRUCTURE AND MONITORING

Form an independent library district or enact (via taxpayer vote or governing-body decision) a library-dedicated tax or portion of property tax. Consider using voter-approved operating funds for capital projects. Employ a rainy-day fund and a 501(c)(3) affiliated nonprofit foundation. Continuously look for revenue savings through productivity measures or revenue generators. Put fiscal guards in place. Monitor local, state, and national economic signals.

In the musical (and later the Academy Award-winning film) *Cabaret,* the up-tempo refrain of the song "Money" (Ebb & Kander, 1966) declares that "money makes the world go around." To the chagrin of many a public librarian, the refrain rings true. Staff, service providers, and vendors alike expect to be paid. "A library is not a business" was a popular exhortation as recently as a decade ago or so. True, technically a public library is not a business. Nevertheless, it is still held accountable by the taxpayers, its stakeholders, its board, and the local media, as well as the local, state, and federal governments. Many public library systems have multimillion-dollar budgets. The library is expected to adhere to all applicable laws and standardized accounting procedures. Thus, a library *is* like a business. And, because money does make the world go around, a good portion of this book is dedicated to this topic.

Financial Structure

Though not always possible, the goal of every library should be financial independence. As in an independent library district, the library can be the steward of its own destiny. Much like funds that flow directly from taxpayers to independent school districts, so do funds flow directly to a library system that is designated as independent. Monies are collected as part of the annual or semiannual property tax billing process. Taxpayers know exactly how much they are individually paying to support the library, as the amount is clearly displayed on their tax bills.

With an independent library district, funds are more stable and they are dedicated. While they can ebb and flow with the economy, they are certainly more stable than the funds in a sales-tax-based system, or in a system in which every municipal department (both city and/or county) has to fight for its share of an often shrinking budget.

In today's sometimes anti-tax environment, forming an independent library district is likely the most difficult initiative a library could take on, but nothing is going to help sustain a library better than a well-thought-out plan to become independent. It will be seen by some naysayers as a new tax, but the funds are for an entity that often has already won over the hearts and minds of its constituents. Additionally, one could claim that other money that once supported the library would no longer be needed, thus technically nullifying that argument. Consultants with expertise are available, as are library directors (both currently working and retired) who have successfully created such entities.

An independent district is often overseen by government officials, politicians, or a commission or board appointed by the communities, council districts, or wards of the municipality. Lobbying by supportive community members may have to take place if current state laws do not yet allow the formation of an independent library district, or if none currently exist in the library's home state. Independent library districts can be made up of libraries that are currently part of a system or those operating independently of one another, even if a city or town council currently governs them. They may also reside in a single city or town, a county, or multiple counties.

Independence will often mean the library needs to provide its own human resources services, legal counsel, maintenance crew, delivery services, and retirement plan. Sometimes the library system takes over the buildings it is using and becomes completely responsible for them. Other times the individual municipality may operate and maintain the building while the library proffers the library services.

Although an independent library district may be the goal, a library that has not engaged in other triple bottom line (TBL) sustainable practices will likely fight an uphill battle to become one. A library viewed as irrelevant, with poor customer service, that is not aligned with community goals, and that has no support organizations such as a 501(c)(3) foundation or "Friends" group in the community will likely not be able to garner enough support to pass an independent library formation initiative at the ballot box. One might argue that the library needs the funding independence in order to make or provide the necessary changes to win over voters; this, however, is a chicken-and-egg problem.

Many TBL sustainable initiatives outlined in this book do not cost money—they just require a paradigm shift, a change in how one approaches the business of libraries. One must usually win over hearts and minds before one wins at the ballot box.

If the formation of an independent library district is simply out of the question, because there is no political will for it or the current purse-string holders will not hear of it, then perhaps getting those same individuals to earmark a dedicated portion of the property tax or other municipal funding stream (such as a portion of sales tax dedicated to the library) is an option. Although such a decision usually must still be voted upon by the electorate, this option may be viewed as more palatable, as it does not incur any new taxes. Library systems around the country have had success in getting such measures passed, though sometimes there is a political cost. City administrators or other municipal departments may grow resentful, and try to get similar measures passed, which could usurp the library's funding. However, if one can exhibit, through primary or secondary research, that the library provides substantial return on investment (ROI) compared to what it costs to operate, and/or that the library is helping to fulfill the community's goals, it is more than possible to pass such a measure.

Yet another possible resource is an additional library-dedicated tax, which charges a flat fee annually to every assessed property in the service area. Often ranging between $25 to $40 per property, such a tax can contribute a great deal of revenue to a library system. It is, however, important that it be clear to the parent jurisdiction that this additional revenue is not monies provided to the library in lieu of other tax revenue previously provided, but instead is on top of the previous revenue in order to meet new or previously unmet community expectations.

Using Operating Funds for Capital Improvements

Library systems often must maintain, add on to, renovate, or build new or replacement buildings. All of these actions are deemed *capital improvements*. Sometimes existing buildings are considered too small, are not properly placed, or are in need of renovation or expansion. TBL sustainable library systems employ a facilities master plan (see Chapter 6) to help manage anticipated growth, population shifts, or changes in service offerings. However, in order to fund such needed capital improvements, a general obligation (GO) bond initiative is often created. A successful voter-approved GO bond allows a government entity to borrow money for a specific purpose (Gamkhar & Koerner, 2002), such as to build a new library, and pay the money back over time. Usually, an aspect of the voter-passed initiative is the right of the governmental entity to additionally tax property owners, or in the case of a sales tax initiative, to additionally tax shoppers; these revenues are used to repay the money borrowed. The initiative is time-bound; that is, it will sunset either after a specific time period or (usually) after all the bond funds plus interest payments have been replenished by taxpayers. The funds can also be used only for the purpose outlined in the language of the ballot initiative. Sometimes this may mean the building is paid for, but not the furniture and fixtures or architectural fees. Certainly, staff cost cannot usually be paid for out of bond funds. Every state and some municipalities have laws about such bond offerings. It is imperative that the library employ the services of a legal expert when it comes to GO bonds and that every rule and law be followed. Otherwise, the library could be subject to lawsuits and funds could be frozen in escrow accounts—and unusable for years—as the library awaits a legal decision. General obligation bonds should not be avoided because of perceived complexity.

This type of vehicle is often used in government finance. They may be the best vehicle for a library to obtain the funds to build or renovate its facilities.

Another source of funding for capital improvements, albeit an odd one, is operating funds. *Operating funds* are funds provided by taxpayers directly or through a parent municipal agency, such as the city or county administration; such monies are typically used to fund the day-to-day operations of the library, personnel, collections, and administrative services. However, at least one Eastern library system uses operating funds not only to operate its library system, but also to make capital improvements to it. *Capital* is often used to describe anything that can be depreciated per current accounting rules. This would include buildings, furniture, fixtures, computers, and physical collections. So why would this library system use operating funds to make capital improvements? The library system in this example builds the cost of needed capital improvements outlined in its facility master plan into its overall budget. The library system goes to the voters at regular intervals to renew and/or raise their tax rate, a millage, to cover its anticipated expenses, including capital needs. Once the system's capital needs are met, the funding does not cease, as it would with a GO bond; instead, the funds flow into the operating budget.

Some library systems are so large that they either have multiple construction projects (both large and small) occurring simultaneously; or, as soon as they complete the last renovation in a series, it is time to begin the whole process anew for the next wave of renovations. In other words, capital improvements are a never-ending story for some library systems: thus, it may make the most sense for those libraries to include capital improvements in their normal operations budgets.

Rainy Day Fund (Deferred Maintenance, Replacement Cost Study)

A *rainy-day fund* is a contingency planning device to cover unforeseen circumstances that have financial implications (Ammar & Wright, 2000). For non-independent library systems, the idea of a library possessing a rainy-day fund might seem nearly absurd, because any "leftover" funds at the end of a fiscal year must often be turned over to the parent jurisdiction, by mandate. However, many government entities possess rainy-day funds; there is even research on the topic that helps entities calculate the right amount based on operating budget levels. Per Ammar and Wright (2000), 3 percent of the annual operating budget is often a good rule of thumb. Of course, to be truly economically sustainable, the percentage would depend on the size of the overall budget and the amount would likely be based on historical need. Unspent funds would of course roll over from one year to the next. Rainy-day funds are not slush funds (i.e., accounts with little to no oversight that management can spend at will and with no accountability). Expenditures paid out of a rainy-day fund would typically be approved by the library's governing board and would be used only for unforeseen emergency expenses. One independent library system management team in the Midwest was criticized by its county's assessor as bad fiscal managers for maintaining a rainy-day fund: He posited that if the library management team was managing their funds properly, they would have no "leftover" funds. (It should be pointed out that county assessors are often elected and not necessarily or always qualified to do the job in which voters have placed them.)

Another reason for a rainy-day fund is the fact that deferred maintenance in government is a real problem. *Deferred maintenance cost* is "the financial sum of the annual maintenance not performed; along with the cost of the compounding effect of deferring the maintenance from one year to the next" (Vanier, 2001, p. 36). One way to maintain a rainy-day fund without being criticized for holding taxpayer funds for allegedly no purpose is to commission a replacement cost study. Such a study is usually performed by a construction firm. It analyzes all the building systems and standard wear-and-tear items found in all the buildings for which the library system is responsible. The firm estimates the remaining useful life of those systems and items, including HVAC systems, roofs, carpets, sliding doors, and paint, among others; it then calculates the cost of replacing those items (including inflation) at the end of the item's expected life. It then rolls all this data up into a spreadsheet year by year, so that the library system can make sure it has adequate funds set aside each year. Certainly, some years can be more expensive than others, but it is better for the library system to be prepared for that eventuality. The library would be well served to look at historical maintenance spending and factor into the estimate items not included in the study. For instance, if bathrooms are remodeled every 15 years, advise the consultant firm so that those estimated costs can be included in the study figures.

501(c)(3) Affiliates (Friends, Library Foundations, and Volunteers)

Library support organizations such as Friends groups and library foundations, as well as volunteers, serve many purposes. Chief among them is giving individuals who care deeply about the library an avenue to support the library via gifts of either their time or their finances. Friends groups can be the library's biggest cheerleaders and advocates. Library foundations can serve as vehicles to raise funds to build libraries or simply support meaningful programs that the library's operating budget cannot afford. Volunteers can help overly stretched staff keep up with demand and provide service to those who struggle with reading or are homebound and cannot get to the library. All serve important roles.

Some libraries have only a Friends group that conducts all these activities, whereas others have a both a Friends organization and a library foundation, as well as a staff-run volunteer office that coordinates the efforts of volunteers. Whatever the library has, it is critically important for these entities to remain separate, with each operating independently of the other(s), and for each to have a defined mission that does not overlap with the others' missions. Additionally, it is imperative that the groups work together to maintain good relations and keep apprised of the others' activities. A typical model would be:

Group	Friends	Library Foundation	Volunteer
Purpose	Advocacy	Fundraising	Proffer assistance to staff and customers

If Friends groups are actively fundraising when the library has its own foundation that also fundraises, it is confusing to community members. If each group in this model chart is examined solely from the standpoint of how it contributes to the library in economic terms, the following is apparent.

Friends:

Purpose: Advocate for the library. Build its reputation and standing within the community. Friends help with ballot initiatives and represent the library at community meetings and the state capitol. They also advocate for the library with friends and family, as well as explain how library services are valuable to the community. They can also demonstrate how to use various electronic resources to their fellow community members. These efforts help the library enhance its reputation and be favored when it comes to ballot initiatives.

Financial impact: Usually small, except when it comes to helping pass voter-based library initiatives.

Political impact: Huge.

Funding: Friends groups may manage an annual or quarterly book sale staffed by library volunteers for the library, or run a used bookstore selling discards and donations with all proceeds repatriated to the library. Many Friends groups sell personal and business memberships. The group should responsibly manage any funds it raises, with a treasurer supplying the group and the library with regular financial reports. Dual signatures should be required on all checks. Consider having the library foundation maintain/invest the Friends group's funds or at least non-petty cash funds.

Operating: As a 501(c)(3) group, with its own board and bylaws. The primary Friends group should act as a parent organization to any branch Friends groups, and work under a memorandum of understanding (MOU) with the library system, with a senior library staff member serving as liaison (nonvoting member of the Friends board).

Library Foundation:

Purpose: Raise funds for the library. As public entities, many libraries can take donations, and the donors can usually deduct the gifts or take them as write-offs. One should check state and local laws to learn more. However, a library foundation exists solely to support the library by raising funds and managing grants that donors see fit to gift to a nonprofit entity rather than a government entity. Sometimes a donor's own charter or bylaws preclude it from giving to an entity other than a nonprofit 501(c)(3) corporation (named for the section of the U.S. Internal Revenue Service (IRS) tax code that governs this specific type of nonprofit). A 501(c)(3) has a wholly different set of rules than a public library, as the latter is usually governed by open meeting and open records laws. Donors may wish for their gifts to stay out of the public eye, or they may wish to control the messaging surrounding their gifts; thus, many prefer that libraries set up and operate 501(c)(3) organizations for fundraising.

One Eastern library, because of its city charter, can only use city funds for collection development, to keep the lights on and hire only librarians and individuals who work with collections, as well as janitors. It uses its library foundation, a 501(c)(3) entity, to hire IT workers, a marketing team, and fundraisers, and to pay for staff travel to conferences. Other libraries may not have such stringent rules with which to contend, but it may be more palatable to stakeholders to use library foundation funds to fund staff travel; bring in a notable author to speak; sponsor a cultural event; or fund a program that, though aligned with the library's vision, mission, values, and goals, might not appeal to every citizen. For example, someone might look askance at summer reading prizes for participants being paid for by public funds. Other such things might just be better funded by donor dollars. Also, expenses funded by donors means that operations money can be used to actually operate the library. One anonymous yet stalwart librarian, who hired her library foundation employees as library staff, would tell donors with confidence, "100%

of your donation goes to providing services, as the books are already on the shelf, staff are covered, and the light bill is already paid."

Financial impact: Usually large, though every library foundation starts somewhere.

Political impact: Usually low. A library foundation often operates somewhat behind the scenes. However, its members should be cultivating powerful friends, who can open financial doors for the library.

Funding: The library foundation should be self-supporting, raising its own operating expenses. One Western library holds an annual fundraising dinner, where it raises its entire operating budget, including staff salaries, in one evening. The remainder of its fundraising activities for the year go to support library programmatic efforts. Still another library, in the Midwest, has utilized foundation donations to underwrite library staff salaries, both full and part time, when the work the staff conducts definitely corresponds to the library foundation's work or projects. The library bills its own library foundation for all or a portion of the employees' salaries and benefits.

A library foundation should properly manage the funds it raises, with a treasurer supplying the library foundation board and the library with regular financial reports. Dual signatures should be required on all checks. Funds should also be professionally managed and invested.

Operating: As a 501(c)(3) entity, with its own board and bylaws, working under an MOU with the library system, and a senior library staff member serving as liaison (nonvoting member of the foundation's board).

Volunteers:

Although some union contracts do not allow libraries to use volunteers, others simply limit the type of help a volunteer can render. It is important to realize that using volunteers can allow the library to fulfill a type of social mission. Seniors may be lonely at home, teens may need work experience, a person may be out of work but wish to stay active, and others may not have the ability to work full or even part-time. Still others just may want to help an organization that they hold dear. There are many good reasons an individual may wish to volunteer.

This said, volunteers should augment employees, not replace them; otherwise you are taking advantage of the volunteers and not being respectful of the library's employees. Volunteers should be subject to a background-check process to safeguard both library customers and staff.

Volunteers should be put to their highest and best use. Having a skilled web designer mend books may not be the right role for this particular volunteer, unless of course this is a high need of the library and the volunteer enjoys mending books and is good at it.

Many wonderful stories are told of individuals volunteering at the library and ultimately being welcomed as employees at that same library. However, an employee of the library should not encourage someone to volunteer as a means of entry to gainful employment. This could be considered unethical at best; nevertheless, if someone wonders if she'd like to work at the library, volunteering might be an excellent way to try it out. The difference is subtle, but important.

Financial impact: Medium, when properly coordinated. Volunteers can help deliver programmatic help (e.g., literacy volunteers, book delivery to the homebound, etc.), or pinch-hit when the library has a huge initiative with a concentrated need for assistance (e.g., teenagers assisting with a robust summer reading program).

Political impact: Small, but use of volunteers does demonstrate a willingness to seek outside help and engage one's community.

Funding: Little funding needed, save for cost of background checks; a part-time staffer (for large systems); perhaps an annual volunteer recognition event, coordinated with the library's Friends group, and small gifts/tokens of appreciation or certificates expressing thanks.

Operating: Usually under a staff coordinator who works with various library departments that make use of volunteers, such as adult literacy trainers, book delivery to the homebound, and after-school tutoring.

Grants, Federal Initiatives

Many large libraries employ a grant writer full or part time; other libraries expect librarians and other staff to apply for and be awarded grants. It is important that grant opportunities align with the mission of the library. The best grant opportunity is for something the library staff wishes to undertake but has not been able to identify funding to accomplish. Successful grant applications usually require a great deal of staff time, and thus applications should be undertaken only if the library has staff and facility to execute the grant. This is usually more easily accomplished when the opportunity is already contained within the strategic plan of the library. There are national, state-wide, and local granting opportunities and many are not published or publicized. Librarians would be well served by using their research skills to uncover such opportunities. One family foundation executive said that her charitable foundation was not in the business of giving money it wasn't asked to give. That doesn't mean the foundation fulfilled every request; rather, it was just that when the local library system didn't submit a grant request one year, the family foundation didn't go knocking on the library's proverbial door in order to hand the library money.

When it comes to other types of grants, state and federal monies are often made available to libraries. These funds can take the form of federal grants to states, grants supporting broadband, and Institute of Museum and Library Services (IMLS) grants won by other agencies that can help fund initiatives the library hopes to enact one day, as well as E-rate funding.

The E-rate program was established in 1996 by the federal government as part of the Telecommunications Act of that year. The E-rate program was meant to help bridge the digital divide by making telecommunications equipment less expensive for schools, libraries, and hospitals (Jaeger, McClure, & Bertot, 2005). For some libraries, accepting E-rate funds is controversial. This is because acceptance of E-rate funding means the library must comply with the Children's Internet Protection Act of 2000, which requires libraries accepting E-rate funds to filter all computers in the library that are connected to the Internet. For some librarians, this brings up freedom-of-access issues, impinging on the right of the public to access any information it wishes. For libraries that are located in more liberal communities, where denying access to a completely open Internet would be controversial, the library administration may wish to forego E-rate funds and discounts if they can afford to. However, for a library that is located in a more conservative community, where complete freedom to access of information (and all that entails) would be equally controversial, the library staff may wish to deploy a filtering service so as to receive the federal E-rate funding and/or available discounts. This chapter presents this option as an economic consideration only, but there are social considerations as well. All public libraries are local, so this decision should be made with the social, economic, and political realities of the local community in mind. Readers should avail themselves of books on the subject of freedom to access information if further interested in the topic.

Fundraising

Many people working in libraries are troubled by the thought of asking for money. It should be noted that library fundraising is not asking for a loan or for money for an individual's personal use, but for use by an institution that is often well-respected and well-loved in the community. Additionally, of particular note, charitable foundations are required by law to give away a portion of their earnings in order to maintain their charitable status with the IRS. If the library staff have done their research, are familiar with the interests of the donor, know when those donors accept requests, and write a thoughtful application, the library is more likely to be successful and staff can rest assured that they are doing good work. Much like a well-navigated reference interview, staff will be helping the donor.

Capital Campaigns

When it comes to capital campaigns for raising large sums of money to remake a building or many buildings, a 501(c)(3) entity is practically a requirement, at least if the library will have to raise outside funds. If public monies can be used to help meet the goal, donors may respond well, knowing that, for example, every dollar they contribute will be matched by a public dollar. Though a full discussion is well beyond the scope of this text, please note that a capital campaign:

- Is well thought out
- Employs experts
- Comprises research, including but not limited to a feasibility study, which is a third-party inquiry of major donors and stakeholders to determine if the community has the capacity and the will to raise the necessary funds to execute the project
- Has a capital campaign coordinator
- Identifies a campaign chair and a campaign committee made up of community leaders
- Uses professional marketing

When it comes to capital gifts such as for buildings (discussed earlier), donors tend to be more generous if they can afford to be because the overall project cost is larger. However, there can be a time lag between when the campaign begins and the day all the necessary funds are raised and in hand. Often gifts come in the form of pledges which can take three to five years to be fully paid. This is valuable time when the building project could be started, but normally all funds must be in place before the general contractor can begin work. Projects cannot stop and start again with the ebb and flow of a bank account. A standard bank loan, secured by the pledges, may be an option; however, another and often better option is a program-related investment (PRI) from a charitable foundation. A PRI is a loan—one hopes with low interest—that a charitable foundation provides to an eligible 501(c)(3) entity such as a library foundation so that it may start its project and see it through to completion; this is possible because the library has the financial backing of the charitable foundation granting the PRI. Most importantly, it signals to the community that this particular charitable foundation has confidence in the project and believes the fundraising will be successful. The charitable foundation is taking a risk with a PRI, and it will not enter into such an arrangement lightly. More than likely, it will offer the PRI after other large donors have made pledges, or perhaps another charitable foundation has made a significant donation, often termed a *lead gift* (which is defined as the largest gift the library hopes to receive).

One must remember that a PRI is a loan. The charitable foundation fully expects to be paid back and there is an enforceable contract to ensure that it is. Although they are not common, there are extremely strong incentives for charitable foundations to make PRIs, as the distribution of the loan monies meets the annual distribution requirements the IRS has set. Thus, a charitable foundation can in theory continuously lend the same money over and over again. It takes a very large charitable foundation to make a PRI that is sizeable enough to build a public library.

Another vehicle for at least partial funding of a library are new market tax credits (NMTCs). NMTCs became available from the federal government as part of the Community Renewal Tax Relief Act in 2000. Per La Franchi (2010, p. 5), these tax credits were "created as a new financing program to provide incentive for private sector investment into economic development projects and businesses located in low-income communities." Though not specific to libraries, NMTCs are a complex financing mechanism which could be used to help fund the building of libraries in low-income neighborhoods or rural areas. The program is administered by the U.S. Treasury Department. Here is an overly simplified explanation of NMTC use: Money is earmarked for certain states and then allocated to approved community development entities (CDEs) within that state. CDEs can be nonprofit or for-profit entities, including banks, real estate developers, city or county agencies, or economic development corporations. The CDE's job is to identify projects with significant social impact, "such as revitalization, job creation or services to low-income residents," for possible provision of NMTCs. Many CDEs look for projects that incorporate environmental sustainability aspects (La Franchi, 2010, p. 7).

If available and if a project is eligible, NMTCs provide some but not all upfront monies for a project. They are usually incorporated into a two-part loan. Part one is a standard loan; part two is a lower-interest loan. The principal on the low-interest loan is forgiven over a seven-year period. The later funds can thus be used to offset the project cost. Where do the funds to write down the principal come from, and why are they called tax credits? In essence, companies that need income tax write-offs buy or invest in the NMTCs. Their tax liability goes down by investing in NMTCs, which in reality are an investment in the library or other NMTC-funded project—which, again, is meant to spur economic development in low-income urban and rural areas.

Because of their complexity, any library management team that is interested in exploring NMTCs should make sure its state has such an allocation and that the allocation is available from one of the CDEs covering the library's state. Sometimes CDEs can allocate outside their own state, but only within an area they have been approved to cover by the Treasury Department. Once the library is aware that an allocation is available, if the library wishes to explore the use of NMTCs to help fund a building project, it is highly recommended (if not imperative) that the library hire a third-party NMTC expert or rely on a library stakeholder who is well versed in complex financial instruments. Given their complexity, is it wise for library management to even explore NMTCs? Perhaps a pertinent question to consider is this: If in broaching a request for a donation to a charitable foundation, a library staffer or capital campaign committee member can state, "we left no stone unturned in looking for alternative ways to fund our project before we came to you," would that library staffer feel more confident about making the ask?

Most library staff members charged with building projects are probably very aware that some, though not all, states provide some monies for notable library projects. Some cities even have project development money available. One Western library funded a massive new central library project via several sources, including but not limited to donor funds, a state library grant, local economic development monies, and a long-term partial building lease, which placed a charter school within the confines of the building. Where there is a will, there is a way to fund new and remodeled libraries.

Relationship Building

One of the most important functions a library leader can undertake is building relationships with well-placed community members. The leader should work to keep the library and its plans forever at the forefront of these individuals' minds. This way, when these individuals hear of opportunities, they think of how that opportunity can help the library. This help might be in the form of a large federal economic grant being made available in the community or a local bond initiative for street and other community improvements that could easily include library improvements, if the library was aware of the potential of such an impending initiative.

Revenue Generators

Library leaders have a few ways to make money to help offset operating costs. These may be as simple as selling computer memory devices such as flash drives, snacks, beverages, used books, or the issuing of passports. Other sources of revenue generation are the running of a library gift shop or the leasing of extra space in the library. For example, unused space located in the library could be leased to a social service agency or a coffee shop. The library may even decide to run its own coffee shop. What is important is that decisions are made carefully, and that the proposed revenue generators are in keeping with or are viewed as a good fit with the library's strategic plan. The partnership the library has entered or item or service the library chooses to sell should be in the best interest of library customers and not take away from their experience. For instance, providing passport services for a fee may seem like a great service for a library to offer (and many libraries do), but one should ask if, in a given community, whether the provision of this service would keep undocumented aliens from using the library. Perhaps a library that offered this service could be mistakenly viewed as a branch of a federal bureau somehow involved in border control. Another questionable situation: Should unhealthy snacks and sugary beverages be sold in a library vending machine if the community is struggling with obesity and juvenile diabetes, while the library is also conducting programming on healthy living and exercise?

If a library-run coffee shop is being considered, one could look to a certain Southeastern library that has trained its circulation staff as baristas. They can take care of an issue on a customer's library account as well as serve her or him up a latte. A Southwestern library has entered into a licensing agreement with a major coffee chain, whereby coffee shop-dedicated library employees sell all the coffee chain's products in a store that exactly matches the major chain's décor package even though it is located in the central library. All proceeds after expenses and licensing fees are returned to the library to help fund library system operations.

Fines and fees are often another significant source of revenue for libraries. One Australian library director stated to her board that, as checkouts move more in a digital direction, the library must prepare for declining revenue in this area. To state the obvious, when always-on-time digital items check themselves in, no fines are collected. Some libraries have moved away from fines, whether not charging fines for children and young adult materials or dropping them altogether. This is clearly an economic decision, as it can have significant financial impact on a library. When fines are partially or completely eliminated, staff labor will lessen due to the significant staff time dedicated to managing and processing fines. If this happen, should a library eliminate or reassign staff positions? These are factors that must be considered when a library system undertakes these changes.

Another discussion around fines and fees has to do with when to write them off as lost revenue and remove them from the financial statements. It is said that "a library never forgets," especially when it comes to money it is owed. Some integrated library systems (ILSs) and library financial statements contain decades-old fine and fee information. A report that any staffer with access to the ILS system could run might indicate that millions of dollars are owed to the library system. These reports can easily be forwarded to and turn up in the media. If not forwarded, the media might call one day and inquire informally or via an open records request. Interestingly, the resulting story doesn't usually reflect the enormous number of "deadbeat" citizens in the community, but rather details what a bad job the library is doing at managing its finances. It's as if there were a giant room full of millions of dollars that the library owns, but it is refusing to access. This can be especially embarrassing or damaging if the parent jurisdiction is in the midst of deciding the library's budget or the library is engaged in a fundraising effort.

Just as a company writes off bad debt and the value of spoiled merchandise, the library needs to remove data concerning fines and fees it will likely never collect. Often states have statutory limitations on how long an entity has to collect funds owed. When the debts are old and are more than likely never going to be collected, those amounts should be removed from the financial fields so they don't paint an unrealistic picture of funds that are still available to be collected. The debt need not be totally forgotten, though: Often the ILS system has a notes field where item information, fines and fees owed, and dates can be entered.

Many libraries do use collection agencies in an effort to collect unpaid fines, reclaim lost materials, or recoup the associated value of those materials. This is a return-on-investment (ROI) decision: Does the financial cost, and the cost of potential lost goodwill, from use of such a service outweigh the benefits and/or financial gains?

Sales
Some larger libraries have begun to sell products that they have developed internally to their fellow libraries. Products include internally developed mobile applications; customer call tracking software; or low-cost, grant-funded social media sites centered on genealogy services. It makes sense for a library to monetize its work product. However, it usually requires that the product be designed upfront with personalization and customization in mind, adding development time. Also, it is important to note that any business transaction requires a contract of some type, whether it is a licensing agreement or a document establishing co-ownership. Details such as technical support, ownership of enhancements, and sharing of information about bugs or customization have to be worked

out and included in the agreement. All of this needs to be taken into consideration when investigating whether a library initiative can be monetized.

Library managers can, of course, hire outside firms (whether existing or new vendors) on a contract basis to develop products that the library owns or is a shareholder of—but only if the library's parent organization or state laws allow this. The library director may be able to negotiate a lower cost for the product if he or she is willing to forgo a revenue share and the vendor is allowed to sell to other interested third parties, whether libraries or other entities. Library directors can also collaborate with other directors to provide seed funding to develop a product. Five U.S. public libraries did just this in 2013, and had an existing vendor they shared develop a customer relationship management (CRM) system. CRM systems are discussed further in the social-external section on customer service (see Chapter 4). The economic underpinnings of the relationship were as follows: Other commercially available CRM systems were beyond the financial reach of the libraries and would take a great deal of customization. The system they collaborated on was built specifically for public libraries, and is now used by more than 50 library systems across the country. In effect, the five initial libraries received their investment back with the waiving of the licensing fee their first year of use. The fee was roughly double their initial investment.

Revenue Savings (Productivity Measures)

Libraries can enact many productivity measures in order to streamline service and save on expenses. One mid-sized Western library eliminated the mailing of paper notices to customers more than eight years ago, instead encouraging the customers to add their email address to their customer record or provide it to staff. The library system staff estimates that more than $80,000 a year was saved by not mailing paper notices. For the customers who do not have an email address, the library system uses the automated telephone-calling feature of its ILS system. One Midwest library system routed all phone calls to a central customer service or customer care department, freeing up time of branch staff from answering nearly all customer phone calls. This decision added the cost of new employees to staff the call center; however, this new staff earned a lower hourly rate and could answer calls at several branches. With fewer branch staff taken off task, staff in branches was more efficient and fewer staff could be scheduled in the branches, offsetting the additional costs. The call center staff were new hires or part-time staff moved to full-time positions. Many have since been promoted to higher paying jobs in the library system.

This same library system automated its customer reserves or "holds" labels, freeing up staff from hand-writing more than a million stick-on labels a year. They also eliminated locking DVD cases, as use required a great deal of staff intervention and took up an incredible amount of staff time—all to protect one of the least expensive media formats the library was purchasing.

Library administrators can also hire process engineers to evaluate workflows and unnecessary chokepoints (those points in processes that slow the workflow). Process engineers note how services and tasks can be streamlined and made more efficient.

Self-service has gained incredible popularity in the United States over the last 40 or more years. Most individuals pump their own gas, conduct banking via an automated teller machine, and order their pizza for delivery online. Library service should be no different. The technology exists to let computer systems conduct routine customer trans-actions in order to free up staff to help customers in more meaningful ways.

It is important for library management and staff to regularly question *why* business is being conducted the way it is currently being conducted, in order to identify cost and time-saving measures. Many organizations allow staff at all levels to contribute more efficient ways of doing business. Some even give out prizes for the best ideas. Libraries should be no different.

Financial Impropriety and Theft Prevention

A chapter on economic sustainability would not be complete without a section on financial impropriety and theft; public libraries have been victims of both. Public librar-ies are held in high esteem and have great public trust. Nothing can damage that esteem or trust more than financial impropriety or theft. Either will likely take the library off mission for a great amount of time, as library leadership must focus a great amount of resources and energy to combat such damage. Better to have proper policies and con-trols in place to stop such matters before they can take root.

Every day, stories in the news media describe businesspeople, nonprofit executives, and church secretaries who are caught, usually because of a slip-up on their part, com-mitting financial misdeeds. Libraries are not immune to this behavior. The director of a sustainable library employs financial professionals, has appropriate checks and balances, and conducts regular and timely (yearly) audits. If a library leader suspects financial mis-doings, she or he contacts law enforcement. Library leaders should be aware that foren-sic auditors can also be hired to uncover suspected fraud, or to help guard against it, for instance, on a multimillion-dollar capital project. In the mid-2000s, one Western library learned a very hard lesson when two employees colluded with one of the employees' spouses to defraud the library they worked for of nearly a million dollars by intercept-ing and inflating maintenance invoices. An employee who suspected that something was amiss and brought concerns to the attention of management was purportedly ignored. Although even timely audits might not have uncovered the fraud, because this library was three years behind with its audits, the library was skewered in the local media and individu-als lost their jobs. The three conspirators were caught, tried, had personal assets seized, and served jail time, but the damage suffered by the library was nearly irreparable.

Though usually less damaging than outright theft, financial impropriety can create a media circus and damage the reputation of the library staff involved in the impropriety, particularly in the eyes of their colleagues. Impropriety can be as blatant as payment for services rendered to a family member, or the hiring of a family member in violation of a nepotism policy or state law, or as subtle as excessive spending on a trip to a work-related convention, or a gift to an employee (no matter how deserved). Often the impro-priety seems small to the offender, and sometimes it's cumulative. A gift to a donor may seem appropriate, but gifts to 22 people over a 14-year period may be regarded by some as inappropriate. It is important that expenditures be board-approved and that a busi-ness case or rationale be associated with each outlay. A good test is to ask how this could play out in the media if only a portion of the information were forwarded to or requested by a media outlet. Weekend work travel approved by the library board is work time—but if the associated compensatory time taken by the library employee is later denied by the library board, it could reflect poorly on the employee or the library. However, if the travel is shown as approved in board minutes, it will not be a problem.

Retirement Plan

If a library offers a pension plan or even a defined-benefit plan (e.g., 457(B)), it is incumbent upon that library's leadership to make sure the plan, whatever type it is, is sustainable, as this is a promise of future benefits to current and past employees. Thus, library leadership should review the plan, make sure it is being properly stewarded, and ensure that it is adequately funded. Outside expertise should likely be called upon to evaluate the plan. Even when the library may be a small participant in a much larger plan, it can still place pressure on the plan's board to ensure that the plan is adequately funded. Library management should ensure that an appropriate employee (perhaps the library's chief financial officer) attends the board meetings or sits for election or appointment to the board. After the recession of 2008–2010, many plans were left underfunded. Because of this, many municipalities are taking prudent—albeit sometimes unorthodox—steps to make sure their plans are adequately funded (e.g., Hiltzik, 2017); still others are placing their heads in the proverbial sand and hoping that the problem will mysteriously and magically correct itself. Regardless, library leadership must ensure that all steps have been taken to assure sustainability of the employee retirement plan.

Monitor Economic Signals

Library staff must also regularly monitor local, state, national, and global economic news for occurrences that could affect their financial sustainability. One Rocky Mountain region library system staff was closely monitoring the price of oil, and noticed when it began to fall. The staff built a conservative budget, as its income was closely tied to the prospects of the oil industry. Fortunately, it did not have to make any budget cuts that year. An independent library system willingly cut $1 million during budget planning because a new state law was going to tax many pieces of property differently in the next year. The actual cuts to revenue ended up not being as drastic as anticipated, so the library system was able to restore most of the funds back to the budget. Nevertheless, this example drives home the point that if library managers do not pay attention to what is being discussed in their state legislature or within local city or county government, they could easily be caught off guard by a funding shortfall.

Library as Economic Engine

One of the top nine features of a great neighborhood, per Realtor.com, is a public library (Colley, 2016). Further, according to a study out of Philadelphia, "homes within one-quarter of a mile of a public library were found to be 7.7% higher in value than comparable homes further away from libraries" (Diamond, Gillen, Litman, & Thornburgh, 2010, p. 13). However, libraries do so much more to contribute to the economy of a community than just raise property values to the handful of homes within proximity to the library. One Southeastern library system staff regularly conducts secondary research, using proprietary databases, to inform economic reports for its city government and local chamber. Several libraries across the country provide in-person and online training classes and practice exams to improve employment prospects for their customers; still others provide résumé and job-coaching services. Many libraries offer small business help, nonprofit resource centers, and co-working spaces. All of these can contribute to driving the local economy. Here is the important question: Is the library staff willing to work to map back these efforts to economic outcomes and report the information out as a ROI by the library to the community?

2. EDUCATION MESSAGE

Market the library as a branch of education for children, as well as lifelong learners, as this is the highest tax-funded sector in the United States. Align internal and external messaging appropriately.

An economically sustainable library markets itself as a branch of local education for children as well as for lifelong learners; doing so makes sense because education is the sector with the highest tax funding in the United States. Libraries and education have always gone hand in hand in this country. Andrew Carnegie referred to public libraries as the people's university. At a time when higher education was available usually only to the elite, the library was a place that invited and enabled people from most walks of life to better their lives. Although libraries and their users suffered through segregation, American indoctrination of immigrants, and censorship (often passed off as maintaining public morals), libraries did help millions of people improve their intellect and find information that was necessary to further their formal or informal education.

Marketing the Library as an Education Provider

Education is something most Americans regard as highly important, despite the problems they hear or read about that are facing today's public schools. Most would agree that schools are essential, but some view libraries as extraneous. Why is this? There is a pervasive false belief that all knowledge is freely available to all Americans, no matter their wherewithal, on the Internet. Librarians report hearing, to their dismay, such statements as, "It's too bad about the library," or, "We're not going to need libraries anymore." Or questions such as, "What's going to become of the library?" Or a potential library donor, who said, "If you asked me, I'd say the downtown library ought to be turned into a homeless shelter." Statements, questions, and attitudes like these are very real threats to the sustainability of public libraries.

When faced with such misguided statements and questions, librarians are quick to cite studies such as one from the Pew Research Center (Horrigan, 2016) which reported that 66 percent of respondents say closing their local public library would have a major impact on their community. However, this indicates that one-third of those responding to the study do not care if their library closes. Even Pew is quick to point out that 33 percent of respondents say closing the library would have a major impact on them personally or on their family. This implies that only 33 percent of households on average are using the library. Is this because many don't know what the library offers or how the library could help them achieve their life goals?

Librarians and those who work in libraries often interact primarily with library users, people who often express their gratitude for the services rendered. However, if the vast majority of a community is not making use of the library, then they also have no idea what the library offers.

The misguided statements and questions just discussed, often expressed in whispered, sad-tinged tones, as if one's dear neighbor Mrs. Library is dying and nothing can be done about it, are illogical and nonsensical. However, logic is likely not the way to combat them. Instead, they should be countered with a smile and statements such as, "Actually, today's libraries are busier than they've ever been!" Or, "The Internet has opened up whole new doors and ways for us to serve our customers." Or better still, "The Internet is allowing us to offer services we never thought possible. Our own online traffic is almost equal to [or if true, surpassing] the physical traffic of xx,xxx per day!"

In addition to individuals thinking the Internet has displaced the library, many think that libraries are simply book warehouses. It is the library director's and library staff's job to educate people in a friendly way—sometimes one by one, sometimes via public speeches to service organizations and others—that this is simply not the case. The library's life literally depends on it.

However, if directors stress that the library offers education, rather than books and "stuff," they have begun to shift the paradigm. Yes, libraries provide access to the Internet, and they help small businesses and job seekers, and they help people apply for government-provided health care. However, isn't the context of libraries always centered on education? In other words, one can also say libraries help bridge the digital divide: they educate small businesses about new markets and customers, or about the Small Business Administration, or how to register a fictitious business; they provide training for job seekers; and they help people learn how to navigate the Web and government websites.

Too many purse-string holders do not use libraries. Perhaps they don't read very much, or perhaps they have enough disposable income to buy everything they could borrow from the library. Perhaps they feel that because they haven't used a library in a long time they don't quite understand how libraries work anymore, or perhaps they had a bad user experience and have turned their back on libraries. Whatever the reason, individuals who work in libraries need to win these people back.

In a talk to university administrators and faculty from across the country, Peter Senge, a Massachusetts Institute of Technology (MIT) professor and author, advised these individuals to stop trying to convince people of something and instead engage with them. Senge is also a big proponent of listening. It is often better to ask individuals for advice than to try to convince them of a particular value or initiative. Perhaps librarians need to better engage with their community to help drive the education message home. Community engagement is discussed in more detail in Chapter 4.

Aligning the Education Message

Education or self-improvement messaging can be key. What do you still want to learn how to do? What's your New Year's resolution this year? How do you want to improve your life or the lives of your family? Customers and potential customers should be advised that the library has the answers to all of these questions and every life challenge, whether positive or negative.

Internally, budgets can be presented as dollars directed toward staff, benefits, collections, and administration, but externally (as in the following case study) they can also be broken out as research assistance, self-directed learning, and the like. If the messaging is always presented as education, libraries move away from being a nice-to-have or luxury item to a need-to-have entity: a critical part of infrastructure.

Education provision and support should be a key component of any library's strategic plan. Once embedded in the plan and the minds of staff, all internal and external messaging should be aligned appropriately.

Economic Sustainability Case Study—The Education Library

Best economic practice: Education message

With respect to economic sustainability, the South Atlantic Library System (SALS) does not have a dedicated property tax; rather, all county departments vie for the same dollars. Each year the library has to make its case for the dollars it needs to operate. By positioning itself as an education provider, alongside public schools and the local community college, SALS gains its parent jurisdiction's (the county's) support for funding. This helps to ensure its long-term viability. The library budget does not break out workforce, collections, and administrative costs as individual line items, as is typically done. Instead, it reinforces the theme of education as its priority by assigning these expenses to categories labeled instruction, research assistance, self-directed learning, and customer service. In fact, 50 percent of the library system's budget is dedicated to instruction. Recently, when a "children's instructor" position was advertised, more than 300 individuals applied. The library is always adding new offerings to these categories, whether it is new technology to aid customer service or classes such as robotics, tai chi, or how to hang drywall. It also has a penchant for making learning fun, while still meaningful. Different library branches in the system contain a teen center, a children's center, an art library, and a historical center. All serve as "centers of learning." The "coolest center of learning," in the library director's opinion, is the STEM learning center located in the county's most disadvantaged neighborhood. These offerings, in the library's opinion, are all part of its portfolio of products.

To read this case study in its entirety, please see Appendix 1.

Discussion Questions:

1. Could your library market itself as an education provider alongside public schools and community colleges? How would your community's residents respond?
2. Does your library see itself as an alternative to public education? Perhaps it is a place that's all fun and nonregimented; perhaps it is the antithesis of public education?

3. CONTINUOUSLY INTRODUCE NEW STRATEGIC INITIATIVES

Continually expand offerings to better align with the parent jurisdiction's goals and maintain relevance. Sunset those initiatives that no longer serve the strategic direction.

Nearly all respondents to the research that prompted this book pointed to continually expanding products, services, or offerings in order to reinforce relevance as a key economic sustainability practice. A library staff may choose to do this to continue to pique customer interest, to better align with the parent jurisdiction's goals, or to maintain relevance. However, if a staff chooses to continually add new products, services, or offerings, it must also regularly sunset those products, services, or offerings that no longer serve the library's strategic direction or customer desires.

Maintain Relevance/Pique Customer Interest

Theme parks are famous for introducing new rides every year (McClung, 1991). This is done to entice existing and new customers back to the park. The park wishes to stay relevant to customers. Without any new offerings, the park can become stale in the minds of its customers. A library too can stay fresh in the minds of its customers by regularly serving up new offerings. There is certainly no shortage of products being offered by library vendors. For an adequately funded library, it might be tempting to add all of them. That, however, would be a mistake. Too many new, disparate products at one time could cause some to be lost in the proverbial shuffle. Although closely aligned products could be successfully launched simultaneously, as they would appear complementary to one another, offering extremely different products at the same time would only cause confusion. The most important consideration when a library wishes to introduce a new product is a positive answer to the question: "Is the product a strategic fit?" In other words, does the potential new product literally map to an area of the library's strategic plan? Try as they might, libraries cannot offer all things to all people or be all things to all people. New product offerings should provide solutions to a strategic problem and/or a customer need.

Align Product Offerings with Parent Jurisdiction's Goals

If a library staff is curious about what types of products to make available to its customers, they often need look no further than the parent jurisdiction's goals, or the goals of community organizations such as the chamber of commerce, local school district, local community impact organization, and/or other leaders. For example, if improving community health measures is of prime importance, the library staff may want to bolster its health collection, add exercise DVDs and equipment for checkout, and offer programming that will help the community improve its overall health. Alignment of the library's strategic plan with that of its parent jurisdiction is covered more thoroughly in Chapter 4.

New Product Offerings

Despite best intentions. libraries do offer many products—so many that it is difficult for even the most active of library customers to know them all. Certainly, they may never make use of certain offerings, but the need for a particular set of knowledge or tools can arise at any time; thus, it is important for libraries to constantly remind customers what they have. The trick is not to overwhelm those customers with product offerings. It is a balancing act at best.

Why do libraries have so many offerings? In part, it's because they serve such a large percentage of the population, especially when viewed in relation to the amount an individual company might serve. Most companies would love to have the 30-percent to 75-percent market share that libraries enjoy (that is, 30 percent to 75 percent of the community's residents or marketplace buying the company's products or services). Some librarians would comment that their "market share" is so high because libraries do not have any competition. Others would argue that this is simply not true. Individuals have a great deal of choice as to where to access information, so libraries do in fact have a great deal of competition. Nevertheless, libraries serve entire populations, from infants to senior citizens. They often offer materials in multiple languages, and often have a presence in most, if not all, neighborhoods. Most of a library's offerings are free to use. To clarify, they cost the community money, usually in the form of tax support, but for individual customers, for the most part they are free to use.

For comparison's sake, consider a chain restaurant. The chain's restaurants also offer many menu choices, yet their television advertising tends to focus on one menu item, a meal combination, or a family of menu items (e.g., a group of pasta dishes) at a time. Why? The advertising is trying to entice customers and potential customers with a new product offering (relevance) or a long-standing favorite (reminder). Often the products also remind customers of other menu items that the restaurant offers. The appetizing-looking product being advertised thus serves as a sort of proxy for a customer's favorite or well-liked menu item. Customers and potential customers know that the restaurant hasn't dispensed with all other offerings just because it is advertising one product during a given time. Instead, they realize this is merely the featured product of the month, or another given time period.

So too should library staff feature their most popular products (reminder) on occasion, either via social media, in-library posters, or news releases, in addition to promoting new products (relevance) in a focused way. A sustainable library is an organized library, one that does not confuse its customers with multiple overarching messages. It lays out the year in advance to the best of its ability.

Library (Semi-Annual) Promotional Chart Example

	Jan	Feb	March	April	May	June	July
Event	New Years Resolutions	Black History Month	Teen Tech Week / Month	National Library Week	Power Product	Summer Reading	New Product
Product	Weight-loss books and audiobooks to exercise by	Genealogy databases / collection	Online homework help	Theme-aligned product	E-books and E-magazines? Training videos? Summer Reading Program ramp-up?	Reading programs	?

While the library's overarching or main messages should be singularly presented, so as not to confuse customers, library staff can still run lower-key "submessages" simultaneously in other venues/media. To clarify, overarching/main messages should be run in similar media month after month, time period after time period. It is up to the library staff to determine where overarching main messages will be presented and where other submessages are allowed to accompany the main monthly message presented in major-partner media outlets (e.g., newspapers, within transit authority busses, in the library's online newsletter, on the library website's home page, and on posters placed in library). Submessages may only be allowed on library web pages that are not home pages, on social media, and/or on minor-partner websites and those partners' promotional vehicles.

Submessages are deployed when the library wishes to take advantage of unique promotional opportunities, such as in-library posters or news releases, that present themselves during the year and are good matches for the library's strategic plan. Otherwise, these would interfere with the major promotion that is running on the highest-priority media platform. For example, if the library has an e-music database that features a major recording artist visiting at a major concert venue in its community, the library would be well served if were to staff promote the artist, his or her concert date, and the fact that the artist's music is available for download today through the library's website. In doing so, is the staff wrongly using taxpayer funds to promote a major artist? In short, no. Instead, the library is riding on the artist's proverbial coattails to promote its relevance and music database.

SUSTAINABILITY FUTURECAST

How can a library with limited staff possibly promote monthly offerings and events in-library and externally, as well as create promotional materials and stay in touch with local media? With a small communications staff, it would have its hands full with the aforementioned alone, never mind adding the promotion of all its minor products to the mix as well. However, a sustainable library could empower a group of existing staff, otherwise deployed in the library, to take on additional duties as product champions. That is, it would assign a given product to one staff member who takes nearly full responsibility for the product's success. What does a product champion do? A product champion looks for unique opportunities to promote the product in the community to groups or at relevant festivals; she or he analyzes its usage and works with his or her manager to set growth goals for it; he or she also promotes the product among staff and trains staff in group settings on how to use the product. A given library system could easily have 30 or more product champions, given the various library products now available, each of whom does much more than work with the library's communications team to create flyers. In fact, the library does not need 30 more flyers or posters with which to paper the walls and counters of the library. Instead, the product champions look for those unique opportunities that come available where they can promote their product: promote online homework help at PTA meetings and with school librarians, promote online training classes or videos at a chamber of commerce meeting, train library staff on how to use the product, promote the library's music database at a festival, and so on. In this way, both the community and library staff learn about the various products the library offers in settings that fit the product. Also, the community comes to learn that the library has a product to fit every one of its information needs. Deploying product champions also gives staff opportunity to develop new skills, take ownership of the library's success, and potentially grow outside their individual comfort zones. Such opportunities are discussed further in Chapter 5.

Economic Sustainability Case Study—"The Meets All Needs Beverage Company"

Best economic practice: Expand product portfolio/customer offerings

When it comes to economic sustainability, this beverage company has many formal practices, such as tight specifications and close monitoring of its procurement policies, and maintenance of its strong market share, among others. However, key among these

Continued

practices is its extension of the product portfolio of beverages. The company had only one product for nearly 50 years, and by the 1970s had introduced only three more. During the 1980s and 1990s, however, it doubled its portfolio through product development and one acquisition. Today its employees believe it is in the "meets-all-needs" beverage business, offering "a beverage for every consumer preference, whatever the time of day or occasion." This is primarily due to reactions to consumer desires, tastes, and preferences. The success of the practice of extending the product portfolio of beverages is measured through sales data, but it is also measured by recording adherence to a specific company policy: everywhere the company operates, it mandates that a low- or no-calorie product be offered.

To read this case study in its entirety, please see Appendix 1.

Discussion Questions:

1. Theme parks seem to introduce a new ride nearly every year. Following this strategy, could your library introduce a new product offering, institute a new service, or repackage an existing service as something new and different on a continuous basis?
2. Do you believe introducing such things would keep your community's interest engaged and convince community members that the library is extremely relevant in their lives?

Sunset Services or Products

Products that are no longer strategic fits, are not used, or take the library off mission should be subject to a careful review. Eventually, all good things must come to an end. Librarians are quick to add new products and services to their cadre of offerings, but are less quick to eliminate those that have fallen out of customer favor or no longer serve the library's strategic plan. The time to end the product or service offering is not when a key staff member retires, as many libraries do. If the product or service no longer makes sense for the library to offer, it should be eliminated. The valuable staff member can be redeployed on a more strategically necessary project. Products and services should not be dependent on one employee. Instead, they should be dependent on multiple internal stakeholders believing that the product or service serves the community and is a strategic fit for the library. Performance goals for products and services should be set and regularly evaluated. If the performance is weak, the library staff should discuss whether to end the product or service, monitor it in a probationary way, or put more resources behind it to give it the best chance for success. After taking these steps, the staff can then reassess and decide how to move forward. A note of caution is in order, though, before terminating provision of a product or service: library staff should analyze the "power users" of the product or service. Even low-performing products and services have fans. Those fans or a sample of those fans should be asked about their use to see what other options or similar products the library might provide. They could also be engaged early on in the review process to see if they can build usage; this gives them ownership and control over the destiny of the product or service. Finally, when the time comes, fans should be given plenty of notice that the product or service will be ending.

CHAPTER SUMMARY

For a library to be truly sustainable, it must also be financially sustainable. It must operate within its means, yet still provide everything that the community in which it operates expects. A sustainable library has or has moved to a sustainable financial structure and its management monitors economic signals to help predict future financial trends. It properly deploys support groups and volunteers to ensure its financial well-being, and it has appropriate financial rules and procedures in place to guard against financial malfeasance. Further, it markets the library with a strong education message, to align the library's services with the initiative that has the highest tax support in the United States. The TBL sustainable library introduces new products in order to display its relevance to the community, better address the community's goals, and help community members improve their collective lives. Lastly, the TBL sustainable library sunsets products and services that no longer meet the community's or the library's needs.

While it is important that the library be economically sustainable, it is equally important that it also be environmentally sustainable as well. Chapter 3 covers the three steps of the environmentally sustainable library: libraries constructed to work in tandem with the environment via LEED practices; reduction of fuel usage and greenhouse gasses, in addition to recycling; and reuse and tracking of progress made in these areas.

FURTHER READING

Andresen, K. (2006). *Robin Hood marketing: Stealing corporate savvy to sell just causes.* San Francisco: Jossey-Bass.

Gross, V. (2012). *Transforming our image, building our brand: The education advantage.* Santa Barbara, CA: Libraries Unlimited.

Holt, G., & Holt, L. (2016). *Crash course in library budgeting and finance.* Santa Barbara, CA: Libraries Unlimited.

Matarazzo, J., & Pearlstein, T. (Eds.). (2018). *The Emerald handbook of modern information management.* Bingley, UK: Emerald.

REFERENCES

Ammar, S., & Wright, R. (2000). Applying fuzzy-set theory to performance evaluation. *Socio-Economic Planning Sciences, 34*(4), 285–302.

Colley, A. (2016, Aug 25). *9 ingredients of a great neighborhood, ranked.* Realtor.com. Retrieved from http://www.realtor.com/advice/buy/neighborhood-features-ranked/

Diamond, D., Gillen, K., Litman, M., & Thornburgh, D. (2010). *The economic value of the free library in Philadelphia.* Philadelphia: Fels Institute of Government, University of Pennsylvania.

Ebb, F., & Kander, J. (1966). *Cabaret.* New York: Sony Music Entertainment.

Gamkhar, S., & Koerner, M. (2002). Capital financing of schools: A comparison of lease purchase revenue bonds and general obligation bonds. *Public Budgeting & Finance, 22*(2), 21–39.

Hiltzik, M. (2017, June 2). Governor Brown wants California to borrow from itself to fund employee pensions. Good idea. Retrieved from http://www.latimes.com/business/hiltzik/la-fi-hiltzik-calpers-funding-20170604-story.html

Horrigan, J. (2016, September 9). *Libraries 2016.* Pew Research Center. Retrieved from http://www.pewinternet.org/2016/09/09/libraries-2016/

Jaeger, P., McClure, C., & Bertot, J. (2005). The E-rate program and libraries and library consortia, 2000–2004: Trends and issues. *Information Technology and Libraries, 24*(2), 57–67.

La Franchi, D. (2010). New markets tax credits. *Economic Development Journal, 9*(4), 5–13.

McClung, G. W. (1991). Theme park selection: Factors influencing attendance. *Tourism Management, 12*(2), 132–140.

Vanier, D. D. (2001). Why industry needs asset management tools. *Journal of Computing in Civil Engineering, 15*(1), 35–43.

3

Environmental Sustainability

As stated previously in this book, the environment is where many people's view of sustainability begins and ends. This is made evident by where the charters of a myriad of governmental departments, purported to be focused on sustainability, also begin and end. One should celebrate any move by any organization to aid the environment; however, environmental sustainability efforts are only part of what makes any organization sustainable.

The good news is that, because of this broad acceptance, environmental sustainability is where most public libraries are excelling. Long ago, many librarians embraced recycling despite the fact that they did not and do not track what or how much they recycle. Although librarians have been less inclined to work toward the reduction of greenhouse gasses (GhG), they have readily embraced environmentally friendly building practices. As this chapter notes, the latter embrace does help to stem the tide of rising GhG emissions. Therefore, although librarians do not claim credit for helping the environment in this way, they do in fact help when they deploy environmentally friendly building practices.

Further, libraries were born green. This is apparent because simply by lending books and having them returned, only to be lent to yet another customer, again and again and again, libraries are the ultimate green venture. Libraries allow their customers to keep from buying book after book after book to be read only once and then sit on shelves and/or later be thrown in the garbage. Yet, beyond this humble beginning, where does a library continue on its mission to be green? Steps 4 through 6 in the 12 steps of triple bottom line (TBL) sustainability are discussed in the next section.

4. LEADERSHIP IN ENERGY AND ENVIRONMENTAL DESIGN (LEED) LIBRARIES

> Begin or continue to add LEED buildings or LEED-equivalent library buildings to the cadre of library-owned/operated buildings. Include solar, wind, and geothermal power; harvest rainwater; and so on. Incorporate LEED technology and practices into existing buildings. Teach practices to interested customers via in-person and passive programs.

Step 4 of TBL sustainability for libraries—the building of libraries planned to qualify for LEED status—has been embraced by governmental entities, public library administrators, and the architects who design libraries. The American building community formed the U.S. Green Building Council (USGBC) and its LEED certification program beginning in 1993. Although the USGBC's work on LEED began in earnest in 1993, the first iteration of the program was not complete until 2000. At the time of this writing, there are more than 101,000 LEED-certified building projects located in more than 162 countries and territories (USGBC, 2017). Currently, registration is voluntary, even though LEED certification has become an industry norm. The LEED standards address sustainable building sites, water efficiency, materials, energy conservation, pollution control, and indoor environmental quality. The cost of a LEED-certified building averages 1.8 percent more than the price of a conventional building (Senge, Smith, Kruschwitz, Laur, & Schley, 2008), although owners can offset the additional expense with savings on energy and operating costs. The USGBC standards also encompass the retrofitting of old buildings.

The first LEED-certified library opened in San Jose, California, in 2002 (Mulford & Himmel, 2010). Today there are more than 620 LEED-certified libraries in the United States (USGBC, 2017). This, of course, includes academic and a few school libraries. Based on data from the American Library Association (ALA, 2017), this would mean that less than 3.7 percent of public library buildings are LEED certified. When compared to the proliferation of LEED-certified buildings in the 30 largest commercial real estate markets in the United States, one finds that 20 percent of commercial buildings in these markets are LEED certified (Holtermans & Kok, 2017). Thus, public libraries still have a lot of room to grow when it comes to their dedication to LEED.

This said, no studies could be identified that looked at why public library governance boards are embracing LEED building practices when they do proceed to seek LEED certification. Anecdotal evidence points to architects convincing library leaders and library boards that a LEED building is an educational opportunity for the community; also, some municipalities are now requiring that LEED standards be incorporated into public buildings of a certain size (e.g., 10,000 square feet and over).

Whether LEED-designated buildings are more expensive to build and maintain than non-LEED buildings is hotly debated. Some library leaders argue that the issue is less about the additional cost of construction and more about the cost of the LEED certification, which in 2010 was reported to cost $80,000–$100,000 per library in fees associated with verification (Mulford & Himmel, 2010). However, given library construction costs that can run from $675,000 for a small branch library remodel to $70 million for the construction of an enormous new central library, the library has to weigh the cost versus the expected derived benefit. Librarians could see a public relations boon from the additional expenditure, with the library being viewed in the community as a truly forward-thinking entity. A library could certainly be built to LEED standards without paying the associated costs for certification and still derive the benefits of a LEED building. A strong reason for a library to seek LEED designation or equivalency, even if upfront costs are higher, is the long-term savings that are realized over the life of the building. While this is a benefit for anyone who constructs a LEED-certified or equivalent building, it is more important to public libraries and public schools and other similarly funded entities: the upfront construction funds are not usually coming from operating funds, but the long-term utility costs are. In other words, when a building is first constructed or remodeled, often the monies for the project are supplied by government-issued bonds or donors, and the additional funds needed for a LEED-certified building are pennies on the dollar. At the same time, lower utility costs over the long term mean more money for books, staff raises, and emergency building repairs over the life of the building. In a recent study of the largest U.S. municipal utility district, the Los Angeles Department of Water and Power, Asensio and Delmas (2017) found that, on average, between the years of 2005 and 2012, commercial LEED buildings saved just under 30 percent on their utility bills versus commercial buildings that did not take advantage of any type of energy reduction program such as LEED, Energy Star, or the U.S. Department of Energy's Better Building Challenge program. However, a note of caution is warranted. Many of the LEED buildings in the study were extremely large, and they were compared to buildings that were likely older and less efficient. The researchers point out that the average energy savings goal set by engineers for the LEED buildings in the study was 20 percent. Thus, this might be a more practical goal for which to aim. However, on a large library building, 20 percent improvement can equate to extreme and substantial savings. Also of note in terms of the study, of the three energy saving programs reviewed, the LEED buildings far and away outperformed the other programs' buildings.

LEED buildings achieve energy savings and help the environment through many means. These include, but are not necessarily limited to:

- Rooftop solar arrays
- Heat-reflecting windows
- Automatic shades that deploy based on the sun's position
- Light-reflecting, white walls
- Deployment of task lighting versus harsh overhead lighting
- Automatic lights that detect movement
- High-efficiency heating and cooling systems
- Features that encourage visitors and/or staff to take stairs; ride bikes; and use alternative-fuel vehicles (such as preferential parking and charging stations)
- Rainwater harvesting and storage for later irrigation
- Low-flow toilets, waterless urinals
- Sourcing of building supplies from the local area
- Use of recycled materials in construction
- Recycling of construction waste
- Passive, always available, programming that educates the public about the environmentally friendly building features

Building a LEED library or remodeling an existing library into a LEED building is not the only way libraries can benefit the environment. Many libraries have implemented cost-saving efforts that also help the environment. One library leader participating in the study started a practice long ago of keeping the branch thermostats at 65° Fahrenheit in winter and 75° Fahrenheit in summer. Other library leaders have set up "green committees" to look at all their library's policies, practices, and procedures in order to help protect the environment, as well as train staff on how they can help in these efforts and educate library customers on ways they too can help the environment. GhG reduction and recycling are discussed at length later in this chapter; other notable practices adapted from Sam Mulford's and Ned Himmel's 2010 book, *How Green Is My Library?*, include:

- Consider virtual meetings when several people have to travel long distances
- Adopt a telecommuting policy for employees whose position allows them to work remotely
- Build a green roof
- Consider a mixed-use building for your next library
- Install low-flow aerators on existing faucets
- Conduct a comprehensive water usage audit
- Layer clothing and ban space heaters
- Use green (nontoxic) cleaning supplies

**Environmental Sustainability Business Case Study—
"The Green Hotel Company"**

Best practice: Efficient operations, LEED-certified buildings

International Hotel Operator (IHO) has instituted many environmental sustainability practices, including targeting specific reductions in energy and water consumption and "greening" its supply chain, as well as other goals centered on reducing waste, educating guests and associates on conservation practices, and building LEED-certified hotels. This extends to development of software applications for meeting planners to control the meeting room environment; light-emitting diode (LED) lighting in all guest rooms; responsible sourcing of hotel furniture, linens, uniforms, and other items; rainforest conservation and management in South America; and water conservation efforts in China, in addition to serving sustainable foods (including fish, and an outright ban on serving dishes prepared with shark fin) in all properties. The company has a Global Green Council made up of internal executives from every business discipline to help identify and provide oversight of these projects.

Inclusive of many of these practices, IHO holds up the building and operating of hotels that are more efficient as its chief best practice when it comes to environmental sustainability. That efficiency has been a part of its business since its founding. Approximately 30 years ago, however, IHO formalized this best practice under its "environmentally-conscious hospitality operations (ECHO)" program. This program evolved into long-term environmental goals that the company adopted in 2007. It then evolved further into the environmental sustainability program it follows today. Today the company measures its TBL environmentally sustainable practices through management reports, including a climate scorecard that is publicly available on the company's website.

Continued

IHO has even gone so far as to introduce gamification[1] into its sustainability efforts by developing and introducing an application (app) that allows property engineers to increase operating efficiency by competing with one another in real time on controlling property HVAC systems.

To read this case study in its entirety, please see Appendix 1.

Discussion Questions:

1. Does your library have plans to build a new structure or renovate an existing library building? Would your community or library board consider building a LEED certification eligible library as IHO has done for its new hotel properties?

2. After reading this short case, would you agree that IHO is really taking sustainability to heart, or do you think it is just using these measures to save money? If the latter, could your library convince stakeholders to "go green" to save money or the environment? Which would be the strongest argument for your community?

5. REDUCE FUEL USAGE AND GREENHOUSE GASSES (GHG)

Add alternative-energy fuel such as electric and natural gas to the vehicle fleet, or insist that delivery vendors move to this model. Monitor and report out fuel reduction and GhG performance via actual reduction, as well as reductions brought about by more efficient operations.

Surprisingly, in the study, no library leaders interviewed cited steps they were taking to reduce fuel usage and GhG as important. Conversely, nearly, if not all of the companies cited their efforts in this area as extremely important. In fact, it was the biggest disconnect between the participating libraries and companies. The *built environment*[2] accounts for double the emissions that cars produce worldwide (Senge et al., 2008). Thus, as every library system participating in the study had at least one LEED library building, all could be credited with making efforts to reduce GhG. Additionally, one library leader did cite incorporating alternative fuel vehicles into her libraries' fleet. Another cited her library's practice of floating its materials collection, whereby books are allowed to be kept at the library where the items are returned by customers rather than having them relocated to a home library location (Van der Noordaa, 2011); this cuts down on deliveries, thus saving fuel.

Libraries are responsible for a great deal of fuel use: there are delivery vehicles; maintenance trucks; staff commuting to and moving between branches; customers needing to pick up, renew, and drop off materials; intermittent shipments of new materials; shifting of materials from one geographical location to another; and customers who are required to visit the library to access certain services, attend classes, and use the Wi-Fi to access the Internet, among others. Library staff should analyze all of these practices and policies with an eye toward lowering fuel usage, as fuel usage is a major contributor to both GhG emissions and cost in the library's budget.

The library leader should also examine the fuel and energy efficiency of its existing fleet. Wherever possible, alternative-fuel vehicles should be deployed. Routing software should also be used to ensure that the most efficient routes are being used to move materials, supplies, and staff between locations. The library administration should offer staff and volunteers incentives to utilize public transportation, bicycles, and carpools when traveling to and from the library. Some other measures librarians have taken include discounted or free monthly passes for public transportation, preferential parking for staff who carpool, and 4-day/10-hours per day workweeks for administrative staff.

Some libraries do not operate fleets, but instead rely upon vendors to make deliveries. Should this be the case for a particular library, that library would be well served, the next time the contract is renegotiated or put out for bid with this vendor, by including requirements to use alternative-fuel vehicles and/or routing software. The library can warn vendors that this requirement is coming so that they can better prepare for it, or the library can work with them to help make it a reality. One Southeastern library uses a delivery vendor to deliver reserve and hold materials to its customers' homes. This library system does so because, by its cost estimations, it is less expensive to deliver the books via this method than to move them around the system and then allow the books to sit on a reserve shelf for up to a week waiting for the customer to pick up—or, as many librarians have painfully learned, *not* pick up—the book. Library staff need to do the math and determine what works best for them and their system. Certainly, it is more environmentally friendly to have one to three energy-efficient delivery vehicles delivering books to a multitude of households than it is to have a (likely) majority of non-energy-efficient vehicles coming to the library to claim materials.

Another effect of such a service would probably be a decline in customers visiting libraries; thus, traffic counts could potentially plummet. The question to be asked is: "Is the library better serving its customers, and are its customers' needs being met? Is the library achieving its hoped-for outcomes?" The library system in this example first worked with the U.S. Postal Service and then switched to a delivery vendor. Customers still have to return the books to the library, but they can do this without entering the building, via a drive-up book return. The library system was able to eliminate all delivery trucks and its bookmobiles by launching this service. This library also eliminated its homebound books-by-mail program, though those customers do get book return mailbags, so the service is, essentially, still offered.

SUSTAINABILITY FUTURECAST

Could a library working with an integrated library system (ILS) vendor save the planet one library at a time by piloting a system whereby items are mailed to a customer in a reusable mail pouch? In this scenario, at the end of the lending period the customer is notified by e-mail that the lending period is up and the item is due to the next customer. A link to a prepaid mailing label is included with the e-mail. The customer packages the item up and drops it in the nearest mailbox; thereafter, it arrives at the next customer's home within a few days, with little to no staff intervention and no time wasted with the item sitting on a hold shelf or in transit from one library to another. Issues of customer privacy must be addressed during use of such a system (e.g., perhaps only an address is used rather than the next customer's actual name), and the occasional loss of or damage to items would have to be taken into account; however, a potentially revolutionary system should not be dismissed because of a few outlier possibilities.

Another envisioned ILS pilot program would allow customers to jump the holds queue by passing an item on to a friend. This only would work in a large system with multiple copies of books and items, though certain popular or new items could be embargoed from the service. In this scenario, customers would get a notice that their lending period is up in three days. They would then go into their customer record, locate the item, and select "lend to a friend." They type in the friend's e-mail address. If the e-mail address matches an e-mail address on file at the library, the library sends an e-mail to the friend, such as "John Smith wishes to share a library item with you. Will you accept it from John, and return it to the library on September 15, 20xx? If yes, please click accept." (September 15 is, of course, the end of the new lending period). John's friend can be given three days to accept; if he or she does not, John is reminded to return the item to the library. If the friend accepts, then he or she has to get the item from John. Again, this service would increase library circulation, decrease library deliveries, and cut down on staff intervention, as well as cut down on the time a popular item sits on a reserve shelf waiting for a customer to pick it up. Cynics may argue that customers will abuse the system in order to extend their loan period, but the customer's friend is now taking responsibility for the item and subjecting himself or herself to any related fines or lost item fees. Also, brief legal language could be included in the e-mail notifying the "friend" and customer that abuse can result in loss of all borrowing privileges. Ultimately, it behooves us to remember that the librarian's mission is to promulgate reading and use of library resources, not to be the library police.

Sustainable library leaders report on how their programs and efforts help the environment. They track how they have lessened their libraries' carbon footprint; reduced use of natural resources such as water, electricity, and gas; reduced GhG emissions; and saved money on fuel; then they can report out how many dollars they have saved and how many fewer gallons of gasoline they have used. Library staff do this by comparing the decline in use or decline in GhG and the like to the base year,[3] as well as to the baseline.[4] If customers are driving to the library less often because they are getting their needs met through electronic delivery or a delivery vendor, these numbers can be calculated as well. Some will be estimates and rely on broad calculations, but this is acceptable. This is especially helpful if in-person traffic is declining while circulation increases. This calculation can show that the library is helping the environment while better serving its customers.

6. RECYCLE, REUSE, TRACK

Recycle all waste, including paper, plastic, aluminum, compost, and discarded books. Report out tons of waste diverted from landfills, including discarded materials sold, recycled, or donated.

Librarians can continue their green journey by stepping up their recycling programs. "Stepping up" is used because it is assumed that nearly every library in the United States has at the very least a basic recycling program. However, can that program be put on proverbial steroids?

All waste should be recycled. It is up to the library whether this is accomplished by setting up four separate receptacles for different kinds of recyclables or by employing single-stream recycling[5] whereby all nonfood waste goes into a single container to be sorted by a vendor later. A library can generate compost, but it needs a place to put or use that compost. This could be done through the municipality, if it collects composted materials; through use in a teaching garden on or adjacent to the library grounds; or through donation to a community or school garden.

In some municipalities, the cost of recycling outweighs the cost of separate collection. To meet its sustainability goals, the library staff may have to pay more than what it would cost to throw the recyclables in the garbage. This is a decision the library director must make, but there is a story to tell if the library staff chooses to recycle rather than causing recyclables to be placed in a landfill where future generations will be forced to contend with them.

Before dumping recyclables in a landfill or paying extra to have them recycled, the library should investigate all available options. Here are some options libraries have employed:

- One Western library system placed a nonprofit-provided container in every branch library where customers could deposit aluminum cans. These were then picked up en masse by the nonprofit and recycled to provide funding for the nonprofit's afterschool programs. This same library, prior to the economic recession, turned over discarded books to a company that shredded the books into a dry pulp that was then used as nontoxic insulation in houses. Unfortunately, once housing starts declined in 2009, the company went out of business and the library had to find another method to dispose of discarded books.
- A Midwest library allowed a recycling company to place paper recycling bins in library parking lots; customers as well as library staff could deposit recyclable paper and cardboard in these bins. The library was sent a monthly check by the recycling company, which it earmarked for its staff association to use. That same library also collected aluminum cans and plastic bottles. Again, those collections and funds were handled by staff, with the funds being designated for the staff association.

Many libraries serve as a drop-off point for spent batteries, used ink cartridges, and various other recyclable or environmentally hazardous items. Again, it is a library's choice about conducting such collections, whether for funding reasons or environmental reasons. The library does not necessarily wish to gain a reputation as a dumping ground. However, beyond selling these items to bolster funding, there are other reasons a library might want to participate in such collections; see the case study on the "Green-Smart Library" later in this chapter.

Book Recycling

Far too many libraries have been taken to task for discarding weeded books, yet standard protocol for proper collection management requires weeding. No story makes the evening news faster than errant librarians throwing caution to the wind by depositing "perfectly good books" in the garbage—yet this story has been reported time and time again. This public relations nightmare must be avoided at all costs and can easily be short-circuited by giving books a second life. Many library branches have a used book sale cart or shelf in their facilities, where they sell gently used books that have been discarded or donated to the library. Many a library Friends group has taken on the project of getting rid of discarded books through an annual or semi-annual book sale or a used-book shop area. A new industry, populated by companies such as Better World Books and Thriftbooks, has debuted in recent years that takes discards off the hands of libraries. These companies attempt to sell the books on the used-book market, typically online. They have also been known to donate some of the books to impoverished school districts for children to take home. The books they cannot dispose of through these means are often donated or sold in bulk to buyers overseas, where a strong demand for English-language books exists. Whether books are disposed of via book sales, taken by third-party vendors, or given new life as insulation, the fact that they have been responsibly recycled should be celebrated and recorded. In other words, these efforts should be tracked and reported.

Just as sustainable library leaders report out the reduction of their libraries' carbon footprint and GhG emissions, so too should they report out the tons they divert from landfills. This includes books sold in used book sales or disposed of through third-party vendors. It also includes recyclable items, including those the public drops off at a recycling dumpster or in a spent battery disposal unit. This is not as difficult as it sounds. Typically, large amounts of waste or recycled materials are measured in tons or charged by the ton. The amounts might be reflected on invoices or check stubs. If not, request the amounts from the vendors or providers going forward. An average weight can be determined for one book; thereafter, for every book sold the amount is multiplied out and added up. Book recyclers can also be asked to provide the weight, as they usually get weight reports from their shipping providers. Ideally, the numbers are collected individually and rolled up into a grand total. This should be reported in an annual report or a quarterly, semiannual, or yearly impact report. This information shows that the library staff are being environmentally and fiscally responsible with the assets of which they have been charged with stewardship. Additionally, as people and employees are positively impacted by this environmental stewardship, the library's social responsibility is showcased as well.

Environmental Sustainability, Library Case Study— "The Green-Smart Library"

Sustainability Best Practices: Working toward reducing carbon footprint/fossil fuel use; Practicing efficient operations and incorporating LEED and LEED-eligible certified buildings; Returning natural resources taken from the earth and/or recycling

This East North Central Library System (ENCLS) does not practice carbon offsetting;[6] however, it has modernized its fleet of vehicles, which has had the effect of improving fuel efficiency and thus reducing consumption. The library also tracks mileage and delivery vehicle routing. The library staff did seek and was granted LEED certification for two recent building projects; however, future building projects, although they will include

Continued

sustainable features, will not be LEED certified, reportedly because of the cost of certification. An additional way ENCLS has improved its environmental sustainability is by converting to a single-stream recycling vendor. In the year leading up to the study, the library diverted 720,000 pounds of recyclable material from landfills, returning the waste to the environment for other uses. Other practices related to environmental sustainability include a single automated control system for HVAC systems across all library branches, which is monitored and can be adjusted centrally. This system also allows the ENCLS facility team to diagnose problems remotely. The library staff has also incorporated many of the latest technologies in environmental building management and even has an employee-staffed "green committee."

To read this case study in its entirety, please see Appendix 1.

Discussion Questions:

1. Is there someone at your library who embraces environmental sustainability, or perhaps someone who is a good "number cruncher," who would enjoy calculating the positive impact your library is having on the environment?
2. Do you believe your community would appreciate and even celebrate your library's environmental success? Could children as well as adults in your community learn how to be good environmental stewards from your library's example?

CHAPTER SUMMARY

Yes, libraries were born green, but they also should live green. In this chapter, the three steps of TBL environmental sustainability for libraries were discussed. These steps include incorporating LEED or LEED practices into existing or new library buildings; reducing fuel usage and GhG emissions by adding alternative-energy fuels such as electricity and natural gas to the library's vehicle fleet, or by insisting that delivery vendors move to this type of delivery model; monitoring and reporting out fuel reduction and GhG performance via actual reduction, as well as reductions brought about by more efficient operations; incorporating recycling; and tracking results for all of the listed steps. Being green is, or can become, literally part of the public library brand promise.[7] This concept, and many others focusing on improving the external social sustainability of the public library, are discussed in Chapter 4.

NOTES

1. "Gamification" refers to a software system that has been designed to have use, design, elements, and characteristic similar to those of video games (reward and reputation systems with points, badges, levels, leader boards, etc.), but is applied in a nongame context (Deterding, Sicart, Nacke, O'Hara, & Dixon, 2011).

2. Saelens and Handy (2008) define the *built environment* as the part of the physical environment that is constructed by human activity (e.g., land use patterns, buildings, transportation systems, and urban design).

3. *Base year* is the historical datum (such as year) against which a measurement is tracked over time (GRI, 2013).

4. *Baseline* is the starting point used for comparisons. However, in the context of energy and emissions reporting, the baseline is the projected energy consumption or emissions in the absence of any reduction activity (GRI, 2013).

5. *Single-stream recycling* (Wang, 2006) refers to a system in which all standard recyclables are mixed in a collection container, instead of being sorted by the depositor into separate containers.

6. A *carbon offset* is a unit of carbon dioxide-equivalent (CO2e) that is reduced, avoided, or sequestered to compensate for emissions occurring elsewhere (Goodward & Kelly, 2010).

7. *Brand promise* is the integrity of alignment of the customer experience with the ethos of the brand, from its packaging, to its advertising, through customer touchpoints, and ultimately the use of the product or service (Mosley, 2007).

REFERENCES

American Library Association. (2017). *Number of libraries in the United States*. Retrieved from http://www.ala.org/tools/libfactsheets/alalibraryfactsheet01

Asensio, O., & Delmas, M. (2017). The effectiveness of US energy efficiency building labels. *Nature Energy, 2*(17033). doi:10.1038.nenergy.2017.33

Deterding, S., Sicart, M., Nacke, L., O'Hara, K., & Dixon, D. (2011). Gamification: Using game-design elements in non-gaming contexts. In CHI'11, *Extended abstracts on human factors in computing systems* (pp. 2425–2428). New York: ACM.

Goodward, J., & Kelly, A. (2010, August). *Bottom line on offsets*. Washington, DC: World Resources Institute.

GRI. (2013). *G4 online glossary: Definition of key terms*. Retrieved from https://g4.globalreporting.org/introduction/glossary/Pages/default.aspx

Holtermans, R., & Kok, N. (2017, Oct.). On the value of environmental certification in the commercial real estate market. *Real Estate Economics*. Retrieved from http://www.rogierholtermans.com/blog/2017/10/4/on-the-value-of-environmental-certification-in-the-commercial-real-estate-market

Mosley, R. W. (2007). Customer experience, organisational culture and the employer brand. *Journal of Brand Management, 15*(2), 123–134. doi:10.1057/palgrave.bm.2550124

Mulford, S., & Himmel, N. (2010). *How green is my library?* Santa Barbara, CA: Libraries Unlimited.

Saelens, B., & Handy, S. (2008). Built environment correlates of walking: A review. *Medicine and Science in Sports and Exercise, 40*(7 Suppl.), S550–566.

Senge, P., Smith, B., Kruschwitz, N., Laur, J., & Schley, S. (2008). *The necessary revolution: How individuals and organizations are working together to create a sustainable world*. New York: Crown Business.

United States Green Building Council. (2017). The leadership in environmental and energy design (LEED) framework. Washington, DC: Author. Retrieved from http://www.usgbc.org/leed

Van der Noordaa, N. (2011). *Will Dutch library collections float?* (Master's thesis). Delft University of Technology.

Wang, J. (2006). *All in one: Do single-stream curbside recycling programs increase recycling rates?* Retrieved from https://nature.berkeley.edu/classes/es196/projects/2006final/wang.pdf

4

Social (External)

Is the public library the heart or the brain of the community? If one had to choose, this author would say the heart. The affection that many hold for the institution of the public library is often without compare. Is it based on the individual's own experience with the library, or is it more profound? Perhaps, it is the knowledge that only at the library can an individual walk in penniless and leave intellectually richer—a place where all are made equal. The community in which a library resides is its very reason for being. How the library supports the community in which it finds itself is the other half of the community member/library relationship described here. Thus, how the library relates to the people who come into its sphere is vastly important, be those people the community at large, a vendor, or a customer. This chapter is devoted to steps 7, 8, and 9 of the 12 steps of public library sustainability outlined at the beginning of this book in Chapter 1. These are the external social sustainability steps.

7. ALIGN WITH COMMUNITY GOALS

Create the library's mission, vision, goals, and values (strategic plan) so that they align with those of the parent jurisdiction, community, and/or collective community leaders. Provide the relevant programming (some via partners, others from all staff) to achieve the goals, and report achievements via outcome measures. Also mitigate risk and continually work to properly manage the library's reputation.

Step 7 in the 12 steps of TBL sustainability for libraries is to align with community goals. Thus, every organization needs to have a strategic plan, defined here as a mission, a vision statement, goals, measurable objectives, and values. Without this formalized document or set of documents, the organization is rudderless: heading nowhere, on no particular path, on no particular timetable, with no concise message that conveys its offerings or what it stands for, and with no stated purpose for its very existence. Libraries are no different from any other organization in needing a strategic plan.

This said, public libraries do not exist in a vacuum. They are often, though not always, a subsidiary of a larger municipal organization such as a city or county government; nevertheless, they are always a part of a community of some sort. Thus, the library's strategic plan should be informed by its parent organization's strategic plan, and/or in conjunction with its community partners and their goals. A strategic plan is developed in part by conducting a needs assessment, perhaps by surveying the community and/or conducting focus groups or planning sessions with community partners, but always with staff involvement. Again, the elements of an organization's strategic plan for the purposes of this book are: mission, a vision statement, goals, measurable objectives, and values.

Community Needs Assessment

The needs of the community may be assessed in several ways. Focus groups, open forums, and stakeholder meetings are all possibilities. One useful way, promoted by the Public Library Association (PLA) and its parent the American Library Association (ALA), is through their joint Libraries Transform Communities program, which was developed by and in collaboration with the Harwood Institute of Bethesda, Maryland.

The Harwood Institute's methodology for engaging one's community is:

Designed to help libraries strengthen their role as community leaders and bring about positive change in their communities. Referred to as, Turning Outward, it is a step-by-step process developed by Harwood. It entails taking steps to better understand communities; changing processes and thinking to make conversations more community-focused; being proactive to community issues; and putting community aspirations first. (ALA, 2015)

Whatever method the library uses to assess its community's needs, it is important that the mission, vision, values, and goals be informed by the community the library serves.

Mission

A library needs a mission statement that the community can support and the employees and stakeholders can get behind. A strategic plan should start with a mission. The management scholar Peter Drucker (2008, p. 14) once wrote:

The effective mission statement is short and sharply focused. It should fit on a T-shirt. It must be clear, and it must inspire. Every board member, volunteer, and staff person should be able to see the mission and say, "Yes. This is something for which I want to be remembered."

Former California State Librarian Kevin Starr (2012), writing on social sector organizations' mission statements, quipped, "Eight words are enough. Do not settle for more." When asked why eight, Starr stated, "It's long enough to be specific and short enough to force clarity."

Vision

A vision statement is typically longer than a mission statement—usually 11 to 22 words—so that it is easy to remember (Kantabutra & Avery, 2010). It serves to motivate and inspire one's colleagues and stakeholders to achieve results. It is typically set by the organization's leader or leadership team, but again must be embraced by staff in order to be successful. A shared vision is, in fact, one of the five disciplines identified by Peter Senge (1990) as necessary to create a learning organization. (See Chapter 5 for more information on creating a learning organization.) Although there is little agreement in business literature on an actual definition of a vision statement, research suggests that strong vision statements are "concise, clear, future-oriented, stable, challenging, abstract and inspiring" (Kantabutra & Avery, 2010, p. 43). One of the libraries reported on in this book relates its vision statement as: "A thriving community where wisdom prevails." Lest anyone be confused, they introduce this slogan with the words: "Our vision: How we see the future." A vision statement is aspirational, in that it will likely never be fully realized and thus will serve the organization for a very long time. It will also not likely ever be made outdated by technological advances. However, to help fulfill a vision, a library leader would "want to align organizational processes and systems to suit the vision and empower others to act to achieve the vision" (Kantabutra & Avery, 2010, p. 39).

Goals

This book defines *goals* as directional and overarching. A goal might read, "The children of ___*[community name]*___ will grow up able to compete globally," or "Cultivate Engaged Employees." Either of these would be an acceptable organizational goal for a public library. These goals would, of course, be aligned with the parent organization's goals, or may have been developed in consultation with community stakeholders or as part of a needs assessment. The goals, while directional in nature, must be achieved or at least responded to or fulfilled. These goals would be achieved by measurable objectives.

Objectives

Per Drucker, "objectives have specific targets, a deadline, a clear statement of who is accountable, and a built-in measurement for feedback from results" (1986, p. 285). Thus, they are measurable. This concept can be further refined by the acronym SMART. SMART objectives are often touted in management seminars and by many, many organizations. SMART objectives are typically defined as being:

S pecific
M easurable
A chievable
R elevant
T ime-bound

A sample SMART objective for a public library might be:

The library youth services staff will visit every school in the county to promote the summer reading program prior to the program's kick-off date.

This SMART objective defines who is responsible; also, the action to be achieved is listed and very specific. The objective is measurable in the sense that it specifies "every school in the county," which for a library would be a known quantity. Only the library staff can ascertain if this is achievable based on their past outreach experience. The objective is certainly relevant, as it aligns with one of the aforementioned goals. It is also time-bound, as it states by when it is to be achieved. As shown in this example, *specific* refers to the goal, but as Drucker adds, the objective must also include who is responsible. In this example, the library's youth services team is responsible.

Every objective should be a SMART objective so that the library is accountable for delivery on its strategic plan. Objectives should also trickle down through the organization, some even from the parent jurisdiction, so that every department is involved and has a stake in the success of the organization.

Values

Organizational values are a unique aspect of the strategic plan in that they define what the organization stands for and how the work is to be accomplished. Staff across the organization, or at least a staff team that is representative of the organization in its entirety, should be involved in defining the values. A new organization with a small handful of employees could set its values, which would then be shared with new hires as they come aboard as part of the onboarding process (discussed in greater detail in Chapter 5). However, a public library tends to have a workforce already in place. If the library leadership team wishes for the staff to truly embrace the values, then it will want to engage a cross-section of employees in drafting the values and any associated statements. The values in draft form can move back and forth between the staff team and the library leadership team and then be shared with the organization at large for staff and governing board input before the values are finalized. This can be accomplished in a somewhat iterative fashion.

One Midwest library laid out its values in an easy-to-remember fashion that also evoked its dedication to good customer service. Its values and accompanying value statements (a short one- or two-sentence statement for each value in order to provide clarity) were developed by a cross-organization team of employees working in tandem with a leadership team liaison. The values and value statements were then shared with the library director, who made minor tweaks to the values and statements. They were then sent back to the staff team for their sign-off. After this, they were shared with all employees for their comments and suggestions. The *Say Yes First* values were then formerly adopted by the library's governing board. They are:

> **S** erving the Community
> **A** dventure
> **Y** our Inspiration
>
> **Y** es!
> **E** thics
> **S** tewardship
>
> **F** un!
> **I** ntellectual Freedom
> **R** espect
> **S** afety
> **T** omorrow's Leaders

Again, in order to build a strategic plan, most libraries need look no further than the goals of their parent jurisdiction, township, city, county, and/or community.

Successful libraries are those that align their services to meet their parent organization's strategic direction (Matarazzo & Pearlstein, 2015). While often this parent may be the official city or county, it isn't necessarily always the case. As previously stated, an active chamber of commerce may have important goals, or a group of powerful stakeholders (well-placed family or charitable foundations) might have initiatives they are looking to have supported.

As an example, one southwestern U.S. city's chamber of commerce, health department, and local university school of medicine were alarmed by the incidence of obesity and early-onset diabetes in their county. A powerful local family foundation was also involved. It was not hard for that county's library system to engage in that partnership as well, especially given the quality-of-life initiative in the library's strategic plan.

Still another library system director read an article in her local newspaper that said an educational forum was taking place. With all the details of the meeting contained in the article, she signed up for the event directly, not waiting for a formal invitation that might not ever have arrived. At the forum, she learned about a community impact program (CIP) launching in her community that was based on a model tried in many other cities. The idea wasn't to launch yet another nonprofit, but instead to have those charitable foundations that were already investing in area nonprofit organizations evaluate those nonprofits that were measuring their success via outcomes measures, and then only invest in those outcomes-based nonprofits that were achieving impact.

The director knew she had heard of outcomes before, but she looked up outcome measures to make sure she grasped the concept. She concluded that what her library was generally using to measure success was output measures (e.g., circulation, visits, program attendance, reference inquiries, etc.). However, it occurred to her that her adult literacy department was measuring outcomes: that is, the number of people participating in the program who were achieving success, such as the number of participants who got a job promotion, the number who passed the citizenship test, and the number who had read their child a story, among others.

Although her adult literacy department was assembling and reporting outcome measures, no other library departments were using outcomes-based evaluation. The director quickly started learning all she could about outcomes measures and started sending staff to outcome measures training offered nationally by the PLA, the division of the ALA focused on public libraries in the United States and Canada (see www.PLA.org). She did this because all the CIP-involved charitable foundations were donors to her library and she didn't want the library to be left behind. She was happy to learn that nearly all the CIP's goals aligned with most of her library's strategic goals. Now her team would just need to start collecting outcome measures regarding the following goals:

Kindergarten readiness	High school and college graduation
Third-grade reading proficiency	Jobs
Eighth-grade math proficiency	

The library's goals had previously differed slightly in that they were focused on eighth-grade reading proficiency versus math and high school dropout prevention. Additionally, the library staff hadn't previously focused on college graduation, but rather college application. However, going forward the library staff decided to assist with and measure their impact on college graduation, because the CIP defined it quite broadly. In the

CIP's view it included completion of a four-year college degree, a master's degree, vocational training, and completion of an associate's degree that led to employment. Even a cosmetology certificate was included in college graduation numbers. As far as the library director's community was concerned, a cosmetology certificate could lead to gainful employment. Today the library measures and reports on outcome measures and the director finds the donor community more engaged with the library because of it. While the library still tracks outputs for planning and staffing purposes, as well as for state reports, she finds her community is more responsive to her outcomes.

Partnership and Collaboration

Nearly every library in the United States would agree that it partners with its local school district or collaborates with a local shelter. Some, for all intents and purposes, are certainly doing a better job at it than others. Additionally, the library has a powerful brand; thus, many organizations, for-profit and nonprofit alike, would like to collaborate with the library. If one likes the organization, does one say, "Yes?" and if not, "No?" If it is a nonprofit, is the answer, "Yes?" If it is a for-profit, is the answer, "No?" The library staff should not answer any of these questions. Instead, they should judge every opportunity, both those which have been presented to the library and those where the library needs to pursue a partnership opportunity based on the merits of that opportunity and through the lens of its strategic plan. A local for-profit newspaper or a local telecommunications/Internet provider might be the best partner with which to achieve the library's goal, despite the fact that these are both for-profit enterprises. A helpful way to ascertain whether an organization is a good fit as a partner is to borrow a business tool called the BrandFit Matrix (Shaffer, 2003).

The BrandFit Matrix was developed to help companies identify other companies to work with on a cross-promotional basis. These companies do not compete with one another; instead, they often sell complementary products. An example is a home delivery pizza company and a local sports franchise that broadcasts its games on a local television channel.

Though built for business use, the BrandFit Matrix can also be used by nonprofit organizations, including public libraries, to build partnerships that further the mission of the library as well as the mission of the partner organization. The BrandFit Matrix is a brainstorming tool that a team of individuals can deploy. It works as follows. Start with the library's mission statement, then complete the following seven steps:

Sample mission statement

"The _____ Public Library is a relevant community gathering place, which provides safe haven and knowledge while promoting life-long learning and recreational pursuit for all."

Step 1: Pinpoint the key words in the mission statement. In the preceding sample they would likely be: *relevant, community, safe haven, knowledge, learning, for all.* Other libraries may have their own key words, such as *culture, diversity, free,* and so on.

Step 2: Order and group the key words, referred to hereafter as the keys of the BrandFit Matrix, in terms of importance and likeness: *for all, community, safe haven, knowledge, learning, relevant.*

Step 3: Identify additional meanings and any double entendres. Often, the antonym of a key word can be helpful.

Step 3 is the most important step in building the matrix, so the team should spend the majority of its time here. In the example case, some words will be subject to substitution: "For all" becomes "democracy." Thus the following example uses: *democracy, community, safe haven, knowledge, learning, relevance.*

Step 4: Construct a matrix and plug in the keys across the top row.

Democracy	Community	Safe Haven	Knowledge	Learning	Relevance

Step 5: Brainstorm.

By plugging the key words/concepts into the BrandFit Matrix, a team can determine subcategories, which will bring focus to strategy discussions and aid in identifying strategic alliance partners and collaborators. Anyone working on the partnership should be involved in this step. In this step, the team has a clear objective and a tool to work with. Using standard brainstorming rules (which include "there are no bad ideas" and "one idea builds off another," among others), the team will be able to conceptualize extremely targeted partners and partnerships. The team should not worry about execution; that will come later. At this stage, they should just let the ideas flow. A good thesaurus is very helpful for this step. A completed matrix for the previous mission statement might look like this:

Democracy	Community	Safe Haven	Knowledge	Learning	Relevance
Freedom for all	Third Place	Sanctuary	Databases	Programs	Technology
Equality	Society	Respite	Books	Educational tools	Programs
Champion	Culture	Escape (through pursuits)	Archives	Literacy	Recreation
For all	Needs	Refuge	Multimedia	Development	Games
Free	Coming together		Memories		Music

Step 6: Now brainstorm potential partners that may meet some of these needs.

Partners may be nontraditional, but because the words brainstormed in the BrandFit Matrix exercise brought them to mind, include them in your list. While the partners will likely be local, national partners can also come into play. They should not be excluded if national, as many may have a local presence as well. As an example, *Sesame Street*® is a national TV show, but it likely is broadcast on a local PBS-affiliated station. Using the sample matrix, the team working on this developed the following potential-partner BrandFit Matrix for the previous mission statement.

The team places the organizations' names in all the applicable boxes.

Democracy	Community	Safe Haven	Knowledge	Learning	Relevance
	District Attorney's Safe Place Program	District Attorney's Safe Place Program	History Channel	History Channel	
	Botanical Gardens		Botanical Gardens	Botanical Gardens	
League of Women Voters	League of Women Voters		League of Women Voters		League of Women Voters
Child Welfare organization	Child Welfare organization	Child Welfare organization		Movie/Book tie-in	Movie/Book tie-in
	Nonprofit after-school tutoring center	Nonprofit after-school tutoring center	Nonprofit after-school tutoring center	Nonprofit after-school tutoring center	Nonprofit after-school tutoring center
		Sesame Street®	*Sesame Street®*	*Sesame Street®*	

Step 7: Refine and define your potential new partnership.

Should the library leader identify a potential partner, how does the staff know how to collaborate with that entity? The BrandFit Matrix has helped to identify potential partners, but it hasn't informed library staff on *how* to partner. The best way to ascertain this is to put reference skills to work and learn as much as possible about the potential partner. If after thorough research the library wishes to move forward, an appropriate person asks for a meeting with the partner at the partner's convenience.

Who should meet? It depends on the size of the partner, its standing in the community, and the strength of the match. It may be most appropriate for a branch manager, the head of youth services, or the library director. Once a meeting is accepted, how should the library broach the subject of collaboration to the potential partner? Much like a potential donor, as discussed in Chapter 2, the potential partner should be approached as one would handle a reference interview. One could ask, "What are your goals and challenges? And how may the library help you achieve these goals?" One library youth services employee learned that a potential partner had the following challenges: No space to conduct what was likely award-winning programming and more volunteers than it knew what to do with. The library system had 58 available meeting rooms! The library system ended up with a unique programming offering that was a fit for both organizations and a slate of volunteers to offer up the programming, all for very little cost to the library system. Best of all, this partnership fit the library system's strategic plan. Twelve years after the partnership was struck, it is still going strong, primarily because it was a good brand-fit.

A true partnership or collaboration has as its basis a formalized agreement. To achieve a good agreement, the partners will have done a proper needs assessment, set out goals, structured a memorandum of understanding (MOU) or contract that is signed by the executive director or the library's financial officer, and outlined how they will evaluate the partnership (presumably via outcome measures). Any other type of arrangement is just a feel-good neighborly event; it is not a true partnership or collaboration. An MOU is a great way to delineate a true partnership from something that is not. After all, allowing a group to place flyers in your lobby should not be judged or looked at the same as co-running an after-school homework club together with codified expectations and measurable outcomes.

Social Sustainability (External), Library Case Study— "The Customer Caring Library"

Best Practices: Programs that promote healthy living; Promoting goodwill; Providing jobs on the lower end of the economic scale; Empowering women

Mountain Library System (MLS) clearly puts its customers at the core of its mission and points to a few programs that promote healthy living as one of its best practices on their behalf. These include a program centered on positive aging and partnerships with nutrition organizations on programs that primarily target the economically disadvantaged. The library promotes goodwill through a multitude of other partnerships it maintains. MLS offers employment to those on the lower end of the economic scale, though two requirements must be met: a high school diploma and customer service experience. The library states that it hires many entry-level people and that they often go on to build careers with the library.

MLS also focuses on programming that empowers women, including programs that promote careers in science to young girls. It also recently hosted a series of lectures on global women's issues, as well as highlighting local domestic violence concerns. The library notes that it has had women in positions of leadership since 1979 and that 37 employees (primarily women) have gone on to get master's degrees in library science, while countless others have received bachelor's degrees in other subjects.

The library system is also engaged in a partnership with the National Issues Forums Institute,[1] an organization that uses a trained facilitator to address controversial topics (e.g., immigration) during community discussions around the identified issue.

To read this case study in its entirety, please see Appendix 1.

Discussion Questions:

1. What challenge does your community face that the library could help address?
2. What organizations in the community might your library partner with to help address this challenge? What are some outcomes you could identify around this issue? How would you measure success?

Manage Reputation

A good partnership choice can enhance the library's reputation, just as a poor choice can damage it. An old adage reads, "Choose your friends wisely, as a person is known by the company she or he keeps." This is true for the library as well. Libraries are held in high esteem. However, this also means they have a long distance to fall in the reputation department. Not every potential partner is a good partner, and that is why one should make sure the partners are mission-aligned.

However, there are many ways to manage the reputation of the public library. One is to make sure the financial house is in order, as covered in Chapter 2. The other is to be as transparent as possible. Nearly all public libraries are government entities. The few that are not are located in communities that have chosen to outsource their library service to private management companies. When an open records request comes in from the media, respond to it. When a citizen wishes to speak to the library's governing board, allow it. Web tools exist that place all the library's finances online. If the library is being properly managed, one should not be worried that something will be uncovered. If a community member has a question, answer it. Place links on the library's Web site announcing the names of the leadership and providing a means to contact them via e-mail. Letters to the editor of the local newspaper about a library concern are not addressed to the library. Thus, library administration needs to decide whether to respond in kind: it is often better to negotiate a one-time guest column if the concern is of substance. The library director could also direct a letter to the individual if the address can be obtained.

Ensure that all senior staff and board members are trained in open meeting and open records laws. All staff should receive a modicum of training on open records. Though unusual, there have been incidents when individual library staff members have been subject to open-records matters (e.g., individual salary information published, internal e-mails swept up in a broader investigation, etc.).

Mark Twain once said, "Never pick a fight with people who buy ink by the barrel" (Negri, 1999). To finish Twain's thought: you will never win. If you fall into your local newspaper editors' sights, they will relentlessly attack you until their notice is captured by another. Politely respond to their requests, continue to advertise with them if you have done so in the past, and wait for it to subside—which it eventually will. If the library has done everything in its power to respond to the particular issue, then that is all that can be done.

Counter any negative publicity with positive publicity. Of course, libraries have a great deal of positive publicity, so the library director and staff should be regularly submitting press releases to the local media about new product and program offerings, awards earned, and the successful impact the library is having in the community. Here the idea is to keep the library top of mind and/or counter what should be rare public controversies or negative impressions.

Libraries are also free to advertise. This can be for trade (e.g., the library allows an organization/publication to distribute quality, library mission-aligned publications such as *Parent Today* in the library lobby, and in turn the publication allows the library to feature a monthly column). Advertisements can also be purchased, if it furthers the library's mission. Although there is nothing wrong with advertising to further the library's strategic mission (nonprofits do it every day), the library could open itself up to criticism for spending tax revenue on advertising. One way to allay this criticism would be to spend only donated funds in this way.

Advertising can be used to improve a damaged reputation as well. This can actually be a morale booster for staff. A library cited earlier had its reputation severely damaged; a three-part advertising campaign was then executed over the course of a year and half. The different phases of the campaign moved the message from an institutional focus, to a customer-institution focus, to a customer-only focus. It is rare that an advertising campaign would focus solely on an institution: Normally, it should focus on the benefits the customer receives. However, in this case, the institutional-only focus was called for because of the damage the library's reputation had suffered. The three phases of the campaign were:

Phase 1: AnyTown Public Library Better Every Day.
Phase 2: AnyTown Public Library Serving You Better Every Day.
Phase 3: AnyTown Public Library Helping You Be Better Every Day.

For those who were aware of the scandal, phase 1 said the library was better. For those unaware of the scandal, the library was improving. In phase 2, a professional photographer was hired and actual staff members were used in the ad campaign (in the other phases, to control costs, stock images were purchased and used). In phase 3, the focus was 100 percent on the customer.

Advertising vehicles used were newspaper inserts, which were also distributed in-branch and to homes that did not subscribe to the local newspaper; newspaper rack placards; bus shelters and bus advertising; and library delivery vehicle wraps. Of particular importance was communicating to staff when the advertising would appear, especially when it came to the newspaper insert and the insert that was delivered in a coupon advertising circular to homes that didn't subscribe to the newspaper. The library administration wanted to be sure staff saw the inserts, which not only featured the slogan, and in one case their colleagues, but also featured a lot of great new services the library was offering.

Another way to help manage the library's reputation is to get the library beyond the four walls of the library. This can be done through traditional outreach, such as visiting schools, retirement homes, and senior centers, and participating in local festivals, but it can also be done in more nontraditional ways. One Eastern library sponsors the Wi-Fi in a section of its local airport. Anyone visiting that area gets a welcoming message from the library. Visitors, perhaps business people, now know that they too have a friend in the form of the 56 branches of the city's library system. This serves as great news to a weary business traveler trying to set up a proverbial shop in this city. In effect, this business traveler has 56 locations of her or his business in the form of the branch libraries distributed across the city. These locations, after all, are likely open every afternoon and even have some "bonus hours" beyond the afternoon, and feature Wi-Fi, computers, perhaps wireless printing, accessible business databases, maybe FedEx boxes nearby, and (most importantly) restrooms. Too bad the library could not afford to sponsor the Wi-Fi for the whole airport, but for this library system in this particular airport the cost was prohibitive. Still, it is clear that this library means business.

Another way to get outside the four walls of the library in a cost-effective manner is to publish a meaningful free publication that promotes reading and library services and distribute it across the library's service area. It must be meaningful, because a self-serving publication that only features library events does not offer any value to people who likely don't attend library events. Often libraries publish a newsletter or event guide but distribute it in the library only. This does not serve people who are not visiting the library. One Southern library that has as a part of its mission to promote reading publishes a monthly book review. Yes, it ensures that all the books in the review are also in its library catalog, promotes its events, includes a map of its locations and hours, and communicates any service changes within the publication. But the book review is just as valuable to a reader who doesn't use the library as to one who does. Perhaps the review will one day convince the nonuser to use the library; but this particular library's mission is to promote reading, not circulation. Its vision statement includes verbiage about a fully literate community, not words about having the highest circulation on per capita basis. Although the book review includes advertising, nearly all of the advertising is for the library. On occasion it does run an ad for a strategic partner, but this is rare. The library has never sold advertising in the book review.

Both of these examples help raise and contribute to the libraries' reputation in the community, and both help keep the library top-of-mind in the community. The message of the airport Wi-Fi example is that this library is about access and it is technologically advanced. The message of the book review example, as stated, reinforces that this library is about promoting literacy and reading.

Unfortunately, local government for the most part is averse to risk (Feeney & DeHart-Davis, 2009). In part this aversion develops because of the scrutiny it often faces. This sometimes makes it difficult to be innovative. However, public library customers and local taxpayers deserve the best. Libraries should be innovative. By planning carefully, looking at every possible scenario, and communicating with staff and stakeholders, a public library can take well-thought out, methodical risks. Feeney and DeHart-Davis (2009) found that it wasn't rules or red tape that caused public-sector employees to lack innovation. On the contrary, they found that these things were necessary. What stifled innovation in the public sector was centralized control. Thus, larger library systems may wish to cut back on centralization where prudent. In other situations, smaller libraries that are held in check by larger city government organization may push for more autonomy, at least when it comes to library-related matters.

Mitigating Risk

Part of sustainability is mitigating risk. Some financial risks were covered in Chapter 2, but there are other risks to which the library is also subject. Many of the risks can be mitigated by keeping library policy manuals up to date, making sure employees keep up to date on the policies, and verifying that they have read them and agree to uphold them. This can be handled by having employees sign a statement to this effect. Other risk factors involving employees are covered in Chapter 5.

Library directors also need to make sure their insurance policies are up to date and adequately cover their assets. Has art the library owns been appraised recently? Is the insurance coverage still adequate? Does the insurance policy cover the depreciated value or the replacement value of assets? If the 75-year old Central Library were suddenly flooded, could the library system afford to make up the difference between the policy payout and the replacement cost? Has a paper conservator evaluated the library's special collection holdings in the last five to ten years? The library acts as a steward of sometimes millions of dollars of the community's assets. The community expects that those assets are receiving adequate care. Disaster plans are covered more extensively in Chapter 6, but disaster preparedness is covered here briefly. Should a natural disaster strike, how will the information technology (IT) infrastructure be restored? How will staff communicate? The community may really rely on its library at this pivotal hour of need; will the library be able to meet those needs? Does the library have an emergency disaster response plan? Are all the library buildings free of safety hazards for staff and customers alike? Are procedures in place to de-ice sidewalks in winter, prior to opening? Are there emergency response plans in place for active shooter, bomb threat, fire, earthquake? Is there a safety manual in every building? Do all staff know where it is? Do branch managers and senior staff have phone numbers of staff and buildings in their personal vehicles? Is there a calling tree in place (that is, a procedure for staff to be contacted by their supervisor or other staff) in case of an emergency or inclement weather? All of these have happened or have needed to be addressed by one public library or another. Many of these things have happened to one or another library several times over the course of a five- to ten-year period. It is always better to be prepared. This too is part of sustainability.

Other risks to be avoided can be brought on by library customers. It seems as though 99 percent of customers have the ability to navigate the library, its policies, and procedures with few to no issues. However, there is a special 1 percent that seems to always have issues using their library peaceably along with their fellow library customers. The sustainable library does not punish the 99 percent of customers who use the library with no issues because of something the 1 percent of problem-behavior customers do. In other words, one does not put a negative policy in place that affects everyone because of a few bad actors. For example (even though writing checks is going out of fashion), a patron might be writing a bad check, and many libraries still accept them. If two customers out of 1,000 in a year's time pass a "bad check"—a check that they have insufficient funds in their account to cover—one should not ban check use from one's entire library system. (It would, however, be appropriate for the library in this example to stop taking checks when so few are used that the bank starts charging an inordinate amount of money to deposit them.)

When it comes to customers behaving inappropriately in the library, laws vary state to state on whether you may ban them from using the library for a period of time. Library administration should get a legal opinion on this. One library system in the Southwest does on occasion ban customers; however, through a grant-funded partnership with a local human services organization, it has a full-time social services caseworker working in the library system. When a customer has to be banned, before the customer can return she or he must meet with the caseworker to develop a plan as to how to make a successful reentry into the library system after the completion of the ban.

8. VENDOR COMPLIANCE

> Create and administer mandatory vendor surveys which provide assurance that all federal, state, and locally mandated labor and ethical sourcing standards are upheld.

A TBL sustainability practice that came up for nearly every company participating in the study, but did not really register with the library leaders who participated, was vendor compliance. However, one library leader did mention that her library had participated in a recall of a summer reading prize or gift that was rumored to be lead-tainted.

They did not distribute the prizes, but instead sent them back to the manufacturer after having to quickly identify and obtain a substitute. For the companies, nearly every one that participated mentioned the Nike sweatshop scandal (Bennett & Lagos, 2007). In the lead-up to this scandal, Nike (and probably every other U.S.-based company using third-party companies to manufacture goods) was shocked to learn that the U.S. public held them accountable for worker conditions in overseas factories that they did not own. At the time Nike was slow to respond; today, nearly every other company is mindful of the conditions in these third-party overseas manufacturing sites.

Many librarians would define themselves as champions for children. Many would even say they are champions of human rights. Yet, in a world where all sorts of items are manufactured a world away, librarians have no idea what the factory conditions are like in the factories that manufacture their books, their summer reading giveaways, and the book bags and flash drives they sell (often at cost). Why is this? Is it safe to say those things are impossible to know, or is it simply "none of my business"? One might posit, "I'd be happy to go visit the factories manufacturing these goods, but I don't think it would be the best use of the library's limited resources." And yet, how tragic it would be to see a picture in the national news of a child laborer chained to a worktable topped by a menacing industrial sewing machine, assembling a brightly colored plastic or canvas book bag for a local U.S. library. What's a library staff to do?

The library director and staff can start by requiring suppliers to sign affidavits stating that items, including components, are manufactured in accordance with the Fair Labor Association (FLA) Workplace Code of Conduct (see Appendix 3 for the text). Per its website, the FLA is a "collaborative effort of socially responsible companies, colleges and universities, and civil society organizations" dedicated to protecting workers' rights around the world (FLA, 2017). Founded at the urging of President Clinton in 1996 in response to the sweatshop scandal crisis, the FLA is headquartered in Washington, D.C., and has more than 350 members. Librarians who think it would be unnecessary to ask library suppliers to adhere to the FLA Workplace Code of Conduct, or that a library would never be held to that level of accountability, might be surprised to learn that the single largest group of participants in the FLA is U.S.-based universities. Apparel emblazoned with university names, team names, and logos are very big business, and no university can afford to have its name sullied by this type of scandal.

Adhering to the FLA Workplace Code of Conduct is especially important when library-purchased items are produced outside the United States. In the future, requests for proposals (RFPs) should include language to that effect, along with the suggested affidavit mentioned earlier. Phones with digital camera capabilities are ubiquitous. No manufacturer can claim it would be impossible to get a picture of factory conditions. In the rare instance in which the library director is dealing directly with a factory representative, the library staff can request photos of the factory, its working conditions, and the factory workers making the items. An ethical factory owner would be honored that any end-customer would take an interest in its factory or workers. The item would further be humanized, and the library could take pride in the fact that it is supporting workers who are well cared for in a far-off country.

This is not the only way in which vendors should be held accountable. One should remember that, although this sustainability step is also about protecting the library's good name, even more importantly it is about conducting business ethically as well as in a safe and caring manner that ensures no one is abused in the name of the library. Vendors should also ensure that they are complying with and conforming to all U.S., state, and local laws and regulations. The library should have a reasonable expectation that the manufacturer is doing this, by spelling these expectations out within contracts, MOUs, RFPs, and on purchase orders. This should become part of the library's standard operating procedures. Further, the library staff should conduct an annual mandatory survey that relates how the vendor is ensuring compliance and, as discussed in Chapter 3, operating in a sustainable fashion. Staff who interact with the vendor should also have a chance to weigh in on the vendor's performance via a survey. All surveys should be taken very seriously.

A staff committee should then review all the collected data. If a particular vendor is shown to go above and beyond the others, and in fact is doing an incredible job, that vendor or its representatives should be invited to the library's staff awards and presented with the library's vendor of the year award. The library may want to have an additional category: the sustainable vendor of the year award. Vendors are partners. They should be making our employees' work lives easier and library customers' lives better. They deserve recognition. It also serves as a potential reward and recognition for their having filled out a survey that (depending on what the library wishes to learn from the survey) could take some time to complete.

Social Sustainability (External), Business Case Study— "The Compassionate Tech Company"

Best practice: Supply chain monitoring/fair and equitable labor practices

In each of the facilities the International Computer Component Manufacturer (ICCM) operates, it deploys a public affairs group that works with the local community and also works with a community advisory group. ICCM characterizes its efforts to protect workers' rights in its supply chain as an external social sustainability best practice. The company is a member of the Electronic Industry Citizenship Coalition (EICC), a nonprofit membership group made up of electronics companies that have pledged to support the rights and well-being of workers and communities affected by the electronics supply chain globally. ICCM strictly adheres to the EICC code of conduct. This activity was driven by the problems that plagued Nike (mentioned earlier in this chapter) and Apple when news of supply-chain abuses were aired in the media. ICCM tracks this activity via regular audits of suppliers.

To read this case study in its entirety, please see Appendix 1.

Discussion Questions:

1. Is your library confident that all materials it lends, all items it sells, and all items it gives away are ethically sourced?
2. Could your library institute a process whereby all vendors are strictly held to international standards as well as local, state, and federal laws when it comes to providing your library with the items it purchases? Would your library consider giving an award to your most upstanding vendor? How about your most sustainable one?

9. EMPLOY EXCELLENT CUSTOMER SERVICE

> Have a customer service philosophy, utilize customer surveys and customer relationship management (CRM) systems, conduct a market segmentation study, employ a chief customer experience officer or advocate, and measure progress against previously mentioned outcomes. Ingratiate customers to the library.

In their book *The Nordstrom Way to Customer Service Excellence*, Spector and McCarthy (2012) relate that at Nordstrom's, the much-emulated department store, new employees are "schooled in the Nordstrom service philosophy and encouraged to work on enhancing the customer service experience one customer at a time" (p. 31). During new employee orientation, these same employees watch a video entitled, *Seeing Your Business through the Eyes of the Customer*. Sustainable public libraries have a customer service philosophy. Like Nordstrom's, this philosophy should be grounded in the action of thinking like a customer: that is, looking at the library and its offerings through the eyes of the customer and with the customer's lifestyle, and likely wants, in mind.

Little academic research has been done in the area of customer service philosophy, but practitioners have much to say on the topic. Rowson (2009) relates eight steps to developing a customer service philosophy. She starts by suggesting that the mission statement have a customer service orientation. She adds that it is important for the philosophy to be embraced throughout the organization. Her steps are:

1. Develop a customer service orientated mission statement.
2. Set standards of what is expected of everyone.
3. Develop and adopt effective communications.
4. Motivate staff for exceptional customer service.
5. Provide ongoing staff training and development.
6. Develop and incorporate a system to measure, monitor, and reward performance.
7. Plan for providing continuing customer care.
8. Most importantly, involve staff in all the above. Foster good teamwork and lead by example (Rowson, 2009, p. 30).

Clark (2012) helps organizations create a customer service philosophy by using what she terms the four aspects of a strong customer service philosophy. In her opinion, these are: "Use common sense, flexibility, solving issues, and recovery." Clark posits that "performing things that seem apparent" is a good place to start. Much like what was related in the Nordstrom example, one should look at any situation from the customer's point of view. For Clark, flexibility means using policies and procedures as guidelines, while staff are be empowered not only to do the right thing, but also to act in the best interest of the customer (2012). For Clark's model, when it comes to solving issues, this would include both handling customer complaints and also solving issues that seemingly have little to do with the library. Doing so helps the library from a public relations standpoint, especially when it is something the library can offer to assist the customer. Last is recovery, whereby the staff is trained how to bring some sort of satisfaction to the customer, when a situation or interaction has not gone well for the customer during his or her interaction with the library.

Finally, Read (2016) states his philosophy, which involves "putting the customer first, focusing on a consistent experience, and implementing the philosophy from the top down." What differentiates Read from the others is his incorporation of the various means by which a customer might interact with the organization, from social media to e-mail to an in-person visit. He stresses that the experience should be similar across platforms. He also balks at customer service philosophies that wish to "delight" customers. He notes that in this self-service age, customers are perfectly happy to find answers on their own (say, on an organization's Web site or user-community group), but when they can't find the answer they will want to communicate with an employee who can solve their problem.

In analyzing all these sources, the commonalities become clear. A strong customer service philosophy is embraced by all employees; it features standards, it empowers employees to solve customer problems, it is always consistent, and it rewards employees for a job well done. Read describes an evaluation component that circles back to the standards, and it most certainly includes a training component. In fact, it can be summed up by the acronym SECRET, as in the "secret" to a strong customer service philosophy:

S tandards
E mpowerment of employees
C onsistent across the organization and its platforms
R eward for a job well done
E valuation of the service
T raining

How does a library know it is deploying good customer service? There are two potential metrics some libraries have borrowed from business: the net promoter score and mystery shopping.

Net Promoter Score

The net promoter score was first developed by Fred Reichheld in 2003. A partner at Bain & Company (2017), Reichheld identified the most powerful survey question in terms of predicting future purchase and referral behavior. The question was: "On a scale of 1 to 10, what is the likelihood that you would recommend Company X to a friend or colleague?" No other question performed as well in terms of correlating to the behavior the company desired. Thus was born the net promoter score. Net promoter surveys can be administered through a link on a Web site, a notation on a transaction receipt, or a verbal request at the end of a call. These surveys should be tied to a transaction via an in-person checkout or after a download or hold request from a library Web site.

A net promoter score is typically calculated as follows: Any respondent to a survey who scores the question at 9 or 10 is considered a promoter. A score of 7 to 8 is considered passive. A score of 6 or lower is considered to come from a detractor. The net promoter score is calculated by subtracting the detractors from the promoters. Hyken (2016) appreciates the brevity of the net promoter score, but he believes a follow-up question or two are warranted. For him, these are: "Why?" and, if the number is lower than a 10, "What would it take to raise our score just by one point?" (in other words, to go from a 6 to a 7, or from a 9 to a 10).

The net promoter score is not a grading of the employee the customer interacted with but rather a grading of the experience. Ultimately, the net promoter score was developed to ascertain loyalty, as loyalty to a particular company is a good indicator of future profit. Although libraries don't profit literally, they do benefit from loyalty. That is to say, they benefit from loyalty at the ballot box, and they benefit from more people using the library, which solidifies the library's importance in the minds of community members.

Mystery Shoppers

Mystery shoppers are used heavily in retail and restaurants, but not so often in libraries. Complaints may arise from public service staff that it is a form of spying on staff. However, one Southeastern library system successfully defended the implementation of the program by linking it to a reward system. A staff member on the service end of a successful mystery shop is rewarded with a gift card or half day off and her or his colleagues are treated to a catered lunch.

Here's how this library system's mystery shopping program works: The library contracts with a local company that hires shoppers for retail locations, restaurants, and now libraries. The shoppers have a script they follow. They are looking for a particular item to check out. The shopper has a list of matters to record on a check-sheet. Some of these are (in no particular order): Time and date of visit. Were they greeted upon entering? Was the entryway free of trash and clutter? Was the location neat and orderly? How busy was the location (ranges of number of people are listed)? Did someone offer to help them? Did a staff member look for an item or offer the shopper help in placing a hold on the item?

Mystery shoppers help staff and thus the library be consistent in their service offering and help all customers to have a better experience when visiting the library. No library director or senior staff member wants to hear from a board member, "Can the staff please acknowledge customers when they enter?" This plea is invariably followed by the information that the board member was not greeted when he or she entered the library that day.

SUSTAINABILITY FUTURECAST

Perhaps one day a public library leader will measure customer loyalty and report back to customers on the value they exact from the library. Many librarians are familiar with the Library Value Calculator (ALA, 2017). Reported to have been developed by the Massachusetts Library Association (MLA), the Library Value Calculator was first put into use by the Chelmsford (MA) Public Library, which was presented with an Ebsco Library Advocacy Award for its effort in 2009. The Library Value Calculator allows a customer to enter how many times he engaged in a particular activity (e.g., borrowed a book, downloaded an article, etc.) and it then calculates a total value for the combined activity. Thus, if a customer tracked all his library use accurately over the course of a year, and then entered it, he would know the value he got from the local library. The library should be applauded for the original effort and be credited for all the libraries that have since put the calculator (freely shared by MLA and the Chelmsford Public Library) on their respective Web sites, so that customers could engage in an opportunity to calculate the worth their library delivers to them.

However, this many years later, can the library community improve upon this initiative? Why not automatically calculate the value for customers and place it within their viewable customer records? Linked library cards could roll up the data for all household members. Over the years, a lifetime value could be calculated as well and also shared with the customer. Might this data also be helpful for staff, to keep them more informed about a particular customer's amount of engagement with the library?

Customer Surveys

The net promoter score survey detailed earlier is not the only kind of survey libraries should be promulgating. There are other customer satisfaction surveys, phone surveys, IT use surveys, jobs surveys. In fact, there are so many types of surveys that customers and staff alike can grow weary of them. That is why the use of surveys should likely be mapped out a year at a time so they don't overlap or run one into the other.

As a general rule, surveys should be mission aligned. What are the results going to tell the library system to help staff further the mission of the library? Surveys can also help directionally. By repeating an extremely similar survey year after year at the same time of year, the library can gauge progress on whatever item the library is trying to measure. This is called a *tracking survey*. Another general rule of surveys is to keep them as short as possible. A common audience libraries do not survey is nonusers or lapsed users. A question to ask them would simply be: Why do they not or no longer use the library?

National Surveys

Libraries can participate in national surveys. A beauty of such surveys is they usually allow the library to be compared to the other libraries taking the survey. One such survey is the University of Washington iSchool's *Advancing Libraries Through Community Insight* (ALTCI) impact survey (University of Washington Information School, 2017). Begun in 2013, ALTCI, per the iSchool's Web site, is "designed specifically for public libraries that want to better understand their communities and how people use their public technology resources and services." It is a low-cost, relatively simple survey to implement.

Another national program is the Urban Libraries Council's (ULC's) and PLA's Edge initiative. Edge is an information technology assessment program/toolkit that has a customer survey as one of its many components. Edge was first developed in 2011 with work from many groups in the public library sphere, including ULC, PLA, ALA, International City/County Manager's Association, the Bill & Melinda Gates Foundation, the University of Washington iSchool, some state libraries, and other nonprofit library groups. "Edge is based on a national set of library benchmarks for public libraries to evaluate their technology services via strategic planning and community engagement" (Urban Libraries Council, 2017). Edge has been described in some ways as similar to the Leadership in Environmental and Energy Design (LEED) program discussed in Chapter 3. Just as the LEED level (LEED, LEED Silver, LEED Gold, and LEED

Platinum) connotes how environmentally friendly a building is, an Edge score connotes how the technology of a library or library system compares against national benchmarks of libraries of a similar size. It is not meant to detract from the library, but rather to give it hard data, which library leaders can then use to advocate for greater technology funding. Edge is accessible to any public library through the Edge Web site (http://www .libraryedge.org/library/register).

Another national survey initiative is PLA's Project Outcome (2017). Outcomes measurement was discussed earlier in this chapter, but users should know that outcome measurements can also be collected via surveys. As of this writing, PLA has created outcome measurement surveys and accompanying training via Project Outcome, an initiative supported by the Bill & Melinda Gates Foundation. As stated previously, libraries may use this data to ascertain how they are performing against their goals and report on their achievements to their stakeholders. Project Outcome has been field-tested and PLA reports that it is easy to use. Per PLA's Web site, Project Outcome helps libraries measure four key patron outcomes—knowledge, confidence, application, and awareness—in seven key library service areas:

- Civic/Community Engagement
- Digital Learning
- Economic Development
- Education/Lifelong Learning
- Early Childhood Literacy
- Job Skills
- Summer Reading

The University of Washington iSchool impact survey, the ULC's Edge initiative, and PLA's Project Outcome give public libraries standardized benchmarked data that allows them to report out data that is used by other libraries to help measure their return on investment (ROI) and to help make the case that not only is the library sustainable, but it is helping the community to be sustainable as well.

SUSTAINABILITY FUTURECAST

In their book *Big Data,* Mayer-Schönberger and Cukier (2013) posited that no longer did researchers have to collect data and then extrapolate the result via statistics, which they nearly likened to an educated guess. Rather, with big data one can collect all the data and report out an exact number for whatever the investigator was inquiring after. Could library leaders do this with their outcomes measures? Could they build a mobile phone application (app) that could be used at, for example, story time, whereby a parent could check in via the app or with a swipe of their child's library card, attend the story time and then be sent a short survey to complete via the app as story time is wrapping up? Better still, could the app track the child's progress on the preliteracy skills outlined in another PLA partnership program, Every Child Ready to Read?[2] Could the app also offer video tutorials and learning games for the child and track the books the child's parent had checked out and read to the child? Last, barring any learning disability, could the app, after all the steps suggested had been taken, inform the parents that they had "built a reader" and their child was ready for kindergarten? Could other, similar apps be developed for other library out-comes to be measured? Could the library then perhaps have a system through which it could track all customer data, survey responses, library program progression, even library use by dollar value gained or some other measure? If so, what would the system be called? Has anyone ever built such a system?

Customer Relationship Management Systems

Customer relationship management (CRM) systems were first developed for the business world in the mid-1980s (CRM Switch, 2013). At that time the systems were databases primarily used for direct response marketing. Companies would build lists of customers, either companies or consumers, and sell the information to other interested companies that wanted to market to them. Robert and Kate Kestnbaum, a married couple from Chicago, first hit upon the idea to track customer sales, interactions (from various sources), and the relationship in general via computer software (Kestnbaum, Kestnbaum, & Ames, 1998). They are considered by many to be the father and mother of CRM. Now, with modern systems relying on cloud-based computing and tracking social media data as well, perhaps today's systems have even exceeded their expectations.

In essence, current integrated library systems (ILSs) are a precursor of modern-day CRM systems for libraries at least. If public libraries only allowed customers to borrow books, the ILS system in effect could act as a CRM. Unfortunately, ILS vendors have not kept up with the modern public library, which offers so many more services than just lending books and other physical materials. A CRM system absolutely does not replace an ILS; thus, something more is needed. Nevertheless, as long as libraries have physical books and materials to lend, a computerized system of some sort is needed that can keep an inventory of all the books and materials and match them up to any customer in the database that wishes to borrow them. The ILS does many other things as well, including but not limited to assigning library card numbers, keeping track of fines, and allowing customers to renew items, among others.

Commercial CRM systems abound, but they are expensive. Often they are set up as software-as-a-service (SaaS) ventures which require steep annual renewal fees. Still, if they can keep track of all customer interactions with a customer, as well as the customer relationship, might they be worth it? Privacy issues certainly come up, but library staffs have always had access to customers' records, and if the proper data protection and access measures are in place there should be no privacy problems. Today's consumer expects Amazon and other similar Web sites to know their interests and track their habits and purchases. They expect Netflix to make recommendations based on their viewing behavior. Often customers may wonder why the library *doesn't* offer recommendations on its Web site, based on their reading habits. "They know what I read!," a customer might posit. Customers also expect a library to know how they are accessing the library. They don't see the library's various vendors that make up the collection as distinct. The relationship they have should be with the library, not a vendor such as Hoopla or Over-drive. The fact remains that last week Ms. X downloaded music, borrowed a large print book, and downloaded a newspaper from the library. Additionally, any staff Ms. X contacts, in the customer's mind, should know what she accessed via the library, especially if she has a problem with any of the transactions and needs help. If a customer says,

"I had trouble downloading an e-book last week," the library staff member may spend a good deal of troubleshooting time trying to ascertain from which library vendor that customer borrowed the book. A proper CRM system would collect all of the information from the various vendors' sites and present it to the staffer.

Library CRM System

Five independent public library systems got together one day in the summer of 2013, in Columbus, Ohio, and asked a library vendor to build a library CRM system. The system is called Savannah and the vendor is Orangeboy.

What Does a CRM System for a Public Library Offer?

A library CRM system, such as Savannah, can help group customers into multiple like-groups. This might be by branch, by how they use the library, by what kind of materials they like to borrow, or because they signed up as jobseekers with the library's jobs program. This information can help the library market to the group or message them.

A message might invite them to attend an author talk by a famous businessperson because they have checked out business books in the past. Or, it could advise them that there is a career fair later in the week. It also might send them an e-mail warning that their branch is going to be closed to effect a repair. The CRM system could also send out a message to all individuals with fines over $15 asking them to make a payment with their specific amount listed in the e-mail and providing an electronic link in the e-mail to do so.

The CRM system would allow a staffer to pull up a specific customer's usage report so that the staffer could see all the ways the customer uses the library. This could help the staff member easily determine a particular type of library product with which the customer was having a problem. If a library system was going to be opening all its branches late the following morning due to a snowstorm, all customers could be notified via the CRM system. The system can also administer surveys and aggregate results or make them available by customer if a library chooses to view them that way. This could be highly helpful in tracking outcomes, as detailed earlier in this chapter. Such a system is probably most powerful or of greatest use to the library when it can aggregate data and crunch through it, providing combined reports across various products, or looking at geographical data or customer penetration numbers. The fact that business has been using such systems for more than 20 years and libraries are only starting to make use of them now might give some individuals pause. However, the fact that libraries are making use of such technology should be heralded.

Market Segmentation Study

If a library system cannot afford a CRM system, perhaps it can afford to conduct a market segmentation study. According to Kucukemiroglu (1999), "market segmentation allows a population to be viewed as distinct individuals with feeling and tendencies, addressed in compatible groups (segments) to make more efficient use of mass media" (p. 473). His colleagues Kaynak and Kara (1996) state: "[T]he basic premise of such research is that the more marketers know and understand about their customers, the more effectively they can communicate with and serve them" (as cited in Kucukemiroglu, 1999, p. 473).

By analyzing how library customers use the library and classifying them into like groups, the library can better market to the groups and better understand how best to deploy limited resources. Of course, catalog data, e-resource usage reports, and public PC data can be analyzed, but yet another way to categorize customers is by adding a listing of 10 or so segments to the library card application. A person applying for a new library card or updating her or his record may elect checkboxes such as "I am interested in: Business, Travel, Home Décor, and Parenting," for example.

Collecting this lifestyle data could go a long way toward how the library markets to this particular customer. Note, though, that if one is going to collect the information, one should do something with it—something, that is, that benefits the customer. Collected data that doesn't benefit the customer could make some customers feel the library is taking advantage of them. A famous marketing adage goes, "If you're going to ask customers for their birthdate, you better send them a card." With e-mail, that is not hard to do. A system could be set up to automatically send customers an e-birthday card, telling them how much you appreciate them as a customer on their special day. This comes with a word of caution: There are federal laws regarding the protection of minors and Web communication with them. Be sure you are aware of these laws pertaining to those under age 13 and abide by them.

Chief Customer Experience Officer, Advocate, or Ombudsman

Sustainable libraries employ a chief customer experience officer, advocate, or ombudsman, whose job it is to look out for the customers' best interest. This individual may be the head of a customer care department that answers all phone and e-mail inquiries, takes care of phone renewals, answers Web chat questions, helps troubleshoot customers' technology issues, monitors social media, posts on social media on behalf of the library, administers surveys, and sends out targeted e-mail marketing messages to customers. This department would also monitor the engagement of new library cardholders to make sure they are making use of the library. The presumption is that the library spent a great deal of time and possibly money recruiting a new customer. If the new customer is not engaging with the library within the first 30 to 90 days, she or he is likely a lost customer, before she or he even got started using the library. At present, the best way to engage such customers is a series of e-mails, each promoting one popular service. The idea is to get customers to use the library early on, so they remain customers for life.

Sometimes the chief customer experience officer is in charge of all of public services, outreach, the Web site, and collection management: any place where the customer is going to interface with the library. Other times the individual may serve as an advocate for customers or as an ombudsman working with the library as the voice of the customer (VOC). The concept of VOC grew out of the total quality management (TQM) framework embraced by many U.S. companies in the 1980s and 1990s (Griffin & Hauser, 1993). TQM was begun in Japan in the 1970s by American management professor W. Edwards Deming (Union of Japanese Scientist and Engineers, 2015). "Firms that adopt and implement TQM tend to experience improved market share, increased profitability and customer satisfaction, as well as improved employee relations" (Stratton, 1991, p. 70). TQM will be covered more thoroughly in Chapter 6, but for now this section touches on this one aspect of it.

VOC is used in manufacturing to bring all departments of a company together (e.g., engineering, research and development, manufacturing, and marketing) to assess what the customer is looking to achieve with the product. The four facets of VOC, as defined within the TQM movement, are: 1) present data, 2) actions the organization can take, 3) implementation decisions, and 4) production planning. If one were to translate this into a library example, it might roll out as follows:

1. Customers have angst about their child's performance on a forthcoming statewide mandated high-stakes first grade-reading test debuting in two years. The library, hopefully working in a statewide coalition of libraries, would survey parents of preschool children to collect data.
2. The library would determine what can it do, what is within its skillset, and what partners it might want to work with.
3. It would implement the decisions.
4. The library would plan out the project, creating a development plan for the reading program, the app, the toolkit, the partnership, or whatever else the library or library community, with the customers' input in mind, decided to roll out to combat the parental angst and help the children be successful on the test.

VOC is more than hearing customer complaints and addressing them. Instead, it is about designing the library's services around what the customer is attempting to achieve. Market segmentation, described in the previous section, helps the library staff prioritize the needs of the customers based on collective groups rather than anecdotal input from one parent or another.

Programs and policies that leading libraries have implemented by listening to their customers include:

- Eliminating fines on juvenile and young adult materials.
- Debuting a library card for youth called "3 to Go," which allows children to check out up to three items without parental permission. Parents were advised that the child had such a library card and were encouraged to trade the child's card up to a regular card. However, with many parents unwilling to allow their child to get a card because the parent did not want to take responsibility for the materials, this new type of card allowed children to use the library and access the library's online homework help tutors and databases.
- Allowing customers to apply for a card online and get immediate access to electronic resources. The card was then activated and mailed to the customer at her or his home address. The act of mailing the card to a specific address verified that the address was legitimate.
- Allowing customers to continuously renew books (for up to one year) as long as no other customer had placed a hold on or request for the item.
- Allowing customers to use public computers for longer than an hour if no one was waiting to use them.
- Setting up parking spaces dedicated for Wi-Fi users and boosting the Wi-Fi to that area of the parking lot.

As part of his library's "Our Library Means Business" campaign, one library director negotiated with Federal Express to place FedEx boxes at all city library locations. This way the libraries could market several freely accessible, business-centric services as follows:

- Wi-Fi
- Wireless printing

- Computers and printers
- Business newspapers and databases
- Business librarians
- Federal Express services
- Clean restrooms

The most important concept when it comes to customer service is to treat all customers with respect and to be friendly to them. One would laugh at a book titled *Customer as Enemy*, yet most people have been on the phone with a company's customer service representative where that's exactly how they felt; customers did feel they were *not* being served. If one thinks of one's favorite restaurant or retail store, what makes it a favorite choice? Now, ask the same individual to think of the last time she or he had a poor customer experience? How did those two experiences differ? The customer was the same individual in both scenarios. Yet, the customer might feel like a completely different person depending on the experience: warm and friendly during the good experience, but during the poor experience . . . probably not. It stands to reason that both good and bad treatment tend to be reciprocated in kind.

Can a library have rules and still be friendly? Yes. Signs on the front door that apply to a small percentage of visitors that read: "NO LARGE BAGS, NO CARTS ALLOWED!!!" are not considered welcoming. The sign should instead read "Welcome to the library. We're glad you're here!" To handle the bags and carts, one enterprising library set up a test holder similar to those used at airport gates. The attached sign read, "Please ensure that all your belongings fit within this space." The library backed up this request by placing a set of athletic gear lockers, made of wire mesh and larger than an average locker, in its attached parking garage. Locks were available for checkout. Customers could store their large items in the lockers free of charge.

One library strove to avoid signs that read "No." It had rules of conduct posted, but not front and center. Instead, it had a sign that read: "Please respect this building, its contents, and all who enter it." The sign included a footnote that referred the reader to the code of conduct, which was also written in a friendly tone.

This same library was subject to a state law that prohibited guns from being brought into the library. The library did deploy a professional-looking sign of a gun within a circle, with a line through it (the universal "NO" symbol). However, the sign referred to the state statute that barred guns from the library rather than any rules the library had about no guns being allowed on the premises. The no-camping sign in the parking lot also referenced the applicable city ordinance.

Staff members were also trained to provide people with options. Rather than saying, "You can't talk on your cellphone in here," staff said, "Would you please take the call in the vestibule? Thank you." Children roughhousing or swearing in the library were told, "You can do that outside, but not in here." Although there is a bit of a "no" embedded in that last statement, it is still an example of saying "you have options." The children invariably stopped the troublesome behavior.

Is the Customer Always Right?

Is the customer always right? Not necessarily, but it usually isn't about who is in the right or who is in the wrong; most often, it's about getting to "yes." Fisher and Ury (1981), of the Harvard Negotiation Project, urged their readers to find out what was the "interest" behind the request when they found themselves in a negotiation. Although better books on negotiating have been published since, this still is a great principle to apply when trying to reach a resolution with a customer. As an example, a customer goes to the circulation desk and says, "I need this book for three months. May I check it out for that long?" The likely answer is "no." If the customer service associate (CSA) at the desk asks why, it may seem intrusive, and library service guidelines may even preclude such a question; thus, the CSA is likely to simply deny the request. Better training would say the CSA's response should be something along the lines of: "That's beyond our normal lending period, but let me see what we can do. Are you a teacher?" (Teacher-customers in some library systems can borrow a book for an extended period of time if it is being used in teaching.) If the answer is, "Yes, I'm a teacher," and the person's customer-type in the ILS confirms this, problem solved. If the answer is "no, but I'm a student," a judgment call can be made. If it is an obscure book that hasn't been checked out in nine months, consider allowing it, if the ILS system permits. If the library system allows unlimited renewals on items for which no one has placed a hold, the CSA can tell the customer, "You're in luck, you can continually renew this book up to [here state the policy], as long as no one else requests it." By learning what's behind a request, one can often find a solution to aid the customer. Customers are *not* the enemy: They *are* the library's reason for being.

CHAPTER SUMMARY

This chapter covered the external social steps toward creating a sustainable library. These include aligning the library's strategic plan with the parent jurisdiction's or community's goals, providing relevant programming via partners or staff, and reporting achievements via outcome measures. Public libraries should also work to mitigate risk and properly manage the organization's reputation, as well as ensure that vendors are upholding ethical sourcing standards and are in full compliance with all federal, state, and locally mandated labor laws. Public libraries should also deliver excellent customer service by creating a customer service philosophy, utilizing customer surveys and when possible a customer relationship management system. They should also employ a champion for the customer experience and measure progress against previously mentioned outcomes. Chapter 5 looks at internal social sustainability, which concerns the workforce and how the library management team should support its greatest asset: its employees.

NOTES

1. Based in Dayton, Ohio, the National Issues Forums Institute (NIFI, 2015) is a nonprofit, nonpartisan organization that serves to promote public deliberation and coordinate activities. Its activities include publishing the issue guides and other materials used by local forum groups, encouraging collaboration among forum sponsors, and sharing information about current activities in the network.

2. Every Child Ready to Read was developed by PLA in partnership with the Association for Library Service to Children (ALSC) in 2001 (Ash & Meyers, 2009). Based on early childhood brain development research, the basic tenets of ECRR were developed by Whitehurst and Lonigan, two well-known researchers in emergent literacy. Their task was to develop a model program that would enlist parents and caregivers as active participants in preparing their children to read.

The researchers created a structure based on the distinctive phases of a young child's emerging literacy: early talkers, talkers, and pre-readers. Within this structure, six pre-reading skills were identified: narrative skills, print motivation, vocabulary, phonological awareness, letter knowledge, and print awareness.

FURTHER READING

The Aspen Institute. (2014). *Rising to the challenge: Re-envisioning public libraries.* Retrieved from http://csreports.aspeninstitute.org/documents/Aspen-LibrariesReport-2017-FINAL .pdf

The Aspen Institute. (2016). *Action guide for re-envisioning your public library.* Retrieved from http://www.libraryvision.org/download_action_guide

Soete, G. (1998). *Customer service programs in ARL libraries: A SPEC kit* (No. 231). Retrieved from http://old.arl.org/bm~doc/spec-231-flyer.pdf

Urban Libraries Council. (2017). Making Cities Stronger. Retrieved from http://www.urban.org /sites/default/files/publication/46006/1001075-Making-Cities-Stronger.PDF

REFERENCES

American Library Association. (2015). *Communities have challenges. Libraries can help: A step-by-step guide to "turning outward" to your community.* Retrieved from http://www.ala.org /tools/sites/ala.org.tools/files/content/LTCGettingStarted_DigitalWorkbook_final010915 .pdf

American Library Association. (2017). Library value calculator. Retrieved from http://www.ala .org/advocacy/advleg/advocacyuniversity/toolkit/makingthecase/library_calculator

Ash, V., & Meyers, E. (2009). Every child ready to read @ your library. *Children and Libraries, 7*(1), 3–7.

Bain & Company. (2017). About net promoter. Retrieved from http://www.netpromotersystem.com /about/

Bennett, W., & Lagos, T. (2007). Logo logic: The ups and downs of branded political communication. *Annals of the American Academy of Political and Social Science, 611*(1). Retrieved from http://journals.sagepub.com/doi/abs/10.1177/0002716206298484

Clark, A. (2012, November 28). Four fundamental aspects of a great customer service philosophy [I want it now: The customer engagement blog]. Retrieved from http://iwantitnow.walkme .com/4-fundamental-aspects-of-a-great-costumer-service-philosophy/

CRM Switch. (2013, September 12). A brief history of customer relationship management. Retrieved from https://www.crmswitch.com/crm-industry/crm-industry-history/

Drucker, P. (1986). *Management: Tasks, responsibilities, practices.* New York: Truman Talley.

Drucker, P. (2008). *The five most important questions you will ever ask about your organization.* San Francisco: Jossey-Bass.

Fair Labor Association. (2017). Home page. Retrieved from http://www.fairlabor.org

Feeney, M., & DeHart-Davis, L. (2009). Bureaucracy and public employee behavior. *Review of Public Personnel Administration, 29*(4). Retrieved from http://journals.sagepub.com/doi /abs/10.1177/0734371X09333201

Fisher, R., & Ury, W. (1981). *Getting to yes: Negotiating agreement without giving in.* New York: Houghton Mifflin.

Griffin, A., & Hauser, J. (1993). The voice of the customer. *Marketing Science, 12*(1), 1–27.

Hyken, S. (2016, December 3). *How effective is net promoter score (NPS)?* Retrieved from https://www.forbes.com/sites/shephyken/2016/12/03/how-effective-is-net-promoter-score-nps/#720adaf023e4

Kantabutra, S., & Avery, G. C. (2010). The power of vision: Statements that resonate. *Journal of Business Strategy, 31*(1), 37–45.

Kaynak, E., & Kara, A. (1996). Consumer life-style and ethnocentrism:. A comparative study in Kyrgyzstan and Azerbaijan. In *Esomar Marketing Research Congress*. Esomar. *49th Esomar Congress Proceedings*, 577–596. Istanbul: Esomar.

Kestnbaum, R., Kestnbaum, K., & Ames, P. (1998). Building a longitudinal contact strategy. *Journal of Interactive Marketing, 12*(1), 56–62.

Kucukemiroglu, O. (1999). Market segmentation by using consumer lifestyle dimensions and ethnocentrism: An empirical study. *European Journal of Marketing, 33*(5/6), 470–487.

Matarazzo, J., & Pearlstein, T. (2015). Corporate libraries: Bellwether of change for the library world at large. *Biblioteca Universitaria, 18*(1), 3–12.

Mayer-Schönberger, V., & Cukier, K. (2013). *Big data: A revolution that will transform how we live, work, and think*. London: John Murray.

National Issues Forums Institute. (2015). National Issues Forums Institute: About. Retrieved from https://www.nifi.org/en/about

Negri, P. (1999). *The wit and wisdom of Mark Twain: A book of quotations*. Mineola, NY: Dover.

Public Library Association. (2017). Performance measurement. Retrieved from http://www.ala.org/pla/initiatives/performancemeasurement

Read, A. (2016, September 29). Empower your team with a customer service philosophy. Retrieved from https://www.kayako.com/blog/customer-service-philosophy/

Rowson, P. (2009). *Successful customer service: Get brilliant results fast*. Richmond, UK: Crimson Business.

Senge, P. (1990). *The fifth discipline: The art and practice of the learning organization*. New York: Doubleday.

Shaffer, G. (2003, October 7). A new tool in the marketing arsenal. *Marketingprofs.com*. Retrieved from http://www.marketingprofs.com/3/shaffer1.asp

Spector, R., & McCarthy, P. (2012). *The Nordstrom way to customer service excellence* (2d ed.). Hoboken, NJ: John Wiley & Sons.

Starr, K. (2012, September 18). The eight-word mission statement: Don't settle for more. *Stanford Social Innovation Review*. Retrieved from https://ssir.org/articles/entry/the_eight_word_mission_statement

Stratton, B. (1991). The value of implementing quality. *Quality Progress, 24*(7), 70–71.

Union of Japanese Scientist and Engineers. (2015). How was the Deming Prize established. Retrieved from https://www.juse.or.jp/deming_en/award/index.html

University of Washington Information School. (2015, April 23). *U.S. Impact Study*. Retrieved from http://impact.ischool.uw.edu/

Urban Libraries Council. (2017). *About Edge*. Retrieved from http://www.libraryedge.org/about-edge

5

Social (Internal)

The library workforce is the costliest part of the library's budget, as well as the library's greatest asset. Without library staff, a library is an unkempt building with disorganized and outdated books and nothing more. School libraries without librarians were recently discussed at a public library staff meeting. The collection management team was asked: How long before these school libraries' collections are completely out of date? They surmised four to five years. That is *completely* out of date; parts of that collection will unfortunately be out of date much sooner.

This book does not distinguish between libraries that are unionized or without a union. The principles by which a library becomes sustainable do not change depending on whether a bargaining unit exists or not. It is in every employee's best interest, whether employees are represented by a union or not, that the library be sustainable.

This said, how does a sustainable library take care of its greatest asset? Start by fully supporting the workforce, by maintaining open communications, and by having the leadership team and all employees interact and recognize their colleagues for jobs well done.

10. SUPPORT THE WORKFORCE

Start with good screening practices in the employee interview process. Provide robust onboarding and training, including leadership development; cross-training; and federal, state, and locally mandated training; as well as safety training. Measure employee satisfaction, and uphold fair and equitable labor practices, including but not limited to hiring minority candidates, veterans, and those on the lower end of the economic scale.

The onboarding process for a new employee starts when the recruiter (a library leadership team member, a human resources specialist, or a fellow employee) first meets a potential hire out in the world. The potential employee in this case has never thought of working at a library. Instead, a library staffer has observed the individual, most likely exhibiting excellent customer service skill in a place of business. The library staffer approaches the individual with a quick statement such as:

"You are really great at handling customers. While you may not be looking for a new career right now, if you're ever in the market, please give me a call," the library staffer says while handing a business card to the customer-service star. "The library offers excellent pay and benefits. My _#_ colleagues and I serve over __#__ customers each and every day. We need great people like you!"

Library staff should always be on the lookout for good talent, even if no positions are currently available. In the preceding example, the potential candidate was already gainfully employed, but the library would want this individual in its candidate pool when a library position opens up.

The Hiring Screening Process

The hiring screening process typically works as follows: A library posts a job and candidates apply. A hiring manager goes through the applications and narrows the pool to the few best candidates for the position, perhaps the most qualified or the best at personal marketing, and a phone or online interview may take place. The hiring manager may also ask the candidates to come in for a job interview. Attention is given to the following:

* Did the candidates fill out the job application in its entirety?
* Did the candidates show up on time or a few minutes early?
* Were the candidates dressed appropriately for the interview?
* Did the candidates come prepared? Had they done their research on the library?
* Did the candidates have concise answers to common interview questions?
* Did the candidates come prepared with a few questions?
* Did the candidates bring all paperwork they were requested to bring?

The library staff has very little to go on in assessing any candidate, especially if it has no experience with the candidate who is an external hire; thus, unfortunately, each action or misstep of the candidate is magnified.

The Most Important Things in the Screening Process

The most important items to cover in terms of the screening process are:

* To convey to the candidate the nature and pace of the work. A common response to the question, "Why do you want to work at the library?" is, "I love books." Too bad the answer isn't, "I love to help people!" This answer reflects the word in the title of the organization that precedes "library": "public," based on an ancient Latin word for *of the people*. Many may want to work at the library because they think the pace is slow or because they think they will be interacting with books all day rather than people. These misconceptions must be quickly dispatched.
* To hire the best candidate. That may not be the one who most resembles the hiring manager. Human resources personnel and library managers do a great disservice to their institution when the staff, which should be diverse and representative of the community it serves, lacks diversity.

Far too often, all the candidates put forward are from the same background, have similar dispositions, went to the same schools, grew up in the same neighborhood, shop at the same stores, and have the same hobbies and interests. When this is the case, it is highly unlikely that the library will be representative of the community it serves.

When it seems difficult to find diverse librarians, a library may have to grow staff from within, encourage promising staff to get an accredited master's degree in library and information science, and even assist them with scholarships. At least one library in the study received scholarship money from a donor in order to help fund both the master's degree in library and information science and bachelor's degrees for employees.

• To ensure that staff conducting interviews are trained in the process, have answers to questions commonly asked by candidates, and are aware of the questions one can legally ask and not ask in an interview.

Employee Onboarding

"Employee onboarding should not be confused with new-hire orientation, which is often a discrete, stand-alone event, conducted by a human resources representative" (Graybill, Hudson Carpenter, Offord, Piorun, & Shaffer, 2013). The goals of onboarding are:

To create an inviting and positive experience for the new employee, outline the importance of communication and how it flows within the organization, align the new employee with key business strategies and outline how the new hire will contribute to the overall mission and vision of the organization. (Workforce Management, 2009)

Best practices in library onboarding identified by Graybill and colleagues (2013) include discussion or documentation regarding six areas: socialization, policies, communication, mentoring/buddy, a checklist for all levels, and the length of the onboarding program.

Socialization—May begin (via LinkedIn, Facebook, and e-mail) before the employee starts, including, possibly, in the recruitment stage to allow new hires to network with colleagues. It also includes introduction to the mission, vision, and values of the organization, along with explanation of the position; training or shadowing; expectations and evaluation criteria; organizational history; culture; language; structure; and politics and people.

Policies—Include leave; attendance; nondiscrimination; eating and drinking rules; phone etiquette; safety and security, including disaster planning and evacuation procedures; and compensation and benefits.

Communication—Explains computer set-up on day one; training on how to use the library's employee portal (intranet); supplying frequently asked questions and answers; supplying an employee handbook or access to an online version of the handbook; training for institution e-mail and a guide for usage; phone set-up; introducing staff to library listservs and automatically subscribing the new staff members; providing business cards when applicable to the position (on the first day); and discussing the employee's and manager's preferred communication styles.

Mentoring/buddy—Officially assign both a mentor and a buddy. Nelson and Sperl say the buddy relationship differs from a mentoring relationship in that a buddy is there to help the new hire become socialized (as cited in Graybill et al., 2013), whereas the mentor is there to answer questions about the work and processes. Both give the new hires someone other than their official supervisor to whom they may turn.

Checklist for all levels—Create checklists for managers, the employee, and the supervisor to ensure that everything that is to take place during the onboarding is happening at the pace (or as close as possible to the pace) at which it is supposed to happen.

Length of the onboarding program—Provide onboarding for a sufficient length of time. The median for best-practice organizations in the Graybill study was from 6 to 9 months, with regular check-ins at 30, 60, and 90 days and again at the end of the official onboarding process. Length depends on what is to be accomplished as part of onboarding. Often a new hire still feels new six months into a new job.

Graybill and colleagues (2013) stress that the cost of bringing on a new employee is tremendous, and that replacing employees is even more costly. Anything that can be done to ease new employees into the workplace and get them contributing to the goals of the organization as quickly as possible is of benefit to the new hire, his or her colleagues, and the organization as a whole. A final strong suggestion: Give every new hire a task on day one that can reasonably be accomplished on that first day, so that new hires can feel as if they are contributing from the very start.

Training

On average, 3 million U.S. workers leave their employment every month (Bureau of Labor Statistics, 2017). When these millions walk out the door, they take a great deal of knowledge with them—not on hard drives or in the form of documents, but within the confines of their minds. One Southeastern library combated this phenomenon by having employees document all the processes they performed. They started with process #1 and at last count were at #456. Each process is 10 steps or fewer, and each step starts with an action verb. If it is more than 10, then in the opinion of this library's staff, it is more than one process. All of the processes are contained in a database accessible to all employees via the library's intranet. If an employee believes there is a better way to execute a process than currently resides in the database, there is a documented process for changing it. All of this was done to ensure that the library's employees got what they were rightly entitled to: the best training the library could deliver. The training is consistent. Trainers are certified. Employees have detailed written instructions for what they are expected to accomplish. If they wish to seek a promotion, they can access what processes are associated with a particular position. Further, when employees retire or leave library employment, they do not walk out with all the institutional knowledge. This said, the library's training system does not stop here.

Training also must include training concerning proper safety; emergency procedures; harassment (up to and including sexual harassment); ethics; and all mandated training regarding local, state, and federal laws. An employee should undergo this training as soon as possible. The best way to handle this is likely through online training that administers a quiz as it progresses, to check for retention of the information. If training is specific to the library, staff could record the training and have it available for new hires to watch in their first week of employment. Although such recordings may not be as professionally produced as some other products that were made for a national market, they will have a certain amount of charm and introduce the new hires to some of their new colleagues. If a live training session is recorded for future display to new hires, be sure to edit it. No one wants to view a recording of employees breaking into small discussion groups or the like. Instead, perhaps break away to a short clip of the library director in a studio having a discussion about the training with the human resources staff.

Group orientations are a wonderful way for new employees to meet their fellow new hires. However, often in libraries months can go by before one is held, leaving the new hire without critical information. Also, some library systems have been known not to require attendance at a group orientation until an employee is working full time, or at least between 20 and 30 hours a week. The problem with specifying a number of hours an employee must be working is that some employees could end up working for the library system for two or three years before they attend an orientation session. While a balance between full- and part-time employees is usually needed at a work location, there is a possibility that a part-time employee could make a career of the library. They need and likely deserve—and it is in the best interest of the library for them—to attend the same type of training full-time employees receive. An option might be a shorter orientation done regionally for part-time employees; or, again, prerecorded training could be used to convey the information.

Cross-Training

Cross-training is a technique whereby team members are trained in the duties of other team members in order to enhance performance of the team overall. Research conducted by Marks, Sabella, Burke, and Zaccaro (2002) indicates that cross-training helps team members:

with communication and coordination, by encouraging team members to understand the activities of those around them; to better understand what information needs to be shared and what activities must be performed interdependently; to better anticipate needs of their teammates and provide assistance to those that are in need of assistance. (p. 4)

Cross-training also assists with empathy building by allowing teammates to walk the proverbial mile in the shoes of their colleagues. When it comes to economic sustainability, cross-trained employees can assist when their colleagues are out sick or on vacation, so that work does not pile up awaiting the absent employee's return. One library that participated in the study allows employees to "try out" another position for which they are considering applying. This is another form of cross-training. The case study on this library is featured later in this chapter.

Cross-training is a win-win for employees, their colleagues, and the library. It helps employees see how different jobs fit together to deliver library service in as sustainable a way as possible.

Leadership Training

"Hidden leaders are those people in your organization who share the belief that what they do matters" (Kouzes, 2015, p. xii). Every organization has leaders hidden within. Some wish to lead and will, unfortunately, rise to their own level of incompetence (Peter, 1969); others are reluctant leaders who have to be pushed and prodded into a role their supervisor, manager, or director feels they were destined to fulfill.

Edinger and Sain (2015) identified five traits employers could look for to identify hidden leaders within an organization. Employers should look for those who:

- Demonstrate integrity
- Lead through authentic relationships
- Focus on results
- Work from a clear customer purpose
- Fulfill the value promise of the organization

Once leaders have been identified, consider formalized training. This could be through a national or state library association, a library cooperative, or a university.

Employee Satisfaction Surveys

Employee satisfaction surveys can be as simple as an anonymized web-based survey (e.g., SurveyMonkey) replete with questions gleaned from a manual on such surveys. They can also be as sophisticated as a validated and normalized survey instrument administered by a professional firm, which allows the organization to compare the satisfaction of the library's employees to the satisfaction of those in other organizations. The cross-tabulated features of such surveys allow incredible insights into the culture of the organization. When surveys are repeated year after year, or every two years, they also allow the library to compare itself to itself to see if certain measures are trending in a positive direction.

Measures of a survey can include, but are not necessarily limited to:

- Overall job satisfaction
- Overall work environment/culture
- Library's progress in last 12 months
- Amount of ongoing training
- Fulfillment of mission, vision, and values
- Level of recognition
- Job definition (requirements and responsibilities)
- Opportunity for advancement
- Perceived workload (challenging but fair, handle comfortably, etc.)
- Performance evaluation system
- Satisfaction with compensation

Although surveys with additional open-ended questions can provide valuable input, three cautions are warranted:

- Employees should be advised not to list information that could identify them if they do not wish to be identified.
- Open-ended questions should be included only if someone is going to read all the comments.
- Questions of an open-ended variety offer some employees a chance to vent anonymously.

However, if the information is not actionable, little can be done with it. The individual reading employee responses should prepare for the worst and hope for the best. Someone with thick skin can read the commentary and separate it into those requiring action (such as "I find the health plan difficult to navigate") and no action (such as personal comments about a supervisor's weight). Action items can then be grouped to streamline them.

No-action items, such as the slur about a supervisor's weight, should be quantified and shared with an independent third party and/or board member to ensure a level of transparency.

Survey results should be shared with staff. However, the amount of results can be enormous and too unwieldy to present to the library's board and staff in their entirety; thus, someone will need to ascertain what will be presented and what will not. A third-party representative along with a library board member should be involved. This third party needs to have access to all the results, so that nothing damning can be hidden or conveniently left on the proverbial cutting-room floor.

A standard survey tool is not the only way to gauge employee satisfaction. TINYpulse (Erikson, 2015) claims to "take the pulse" of an organization's workers through a weekly, one-question survey. When the information technology (IT) department of a particular company wished to address high employee turnover, it started using this tool. "The department manager would discuss the results of each week's survey with the entire department. He openly addressed the issues they raised. This step proved to be pivotal in improving morale." This reiterates the importance of doing something with the feedback gained, no matter what tool is used to gain that feedback.

The results of the employee satisfaction study could be abysmal or stellar, or anywhere in between. Regardless, there is always room for improvement. The responsibility for acting on any recommendations that come out of the survey should not fall only at the feet of library leadership. A staff committee should be formed, the recommendations should be divided up among the leadership and staff teams, and the findings should be tackled together. Staff and the library leadership must meet halfway on this. The state of the workplace is everyone's responsibility and everyone contributes to it. It is also in everyone's best interest to improve the culture of the organization, no matter how wonderful or lacking it might be. If everything is negative, the library has only one way to proceed—and that is up.

A Western library that had gone through a particularly tumultuous time for many years was faced with such a situation. The services of a third-party company that specialized in administering normed cultural surveys were employed, and the results proved that the situation was incredibly lacking. A retired city manager, who specialized in troubled organizations, was brought in to act as interim director. He worked with employees to identify a to-do list of more than 100 measures, which was updated monthly. Each measure was assigned a due date and was assigned to a specific individual, group of individuals, or a department. Over the course of 18 months, the library staff turned the library system around by tackling every item on the list. The important factor here was that employees had a hand in identifying the measures, as well as a hand in resolving any associated issues. The library could only progress in one direction. Morale improved, presumably because of the employees' involvement in identifying needed changes that were in fact undertaken.

Social Sustainability (Internal), Business Case Study

Best Practice: Measuring employee satisfaction

ASDIM is an airline serving domestic and international markets. ASDIM cites the work it does in the community and the positive impact this has on employee morale as

Continued

evidence of the internal social component of its TBL. Additionally, many company employees participate by donating their time to these company-supported enterprises. The company measures these practices via output measurements (e.g., how many tickets are given
away, how many volunteer hours employees log, etc.). ASDIM's internal social TBL sustainability is evident by high marks received on employee satisfaction surveys, which are
administered regularly.

TBL best practices are part of how ASDIM does business. The company does not have
to incorporate specific TBL language into everyday practices because the employees see
it as the way business is done. Public libraries can learn from how this airline has incorporated the TBL approach into its DNA.

To read this case study in its entirety, please see Appendix 1.

Discussion Questions:

1. Do you and your colleagues volunteer in the community? If yes, do you tally all the hours
   into one number to illustrate to the community how everyone working in the library
   makes a difference, even outside of the work everyone does at the library to help the
   community?
2. Does your library measure employee satisfaction via a survey? If yes, what happens
   with the results once the survey is completed?

Employee Compensation and Classification Studies

Compensation is not everything, but it is important. While a workplace satisfaction study
of some type is incredibly important, the library administration also needs to make sure it
is adequately compensating its workforce, and also needs to make sure the duties each
employee is performing falls in line with those of others who are within the same job classification. Thus, the sustainable public library occasionally performs a compensation
and classification study. Little scholarly work has been done in this very important area,
and a detailed explanation of the process is beyond the scope of this book. Needless to say,
such a study should be performed by a skilled professional or team of professionals.

Typically, a library would contract the services of a firm specializing in this area via
a request for proposal (RFP). The firm, working with library management and likely a
team of individuals from across the organization, would direct the organization to update
the job descriptions of all employees to better match their current duties. These would
be compared with the current job descriptions and current salaries. The job descriptions
would then be grouped into similar groups based on like duties and similar levels of
responsibility. Similar-position salaries in the community would be studied along with
salaries in other similarly sized libraries. Geographic salary factors would be considered as well (that is, salaries in a dense urban area are likely higher, because of cost-of-
living factors, than salaries in less-populated areas). After all data have been gathered,
the hired firm would take all the information under consideration, including the library's
available budget. Positions are then assigned to particular levels or grades and the hired
firm reports on how individual compensation should be changed. The hope is that no
one is reclassified as making less pay, though that does happen on occasion. In one case,

when a few staff were identified as being overcompensated based on the analysis, one library director whose library participated in a compensation and classification study carefully explained the situation to the affected employees. Once the employees understood the situation and what was to be done about it, the library froze those few employees' pay until they "caught up" to their current pay level. That is, they received no automatic pay increases, despite the fact that other employees were receiving performance increases, time-of-service increases, and/or cost-of-living increases. Although this took a few years, at least the employees never had to experience a pay cut.

Library administrators have also faced situations where they would like to raise compensation but have been unable to, based on budget constraints. Given the third-party analysis, they do have evidence on which to base a request to their governing agency or voters about the need for staff pay raises.

Many private sector companies and a few libraries adjust salaries based on merit. Again, a detailed explanation of this process is beyond the scope of this book, but should the library wish to enact such a system, it needs to ensure that the system is fair and equitable, that details and expectations are clearly outlined in advance, and that employees understand how the system works and how they can become eligible to earn a merit increase.

Fair and Equitable Labor

Many federal and state laws protect workers in the United States and other countries, and it is incumbent upon every manager, supervisor, and employee to be aware of them. The sustainable library ensures that adequate training is provided to all employees, dependent on their level within the organization. If libraries are employing workers under the age of 18, they should also make sure they adhere to the Fair Labor Standards Act (FLSA; U.S. Department of Labor, 2017) which states, in part:

Rules vary depending upon the particular age of a minor and the particular job involved. As a general rule, the FLSA sets 14 years of age as the minimum age for employment, and limits the number of hours worked by minors under the age of 16.

Many libraries today have human resources professionals because of the complexity of regulations and standards, as well as the possibility of lawsuits or other legal actions when regulations are not upheld. Not only must employees be trained, but their training must also be tracked, especially if they will be serving in a supervisorial capacity. All employees must be trained so that they are aware of the elements of a hostile workplace and how to avoid creating or participating in one. However, mandatory training based solely on legal requirements should not be the only training employees receive. The sustainable library looks to its workplace needs and provides training to answer those needs.

Just as vendors should be held to the standards of the Fair Labor Association (FLA) Workplace Code of Conduct (see Appendix 3), as discussed earlier, so should the library itself. Although posting is not required by federal law, library administrators may wish to consider posting this code in a staff room, if doing so is not redundant; at the very least, all supervisors should be made aware of it.

Hiring Diverse Individuals (Ethnic and Others), Veterans, and Those on the Lower End of the Economic Scale

Both the companies and the libraries participating in the study reported in this book were proud of the inclusive work they had completed in order to attract diverse individuals (ethnic and other), veterans, and those on the lower end of the economic scale into their workforces. The sustainable library has a staff that is reflective of its community and lifts all community members.

The librarian profession, in general, is considered to lack diversity. This, however, does not mean that no steps can be taken to diversify employee ranks. As discussed previously in this chapter, diverse candidates may be identified within the library and given help to attain additional training or formal education to fulfill job requirements for advanced positions within the library. Again, it is important to advertise positions in places where diverse populations will have greater opportunity to view them. Ethnic diversity is of course important, but libraries should not overlook other diverse populations: gay, lesbian, bisexual, transgender, and queer (GLBTQ); religiously affiliated individuals; returning veterans; and those, often through no fault of their own, who find themselves at the lower end of the economic scale.

II. MAINTAIN OPEN COMMUNICATIONS

Have an open-door policy and a pathway for employee feedback and input (not necessarily anonymous, the latter because many of the libraries participating in the study have moved away from anonymous feedback). Conduct performance reviews in a timely and thorough fashion. Create a learning organization.

Communication within organizations is often challenging. Thus, librarians need to work to facilitate it in every way. This should be done through a myriad of ways, such as postings on an internal intranet, employee newsletters, regular video announcements from library leaders, and standardized update reports that quickly communicate urgent need-to-know items, among many other possibilities.

Open-Door Policy

An open-door policy applies not only to the director of the library, but also to supervisors up and down and throughout the organization as well. The phrase is a bit of a euphemism which stands in for making oneself available to engage with employees. This said, a library leader who constantly has his or her door closed invites suspicion, regardless of whether or not anything nefarious is afoot.

An open-door environment can be brought into being in many ways. These include, but certainly are not limited to:

- Open calendars that allow others to view one's availability. Private appointments can be marked as private.
- Regular supervisor check-in with employees.
- Weekly written or video updates from the library director to staff.
- Five-minute morning check-in meetings before a facility opens, which everyone attends. (The team reports who is off; who is coming in later that day; any group, community leader, or outside colleague visits that are expected; who is out on an outreach call; whether all the equipment is working; and perhaps a joke or thought for the day.)
- News reports when the library is expected to be in the news that day; it is nice for employees to have advance warning of these occurrences.

- System-wide change alerts or down-reports, such as equipment or software that is not functioning fully or properly.
- Monthly or quarterly statistical reports that share how a location or department is contributing to the overall goals of the library; these could be prepared by the department itself and shared organization-wide.
- Staff intranet (perhaps entitled *In the Hopper*) with postings about policies, procedures, and new product or service offerings the library is entertaining the possibility of incorporating into its service offerings; employees should be able to offer feedback through this same medium.

Finally, the open-door policy can be fulfilled, as outlined in the following PLS Library case study, by having the library director be available in fact to meet with any employee via appointment. This erases a concern that the library director would need to drop everything to speak to any employee who happened by her or his office in order to have a true open-door policy. Interestingly, even with a policy that allows drop-in guests, experience shows that few employees will take advantage of this "open door"; most are extremely respectful of all their colleagues' time, including that of the library director.

These last few points do highlight the importance of two-way communication. It is critically important that libraries set up formal channels for employees to communicate among themselves, with their supervisors, and with leadership. This can be achieved online, via an employee staff group, or through union shop stewards.

Anonymous Employee Feedback

Anonymous employee feedback was not discussed by any of the companies participating in the study, but it did come up with the libraries. Surprisingly, most received very little. Those that occasionally did were, for all intents and purposes, ignoring it rather than accepting; however, they had very good rationales for doing so. The library directors in the study simply said it was impossible to ask for clarification or respond to anonymous feedback. Often, the concern affected less than 1 percent of the workforce, so it didn't make sense to share a response with the other 99 percent. Also, the library directors pointed out that they have mechanisms and policies in place to receive feedback via a union representative or employee ombudsman.

One Western library does in fact make use of an employee who, in addition to other duties, acts as an employee ombudsman. Much like the customer ombudsman discussed in Chapter 4, the employee ombudsman is also looking out for the best interests of a segment of the population; however, in this instance it is the employees. This Western library recruited a highly respected, long-serving employee who worked in middle management of the library. She had no higher aspirations and she likely will not, by choice, ever be serving in library administration. Any employee can call or e-mail her or make an appointment to meet with her if they have a concern for which they feel they cannot go to their supervisors. She will consult with those employees. Sometimes the concerns have to do with library administration, though often they are just as likely to have to do with a problem at an individual's branch or with a colleague at a particular work location. The employee also might just want advice on how to get ahead in the organization. The ombudsman turns in quarterly reports to human resources and the library director of activities related to the role; of course, these reports do not include names. The ombudsman is also free to meet with the library director if something requires her attention. This procedure respects employees' anonymity, but because the ombudsman knows their identities she can provide feedback or act as an intermediary.

Social Sustainability (Internal), Library Case Study

Best Practices: Workforce training and leadership development; Nonhierarchical environment/open-door policies that attract and retain employees

The Pacific Library System (PLS) does not participate in a formalized workplace cultural survey to measure employee satisfaction. It does, however, believe it listens to employee concerns by having library leadership constantly out in the branches talking with employees. PLS offers no anonymous feedback procedure for staff, as it feels this is unproductive. If employees have a grievance, there is a mechanism for them to pursue it via their union representatives.

Upon arrival in 2005, the current library director immediately set about "making friends with labor." PLS is a union environment. Like nearly all library systems, staffing is its biggest expense. When the 2008 economic downturn occurred, staff appreciated the importance of a director who put their concerns first. While other county departments were experiencing layoffs, there were none in the library. In fact, during the downturn, customer usage went up and many rather than fewer well-trained employees were necessary. PLS management knew they needed to capitalize on this upward trend and not turn customers away with fewer hours and less staff to help.

Both the county and the library offer staff leadership training, as well as other training opportunities. The library also allows employees to try out new positions on a temporary basis. This allows the employee and the library a chance to evaluate whether an individual is a good match for a position. This includes positions at a higher pay grade than the one in which the employee is currently working. This sometimes allows the library to see if the person has management potential. This type of recognition carries through to the many employee awards the library gives at quarterly staff training events. The number of awards given reflects the fact that every employee is cross-trained. Anyone can make a library card, check out a library book, or conduct a program, provided in the latter case that they have the expertise to do so.

When it comes to a nonhierarchical organization and open-door policy, any employee is free to make an appointment with the director. Management believes it is very approachable and that it runs a very lean organization. It also feels that it offers great benefits, including a pension plan available through the county, which it cites as an increasingly rare benefit, even among government agencies. PLS management also believes the library is extremely humanistic in how it treats its employees. The director regularly sends cards to staffers and in one case, when an employee had a severe family crisis, the library allowed the employee to work extra available shifts so the individual could better assist her family. Employees are also allowed to make mistakes: that is, they are often given a second and sometimes third chance when a mistake that is rectifiable occurs. The

Continued

management team always wishes for employees to know that they are making decisions with staff in mind.

To read this case study in its entirety, please see Appendix 1.

Discussion Questions:

1. Does your library director have an open-door policy? Could you see the director honoring this in the way the PLS director does? How about others in supervisory roles? Is there a mechanism whereby staff can meet with them as well?
2. Can employees in your library try out new jobs within the library on a temporary basis? What if the position is at a higher pay grade?

Performance Reviews

Employees deserve to know where they stand in their workplace. Thus, it is incumbent upon the library to conduct performance reviews in a timely, regular, and thorough fashion. No employee should be surprised by the results of a performance review. Their supervisors should be in constant communication with them, applauding their accomplishments publicly and coaching them privately on areas where they need to strengthen their performance. Expectations should be crystal clear. Not conducting regular performance reviews is akin to leaving an employee out at sea without a life raft. Further, filling a performance review with irrelevant niceties such as, "I love how you bring flowers from your garden to the library, it really brightens up our day," instead of documenting the individual's poor performance does not serve anyone. Not documenting problematic issues and events could also set the library up for legal challenges. Thus, it is in everyone's best interest to complete performance reviews. Many libraries have started incorporating 360° reviews into their performance management policies. In brief, a 360° review includes more than the supervisor and direct reports, instead calling on all individuals working with the individual to weigh in on the individual's performance. Still other libraries have begun using performance review software that sends reminders when reviews are due or overdue and also flags potential inflammatory language in the review before it is submitted or sent. Whether 100 percent paper, 100 percent digital, or somewhere in between, a sustainable library has regular reviews and provides feedback to its employees.

Create a Learning Organization

A *learning organization* is defined by Peter Senge (1990) as an organization working in teams, using a combination of systems thinking, personal mastery, mental models, and team learning, to achieve a shared vision. He goes on to state that "a learning organization is one that can continually enhance its capacity to realize its highest aspirations" (p. 6). A library that is a learning organization uses teams, along with continuous improvement, to work toward its shared vision. Senge describes the components of a learning organization as follows.

Systems-Thinking

"Systems-thinking is a discipline for seeing things in wholes; a framework for seeing interrelationships rather than things" (Senge, 1990, p. 68). In other words, with systems-thinking, one sees the library not just as a branch where customers borrow books, but as all the departments—from collection management, to IT, to accounting, to the 501(c)(3) that made the improvements to the branch where the book was borrowed financially possible—interrelated or as related in such a way that they allow for a book to be borrowed by the customer. This viewpoint also looks at the staff member as a whole individual: not just a person who works at a library performing transactions, but rather as a whole person with hopes, dreams, aspirations, and ideals, along with an accompanying family and family history.

Personal Mastery

In contrast to systems-thinking, personal mastery relates to the individual and how each individual employee of an organization develops skills via a commitment to his or her craft via lifelong learning. Senge (1990) likens it to how a skilled artisan works to improve her or his skill continuously over time. He speaks of the motivated worker, who is inspired by the vision the organization wishes to achieve, and how that worker believes in her or his heart-of-hearts that she or he makes a difference. He speaks about the commitment an organization needs to make to the employee and vice versa, and the connections between personal learning and organizational learning.

In the library, this could be exemplified by a youth services librarian who stays abreast of the professional literature, sharing back and forth within professional associations, collaborating across the country with her or his peers and internally with her or his colleagues, and preparing exhaustively for story times and programs, as well as sharing program designs freely with others. In this example, the youth services librarian fully embraces the mission of the library and remains passionate about her or his role within the bigger picture and the community.

Mental Models

Mental models are often entrenched thinking, assumptions, and generalizations about how people and in particular like-minded individuals view the world. Senge relates that the continuous adaptation of growth in a changing world is necessary. Managers and employees have to work hard to identify or challenge their mental models. Senge challenges his readers to "turn the mirror inward and learn to unearth one's internal pictures of the world" (1990, p. 9).

A mental model most public libraries must contend with is that homeless persons are a library problem: that their situation is primarily a challenge with which the library alone must deal. In fact, the situation of homeless persons is not just a library problem, but rather a community problem, one that the entire community must work together to solve. There are, however, other mental models, which involve library staff only, that must be reflected upon and corrected. An example of such a model is that librarians are the keepers of materials, rather than persons working toward the eradication of illiteracy; another is that in a day when much of the materials to which libraries offer are electronic, some would have libraries deny access to an individual who did not return a physical item years ago.

Building Shared Vision

A shared vision was discussed in Chapter 4 in the section related to strategic planning and vision statements. However, Senge describes it as "a shared picture of the future we seek to create . . . that [serves to] galvanize an organization" (1990, p. 9). He shares that most individuals will opt for pursuing lofty goals, both in good times and in bad. He speaks of genuine commitment and enrollment versus forced compliance. For a library, a shared vision could be a short statement that the whole organization buys into, can get behind, and support, such as: A future where all are meeting their full potential.

Team Learning

Team learning happens in sports, orchestras, and theatrical performances, but often not in organizations. A team, however, should be greater than the sum of its parts. Senge relates that team learning starts with dialogue rather than discussion, "a free flowing of meaning through a group, allowing the group to discover insights not attainable individually" (1990, p. 10). Team learning continues in identifying the shared picture and evolves through harmonization and alignment.

Managers describe meetings where the time flew by, in which no votes had to take place, yet everyone left with a shared understanding of the steps that were to be taken thereafter. In a library setting, this might be accomplished through meetings that have set start and stop times, where an action agenda is developed during the meeting, and where brainstorming took place while no individual was jockeying to curry favor. The action agenda would then be posted to a commonly accessible drive, so others who did not attend the meeting could share the knowledge gleaned therefrom.

Senge sums up his thoughts on learning organizations by saying that to build them "involves developing people who learn to see as systems thinkers see, who develop their own personal mastery, and who learn how to surface and restructure mental models, collaboratively" (1990, p. 367). A library that is not a learning organization simply does not practice what it preaches. After all, a library is all about learning. The interrelated disciplines Senge describe are truly components not only of great organizations, but of sustainable ones as well.

12. RECOGNIZE AND INTERACT WITH EMPLOYEES AND TEAMS OFTEN

> Leadership teams should visit branches often, give out employee recognition awards, nurture employees, and encourage them to take on new challenges. Promote from within when possible and appropriate.

Visit Branches Often

One Southeastern library worker described a former library director of hers as the "ice princess." She said the director would visit the libraries in the system once a year to inspect them . . . not exactly the best way to warm to one's employees! Tucker and Singer (2015) conducted a randomized survey in hospitals where they observed management-by-walking-around (MBWA), which they define as

a widely adopted technique that involves senior managers directly observing frontline work. They examined an improvement program based on MBWA in which senior managers observe frontline employees, solicit ideas about improvement opportunities, and work with staff to resolve the issues (p. 253)

The researchers found that improvements came only when senior managers were assigned responsibility for ensuring that problems got resolved. In other words, "senior managers' physical presence on their organizations' frontlines was not helpful unless it was immediately followed up by active problem solving" (Tucker & Singer, 2015, p. 253).

For library leaders this means that although visiting branches is important, just a visit is not enough. Library management needs to engage with employees, learn of their challenges, and then address these challenges. Sitting in one's office reading reports, though necessary, is not going to get frontline issues resolved. Actively getting out into the facilities and talking to staff will. Library managers need to spend time in the field.

Employee Recognition Awards

As stated earlier, compensation is important, but it is not everything. Employees also wish to be recognized for a job well done. One Midwestern library, which is likely not unique, makes available a myriad of awards, starting with five-dollar gift cards that any employee can give to another employee instantly when they observe a job well done. This same library systems also allows employees to nominate a colleague for a large cash prize awarded by a committee made up of their fellow employees. The gift cards and cash prizes are provided by the library's associated 501(c)(3) fundraising group. The associated certificate and prize are presented in the middle of the day, in front of present colleagues and customers, at the awardees' work locations. This same library also has a noncash prize consisting solely of a library system-wide award that is presented to a work team (such as a branch staff group) or cross system-wide library team in recognition of a job well done and exemplary teamwork.

Staff recognition does not, however, have to involve cash prizes or gift cards. A simple thank-you note from the director or a statement of, "You're doing a great job, Heidi," from a supervisor goes a very long way. Acknowledging a teamwork project on a staff intranet, in an employee newsletter, or at a staff gathering goes a long way, too. As stated earlier, the library's greatest asset is its employees. They not only deserve recognition, they have also earned it.

Recognize often and in many ways. Track the recognition and be sure to spread it around.

Nurture Employees and Encourage Them to Take on New Challenges

As the number one asset of the library, employees should be nurtured in their careers and in the workplace. *Nurture* means different things to different people, and no two people are the same. It is incumbent upon a supervisor to understand what motivates each employee and what those employees need to get from their supervisor in order to create the best work product they possibly can. Some employees need strict guidance and step-by-step instructions, whereas other employees prefer loose guidelines but still deliver a great work product. Gallup developed a low-cost survey instrument that allows an employee and a manager to learn the employee's strengths and how best to motivate the person. A total of 16.3 million people, including some who work in libraries, have already taken advantage of the Clifton StrengthsFinder (Gallup, 2017). Other libraries would likely be well served by having employees take advantage of this relatively low-cost tool.

Managers of sustainable libraries occasionally push their employees out of their comfort zones in order to demonstrate to employees their personal potential. Many library workers will admit that they had no desire to take on a certain task or rise to the call of taking on a management role. They may go so far as to say that they didn't believe they could do it—but a manager saw in them something they did not see in themselves.

SUSTAINABILITY FUTURECAST

The PLS library case study, presented earlier in this chapter, described how staff could temporarily try out a position. This may be an excellent way for staff to temporarily leave their comfort zones. Something not in place in most organizations, outside of academia, is the opportunity to work in a position for a time and then rotate back out of the position. If this opportunity were commonly present in most workplaces, there would be no shame in someone leaving a position that did not suit them and returning to a previous position if the trial job was not what they expected, did not fit well, or they grew tired of it. Often, an individual may find that she or he needs to leave a library system completely if a promotion turns out not to be what she or he expected or if she or he does not live up to the expectations of management. This could be a heavy loss for both the library and the individual. Forward-thinking administrators should consider building a culture that encourages job rotation and experimentation.

Promote from Within When Possible/Appropriate

Library managers who have not developed their talent within may feel they have no choice but to recruit from outside the organization. This can be disheartening to the existing staff. Individuals need to be developed. A library organization that thinks only the leadership team is capable of taking on particular projects is denying its staff colleagues the opportunity to grow in their careers. A good manager delegates every task that it is possible to delegate, so as to develop her or his employees.

As discussed earlier, in a true learning organization staff teams take on projects. They certainly can have a leadership team liaison: someone to help move things through the organization or unblock or direct workarounds when an initiative becomes stuck. By constantly challenging its workforce, the organization is developing its colleagues, so that one day they can, collectively or individually, take on even greater challenges. A library described earlier in this book documented all the processes related to various positions. In doing this, it laid out a path for individuals to move forward in the organization. They truly could identify everything they needed to master in order to be eligible for a particular position. An old adage goes, "In order to be promoted, one must train one's replacement." It is the responsibility of everyone in an organization to move the organization and its employees forward. It is said that there are only two directions in which an organization can move: forward and backward. Thus, an organization that is not moving forward is not standing still; instead, it is going backward.

A note of caution: If the organization never hires anyone from the outside, it may grow incredibly singular and insular in its focus, with no new thinking. Certainly, someone from the outside can bring a fresh or different perspective. However, there are few organizations in existence today that have never hired from the outside. The point of this section is to emphasize the importance of providing opportunities to the employees who have gotten the library to where it is today.

CHAPTER SUMMARY

Sustainable libraries need to support their workforces, via robust onboarding practices, training, the solicitation of feedback, fair and equitable labor practices, and diverse hiring that is reflective of the community served. They also maintain open communication, create a learning organization, and conduct performance reviews on a regularly scheduled basis. Managers, directors, and other leaders recognize and interact with employees and teams often. Last, they take care of their greatest asset: their employees, so that the employees will take care of the library's customers and thus carry the library sustainably into the future. Chapter 6 discusses planning, including facility master plans, succession planning, and disaster planning, as well as freely available tools to help with sustainability planning and reporting. It also explores available tools and processes libraries can use to fulfill their sustainability goals.

REFERENCES

Bureau of Labor Statistics. (2017). *Quits levels and rates by industry and region, seasonally adjusted.* Retrieved from https://www.bls.gov/news.release/jolts.t04.htm

Edinger, S., & Sain, L. (2015). *The hidden leader: Discover and develop greatness within your company.* New York: AMACOM.

Erikson, R. (2015). *Getting to the heart of engagement.* Retrieved from https://cdn2.hubspot.net /hubfs/443262/UPDATED_Bersin_CS_GuideOne_RE_Final.pdf

Gallup. (2017). *Gallup created the science of strength.* Retrieved from https://www .gallupstrengthscenter.com/Home/en-US/About

Graybill, J., Hudson Carpenter, M., Offord, Jr., J., Piorun, M., & Shaffer, G. (2013). Employee onboarding: Identification of best practices in ACRL libraries. *Library Management, 34*(3), 200–218.

Kouzes, J. (2015). Foreword. In S. Edinger & L. Sain (eds.), *The hidden leader: Discover and develop greatness within your company* (pp. xi–xiv). New York: AMACOM.

Marks, M., Sabella, M., Burke, C., & Zaccaro, S. (2002). The impact of cross-training on team effectiveness. *Journal of Applied Psychology, 87*(1), 3–13.

Peter, L. (1969). *The Peter principle: Why things always go wrong.* New York: HarperCollins.

Senge, P. (1990). *The fifth discipline: The art and practice of the learning organization.* New York: Doubleday.

Tucker, A., & Singer, S. (2015). The effectiveness of management-by-walking-around: A randomized field study. *Production and Operations Management, 24*(2), 253–271. doi:10.1111/ poms.12226

United States Department of Labor. (2017). *Age requirements.* Retrieved from https://www.dol .gov/general/topic/youthlabor/agerequirements

Workforce Management. (2009). Onboarding: a critical element in strategic talent management. *Workforce Management, 88*(7).

6

Triple Bottom Line (TBL): Bringing It All Together

Many cities and counties in the United States have a sustainability department. As related earlier, many of these departments focus only on environmental sustainability. The efforts these departments make each and every day are to be applauded. However, as outlined throughout this book, sustainability is bigger than the environment alone. Public libraries should take advantage of the existence of such departments when they are housed within a city or county government parent organization, but the library itself should also have a chief sustainability officer who embraces and is the champion of the TBL. This individual should be a member of the library's executive team and work in consort with or oversee finance, human resources, facilities, and public services. It is a big job; but, with a champion in place at the highest level of the organization, a paradigm shift can take place whereby the entire organization begins to embrace TBL.

The *Fortune* Most Admired Companies that participated in the study reported in this book had moved beyond the nomenclature of TBL; they knew what it was, but in their worldview, sustainability was just the way they conducted business. Sustainability must be embraced at the highest level in order to proliferate throughout an organization. The library director, the chief operating officer, and/or deputy director must be on board and work in tandem with the individuals who are charged with taking the organization through its sustainability journey. The library's mission, vision, values, and goals must reflect a sustainable mindset, and the employees must be indoctrinated into the sustainability mindset so that they can move in the same direction the library will soon be embarking on or has already embraced.

Also, it should be noted that a library staff may engage in many practices that evoke more than one facet of sustainability. For example, the library's retirement plan should be both economically and socially-internally sustainable. Is the staff engaging in work that aids the community's economic development efforts, or helps community members brush up on their job skills so that they are economically and socially-externally sustainable? These aims should be pursued if they align with community goals or fiscal responsibility. Even when the retirement plan is run by another entity, this does not excuse administration from inquiring about or funding an actuarial study of the plan. Such practices do not fit neatly under one facet of the TBL program; however, as discussed earlier, sustainability incorporates organization-wide systems-thinking. One should always be looking at the organization holistically, not as a collection of vaguely related silos. Additionally, it should be clear by now that initiatives need not embrace all facets of sustainability in order for them to be "truly sustainable" or reflective of TBL thinking. In one major U.S. city, it appeared that all three facets (economic, environmental, and social) had to be present in any initiative before the city would agree to undertake it. This is misguided and unfortunate. An initiative that supports only one facet of TBL may still be undertaken as long as it is aligned with the strategic plan of the library or organization.

Libraries have embraced many other sustainable practices beyond LEED buildings. Often personnel may not think of them as related to sustainability, but in fact practices such as the creation of a facility master plan, succession planning, and the creation and promulgation of a library-wide disaster plan all align with the drive toward sustainability.

FACILITY MASTER PLAN

A proper facility master plan (FMP) embraces all three facets of sustainability: economic, environmental, social-external and social-internal. As librarians often manage large buildings or a multitude of buildings for extensive periods of time (usually the life of the building and its site), they must plan for the future of both. Typically an outside firm, usually an architectural firm, ideally working in consort with a library consultant and a construction company, assembles the plan by looking at each building and all real estate holdings to determine not only whether each building is meeting current needs, but also, based on projections based on population trends and the like, what changes will be needed to meet future needs. The plan will have founding tenets that should be carried throughout. Each new building will be sized equally, on a square-foot basis, with the planned square footage tied to projected population; buildings and sites will be built, expanded, or rehabilitated with sustainability in mind. A new service model may be incorporated after being tested to ensure that the space planning allows for how the library will operate in the future, which is not necessarily as it does today. The library system administration, working with staff work groups, may decide to design the library with more people spaces than book spaces. New or expanded offsite storage or offices may be recommended. Consolidation of libraries may be planned, while noting that this may have political ramifications that may surface if the community, which should be engaged, is in fact engaged in the process. In a proper study, work and customer flow/usage will be analyzed to ensure that the buildings are designed to suit how staff and customers use the building.

Once the FMP is complete (which is an extensive process), library administration should regularly keep it updated, giving annual or semi-annual reports to the library's board and community on progress toward achieving the plan. Administration can also set about acquiring, deaccessioning, or swapping real estate in order to realize the plan. Keep in mind that it could take years to acquire or raise the necessary funds and decades to fully realize the complete vision of the plan. Thus, it is important to take the long view with regard to projections and anticipated construction costs, the latter of which inevitably rise.

SUCCESSION PLAN

As stated previously in this book, employees are a library's number one asset. Nevertheless, beyond a start date, one thing that is 100 percent predictable is all employees will have an end date to their employment with the library. Thus, it is important for a library to have a formalized succession plan: one that is multifaceted and tracks employees' proposed retirement dates, predicts their replacements, and ensures that the retiring employees' knowledge of their duties and community contacts has been captured in a knowledge management system. Succession planning can also be about growing the organization's own leaders. A proper succession plan looks at the organization holistically, not vacancy-by-vacancy. A proper metaphor for the workplace might be a giant chessboard, where moves are planned out two and three in advance, with scenarios thought out for the somewhat, though not always, unpredictable nature of the opponent, which in this case might be deemed the future.

Another term for succession planning, which is being used more and more in corporate circles, is talent management. *Talent management* is defined by Cappelli (2008) as a matter of "anticipating the need for human capital and then setting out a plan to meet that need" (p. 1). Note that this may be where libraries and corporate America differ. Cappelli would argue that succession planning is dead and talent management is the new order—but this could just be semantics. In the same article, he tells of a medical device CEO who once quipped, "Why should I develop people when our competitors are willing to do it for us?" This sentiment, of course, refers to the corporate practice of hiring one's competitors' best people. Though libraries are not immune from this practice, it happens less in libraries. In fact, at the moment libraries more closely resemble the larger companies of the 1950s and 1960s, who offered pensions and often almost a guarantee of lifetime employment. Of course, no library today guarantees anything of the kind, but they are still filled with long-serving employees, and more closely resemble the workplaces of our forefathers.

However, just as corporate America is changing, so too will libraries need to change. Today's millennials, born between 1979 and 1994 (Smola & Sutton, 2002), who work in libraries are no different from those millennials working in the private sector. They purportedly have an outsized sense of entitlement and value, as well as unrealistic expectations when it comes to "putting in the time" or earning a promotion (Myers & Sadaghiani, 2010). This said, millennials have many positive attributes: "they work well in teams, are motivated to have an impact on their organizations, favor open and frequent communication with their supervisors, and are at ease with communication technologies" (Myers & Sadaghiani, 2010, p. 225). The point is that the entire library staff will need to adapt to the new workforce, lest it becomes necessary to train employees to prepare them for work elsewhere. The old model of "doing time," such as waiting seven years for a promotion, is likely not going to serve the library for much longer. Note that the next generation, Generation Z (the generation following the millennials) is on average age 24 and counting at this writing. They too have already begun to enter the workforce. The library's succession or talent management plan will need to take these realities into account.

SUSTAINABILITY FUTURECAST

So, how does a library staff manage talent or manage for succession in this environment? Likely, by making it crystal clear how one gets ahead in the library, what skills are valued and what education is needed, ascertaining which staff members are interested in promotion (not all are), and supporting all employees through knowing and addressing their individual needs. In a large organization, this is not as impossible as it sounds. Employees could be classified into like-groups and supported in ways that acknowledge and value them in a way that is most suitable for and acceptable to them.

The sustainable library would be well served by creation of a workplace that maps to the traits of the millennials and subsequent generations. In short, the library staff needs to evolve its workplace practices just as it evolves its service offerings. In the words of Peter Senge, it needs to become an adaptive learning organization.

DISASTER PLANNING

A sustainable library also plans for the unlikely event of a disaster. This could be a flood, fire, hurricane or tornado, earthquake, or other occurrence. No area of the world is immune from natural disasters. The professional literature is full of examples of libraries that have been destroyed by natural disasters; for example, several libraries were destroyed during Hurricane Katrina and the flooding aftermath thereof. Again, protection of the library's number one asset should be paramount: employees must be kept safe. Ensuring that managers have staff phone numbers with them at all times, and that such lists are routinely updated, is important. Should the system not open because of excessive snow or threat of natural disaster, employees must be notified.

Additionally, it is vitally important that redundant computer systems exist and that data be regularly backed up offsite. It is also equally imperative that data be accessible by more than one staff member. Phone numbers for restoration companies that specialize in damaged buildings and those that specialize in library collections should be readily accessible as well. The library should also have its insurance policies analyzed by a third-party professional to make sure it has adequate coverage, that all type of disasters are covered, and that replacement value is part of the policy if the library cannot afford to cover the difference between the cost to replace and the depreciated value of its assets. Remember, disaster more often comes in the form of a broken pipe than in the form of a flooding river or tsunami.

When it comes to communitywide disasters, the library may be the second place the community turns to for assistance after hospitals. The library should be designated a vital community resource by the city, county, or local emergency response community (ERC). Five years after Hurricane Katrina, the Federal Emergency Management Agency (FEMA) took the important step of recognizing libraries as essential community organizations, thereby making them eligible for special provisions (Malizia, Hamilton, Littrell, Vargas, & Olney, 2013). However, if this is not widely known by the local ERC, it might be for naught. Getting the library designated as such will ensure that the library and its needs are addressed early in the recovery process so that the library resources can be made available to the community as soon as possible. Having a nonredundant server in a flooded basement will not exactly make the library fully usable by those seeking help and relief.

Instead, library staff should have access to a server that is routinely backed up and likely housed in the cloud.

Many U.S. cities have designated cooling centers in the event the city is beset with a prolonged heat wave. Having the library designated as such a place is not only good for business and public relations purposes, but could also save lives. If the library is designated as an official cooling center, should rolling blackouts cause an electricity shutdown, the library should be spared because of its designation as an official cooling center facility.

INTERNATIONAL CITY-COUNTY MANAGEMENT ASSOCIATION

An organization called the International City-County Management Association (ICMA) is the professional association for city and county managers. Most, though not all, library directors report directly to or ultimately to the city or county manager of their jurisdiction. Should they work in an independent library district, they may not report to such persons, but they are certainly in the sphere of influence of those managers. Thus, it is important for library staff to know that the ICMA is a huge proponent of TBL sustainability—to the point of holding numerous sessions on the topic at its annual and regional conferences, as well as dedicating a portion of its website to the topic. While one might think that ICMA and its members do not consider libraries as important, at this writing ICMA is preparing a nationwide webinar in order to garner interest in exactly that. They are promoting it with the slogan "Ready to Re-envision Your Library?" (ICMA, 2017). The webinar appears to be less provocative than this "hook" might portend. However, it promises to investigate the following (ICMA, 2017):

1. In what ways is your library supporting local community goals?
2. What capacity and resources does your library have to plan and implement new technologies as the information environment and content industries continue to evolve?
3. How do you build a more sustainable future on the strengths and priorities that are in place? Public libraries need to transform their service model to meet the demands of the knowledge society, while securing a sustainable funding base for the future.
4. In what ways are you cultivating leaders in the community to support your library?

If city and county managers are having these conversations among themselves without engaging the library administration, it does not bode well for their leadership style. Further, if they are having these conversations in order to confront library leaders, it bodes even worse. This said, there is nothing horrifying in the questions posed here. In fact, all of them align perfectly with the sustainability premise of this book. The hope is that library leaders are coming to their city or county managers with answers to these questions, before they are even asked.

In a survey conducted by the Aspen Group, in conjunction with ICMA and the Public Library Association (ICMA, 2016), 22.4 percent of city/county managers replied "very rarely or never" when asked, "How often do you have contact with the chief librarian/library director?" Whether the library is a city or county department or simply independent, that answer needs to change, lest an old adage, attributed to no one in particular, becomes truth: "If you're not at the table, you're probably on the menu."

The point of this section is to advise library leaders and staff that TBL sustainability has been embraced by ICMA and its membership for at least five years (ICMA, 2012).

Now those conversations have evolved to include and discuss the library. Thus, it is incumbent upon the library and its staff to investigate and prepare for a TBL-sustainable future.

TOOLS TO HELP WITH THE JOURNEY

Where does one start on a sustainability journey? The previously outlined 12 steps are one road map, but no framework incorporates them all. Fortunately, there are a couple of good working frameworks and the good news is that, for the most part, they are free to access. Also, a wealth of experts can help one's library, and statewide organizations can help as well.

What is surprising is how readily public libraries have embraced the LEED framework for building projects (which is to be applauded), when they have not so readily embraced other frameworks for library-wide sustainability. Perhaps these other frameworks are just not as well known as LEED, despite the fact that two of the three have been around longer.

THE QUALITY MOVEMENT AND BALDRIGE AWARD

In Chapter 4, the author touched on Total Quality Management (TQM). In the 1960s and 1970s, this methodology was brought to the United States from Japan where it had been heartily embraced. In the 1970s, the United States was mired in recession and the auto industry was being abandoned by U.S. auto consumers, who were buying foreign-built cars in greater and greater numbers (Zarnowitz & Moore, 1977), purportedly because of the perceived lack of quality inherent in American-built cars. The manufacturers were accused of incorporating planned obsolescence into their designs: that is, the production of goods with uneconomically short useful lives so that customers will have to make frequent repeat purchases (Bulow, 1986). In other words, the cars and/or their parts were wearing out in a short amount of time, requiring purchasers to put up with numerous repairs and/or downtime unless they were willing to purchase a new car. Meanwhile, foreign-made cars, notably those from Japan, Germany, and a few other countries, were building reputations for being well-built, long-lasting, low-maintenance vehicles.

To combat this, the-then Secretary of Commerce Malcolm Baldrige, a practitioner of TQM, introduced the concept of a national quality award for businesses (NIST, 2017):

After his untimely death, the Malcolm Baldrige National Quality Improvement Act of 1987 was introduced. Its goal was to enhance the competitiveness of U.S. businesses through an award program. Its scope has since been expanded to health care and education organizations in 1999 and to nonprofit/government organizations in 2007.

Although the Baldrige award is not geared specifically to sustainability per se, a perusal of its measures (see Appendix 5 for a copy) will quickly illustrate how relevant it is to the principles and practices discussed in this book. It does not focus on the environment, but it does heavily focus on the economic and social practices discussed in the previous pages. Further, the Baldrige reporting criteria are not 100 percent prescriptive, meaning that if an organization wishes to focus on environmental measures in addition to the standard report measures, it can certainly do so. Because the report has to work for many different types of organizations, from manufacturers to schools to hospitals, it is fairly flexible.

The beauty of the Malcolm Baldrige program for libraries is that nearly all the tools are freely available and that every state and possession in the United States is party to a one-state, multistate, or territorial consortium of practitioners to help or advise the library on its total quality journey. In other words, there is a method and it is free to use. Should your library wish to train staff as examiners or stand for a state award (which is a requirement before submitting an application for a national award), some small costs are assessed for participation. These costs are minimal considering the performance enhancements and thus cost savings the library will reap by participating. Many school districts have participated in the program and won awards, but to date the author is aware of only one public library that has done so. However, incorporating the practices does not require one to stand for an award. In fact, the preferred first step is to have employees be trained and serve as examiners and then report back on what they learned to the organization. This is an excellent way for the library staff to serve the statewide community and become known and appreciated outside the four walls of the library. It will also start to familiarize library staff with TQM thinking and practices, which can later serve the library well. Should the library staff submit an application, be chosen to be visited by a team of examiners, and be awarded a state award, the library will be held up to the community as a proper steward of the funding the library has been awarded, in addition to providing proof of an appropriate return on investment. Should the library win, however, TQM demands that there be no resting on one's proverbial laurels. Instead, TQM is about continuous improvement. Yes, the library may celebrate for a day. However, after that one day of celebration, staff should ask themselves, the very next day: How can we improve upon this success?

THE GLOBAL REPORTING INITIATIVE

A comprehensive sustainability report for organizations of all types and sizes does exist: the Global Reporting Initiative (GRI). It was founded 20 years ago in Boston, but its headquarters are currently located in Amsterdam (GRI, 2016). Early on, the organization incorporated the 10 principles of the United Nations' Global Compact (n.d.), which cover the areas of human rights, labor, the environment, and anti-corruption. In fact, the GRI was co-developed by the United Nations (UN) World Commission on Environment and Development. The United Nations posits that "sustainability begins with a principled approach to doing business" (UN, n.d.). The GRI is presently in its fourth iteration (G4; GRI, n.d.), a copy of which may be found in Appendix 4. Trainings are available around the globe, and those who have attended a training session may sit for an exam to be certified on their ability to use GRI's G4 Guidelines. All the businesses that participated in the study reported in this book annually complete a GRI report. However, these organizations have a director of sustainability and often a whole department dedicated to sustainability. The smallest company participating titles its document *The One Report,* as it is the only annual report the company prepares. They have wrapped up all of their required reporting into their sustainability report. This is likely a reflection of the fact that this company has embraced sustainability so wholeheartedly that it seems unnecessary to look at the world and thus report on the company's place in it in any other fashion.

Library staff, however, should not be put off by the GRI G4 Report. It is a self-report, and thus they can build toward completing the report in its entirety over the first few years of adoption. GRI makes available free publications to assist organizations that are just starting out, as well as publications to assist small to medium-sized enterprises; all are freely available on the GRI website and listed in the "References" section of this chapter. The GRI is by far the most wide-ranging and most widely used sustainability reporting tool available today. Unlike the Baldrige Quality program, there are no state-wide groups or awards and no national or international recognition. Nevertheless, any organization that completes and publishes a GRI can claim to be on a sustainable journey, as well as a practitioner of transparency.

THE NEW YORK LIBRARY ASSOCIATION (NYLA) LIBRARY SUSTAINABILITY INITIATIVE

At this writing, the New York Library Association (NYLA) is testing a sustainability tool in a handful of libraries (large and small), which promises to help libraries on their TBL sustainability journey. The pilot libraries, which range from small rural to large urban libraries, will inform the design of the tool so that adjustments can be made to the final product before it is launched to New York libraries, statewide, and eventually made available to libraries across the country and around the world. The tool is being designed with ease of use in mind, as it is hoped that the tool will be welcomed and used by the library community at large. NYLA is to be applauded for taking a leadership role with sustainability and this important initiative.

CLOSING

Malcolm Baldrige, referred to earlier in this chapter, said, "Success is finding something you really like to do and caring enough about it to do it well" (NIST, 2016). Presumably, those working in public libraries like the work they do. There is also a general belief that libraries help improve people's lives. However, another prevalent—though false—belief is that everything that can be found in a public library can be found on the Internet.

Libraries and the people who work in them cannot afford for this notion to take further root. The way to stop it from getting further cemented in the public consciousness is not to argue its fallacy but rather to prove beyond the shadow of any doubt that the public library returns more than is invested financially into it. That is not only the library part of the solution; it is, in many ways, the solution to a more sustainable community. For the community to survive and thrive, the library must survive and thrive. The library must prove that everything the community desires for itself, the library can help deliver.

At a United Nations Conference in 2012 in Rio de Janeiro, Brazil, the countries present adopted a resolution titled, "*The Future We Want*" (UN, 2012); they then set about creating a framework to achieve that desired future. Public libraries and their staffs must outline the future they want. If libraries want to be present in the future, staff must start building a sustainable framework that ensures their libraries are present in the future: not just surviving within it, but instead thriving.

REFERENCES

Bulow, J. (1986). An economic theory of planned obsolescence. *Quarterly Journal of Economics, 101*(4), 729–749.

Cappelli, P. (2008). Talent management for the twenty-first century. *Harvard Business Review, 86*(3). Retrieved from https://hbr.org/2008/03/talent-management-for-the-twenty-first-century

Global Reporting Initiative. (n.d.). *An introduction to G4: The next generation of sustainability reporting*. Retrieved from https://www.globalreporting.org/resourcelibrary/GRI-An-introduction-to-G4.pdf

Global Reporting Initiative. (2016). *GRI's history: Enabling positive change*. Retrieved from https://www.globalreporting.org/information/about-gri/gri-history/Pages/GRI's%20history.aspx

International City-County Management Association. (2012). *2012 annual conference program: Milwaukee*. Washington, DC: Author.

International City-County Management Association. (2016). *Local libraries advancing community goals, 2016: Summary of survey results*. Retrieved from https://icma.org/sites/default/files/308908_2016%20public%20library%20survey_ICMA%20summary%20report.pdf

International City-County Management Association. (2017, June 19). Ready to re-envision your library? Retrieved from https://icma.org/articles/ready-re-envision-your-library

Malizia, M., Hamilton, R., Littrell, D., Vargas, K., & Olney, C. (2013). *Connecting public libraries with community emergency responders*. Retrieved from http://publiclibrariesonline.org/2013/04/emergency_responders/

Myers, K., & Sadaghiani, K. (2010). Millennials in the workplace: A communication perspective on millennials' organizational relationships and performance. *Journal of Business and Psychology, 25*(2), 225–238.

National Institute of Standards and Technology. (2016). *Malcolm Baldrige biography: Malcolm Baldrige 26th Secretary of Commerce*. Retrieved from https://www.nist.gov/baldrige/how-baldrige-works/about-baldrige/history/malcolm-baldrige-biography

National Institute of Standards and Technology. (2017). Baldrige performance excellence program. Retrieved from https://www.nist.gov/baldrige/how-baldrige-works/about-baldrige/history

Smola, K., & Sutton, C. (2002). Generational differences: Revisiting generational work values for the new millennium. *Journal of Organizational Behavior, 23*(4), 363–382.

United Nations. (n.d.). *The ten principles of the UN Global Compact*. Retrieved from https://www.unglobalcompact.org/what-is-gc/mission/principles

United Nations. (2012). *The future we want: Outcome document*. Retrieved from https://sustainabledevelopment.un.org/futurewewant.html

Zarnowitz, V., & Moore, G. (1977). The recession and recovery of 1973–1976. *Explorations in Economic Research, 4*(4), 1–87.

Appendix 1: Selected Case Studies

Airline Serving Domestic & International Markets (ASDIM)

Company History

Founded: Mid 20th Century

This airline serving domestic and international markets (ASDIM) began as an intra-state airline serving geographically far-flung, high-demand locations where car and bus travel were impractical. Service then expanded to out-of-the-way airports in other states and markets not served by other airlines. Thereafter, ASDIM developed a networked, cross-U.S. system serving nearly all states. Now, it has additionally expanded to serve some international markets popular with vacationers.

Present Situation

Revenue (2014): $18.6 billion[1]

Income (2014): $1.1 billion[1]

Number of employees: 46,278[1]

Adopted triple bottom line (TBL) practices formally in: 2008

Sustainability function reports to the Senior Vice President of Culture & Communications

Interview

Subject: Sustainability practitioner, bachelor's degree in English language and literature, 19 years with company.

The TBL: Part of ASDIM's DNA

Summary: In retail, it is said the key to success comes down to three things: location, location, location. For this U.S.-based airline, serving domestic and international markets, the key to success appears to be people, people, people. Giving back to the community, being environmentally friendly, and treating employees well were among the tenets upon which the company was founded in the late 1960s. Later, when investors approached the executive team about the possibility of measuring and reporting on the company's environmental impact, it was second nature both to say yes and to expand on the request.

In the late 2000s/early 2010s, ASDIM consolidated its various efforts related to TBL reporting. Starting with the request from investors to measure environmental impacts, the company went further and adopted the internationally accepted Global Reporting Initiative (GRI). Later, ASDIM incorporated these activities into its required United States Securities and Exchange Commission (SEC) financial reports. This resulted in aligning all these measures, along with the related work the company had been doing since its founding, under one reporting structure, as well as enabling a more complete capture of the company's TBL. In ASDIM's case, no one event caused the company to embrace TBL; rather, it was an evolution.

Economic Sustainability

Best practice: Put people (employees) first/strong labor practices.

ASDIM attributes its financial sustainability to how it treats its employees. Whereas most companies put customers first, ASDIM puts its employees first. It believes if it takes care of its employees, they will be happy; this results in employees treating customers well and creates happy customers. In addition, the cost involved in attracting and retaining employees can be staggering for most companies. Given that ASDIM is 82 percent unionized, it can be presumed that high levels of employee satisfaction will result in fewer union actions. Happy or content employees result in lower turnover. The cycle is complete when all this results in satisfied stockholders.

ASDIM's top two expenses are employees and fuel; these trade first and second place as costs such as oil prices vary. Additionally, many members of today's workforce, certainly those just entering the workforce (millennials) wish to know how their company is helping or hindering the planet. TBL practices are more aligned with help than with harm. ASDIM measures its success in terms of employee satisfaction by conducting biannual employee surveys and looking at what it terms its "retention rate" versus what some companies would call their turnover rate.

Environmental Sustainability

Best practice: Reduce carbon footprint/fossil fuels; practice offsetting
(e.g., managing fuel properly).

Fuel is ASDIM's most unpredictable expense, so measures have been put in place to reduce its use as much as possible. Best practices related to the management of fuel consumption, which positively affect the company's environmental bottom line, include: keeping planes tethered to electricity as much as possible when on the ground, using electric-powered tugs and carts, routing planes in the most efficient way possible to minimize fuel consumption, and the like. The critical event that contributed most to

ASDIM incorporating such practices is the ongoing volatility in energy prices, particularly when prices spike precipitously. Obviously, these practices are not suspended when prices go down, so they have been adopted as general operating practices. No matter the price of fuel, these practices continue to save ASDIM dollars. This is one way the company measures its reduction of fuel use. Because low fuel costs could potentially mask abuse or carelessness, the company also measures its energy use in many additional ways, including dollars spent, fuel used, and completion of a company-wide carbon disclosure report.

Social Sustainability (External)

Best practice: Promoting goodwill in the community.

Regarding external social TBL, the company uses its rankings against its competitors to measure goodwill, for which it attains high marks. This goodwill is the result of many factors, including the airline's safety record, its low fares, its lack of customer fees (which have become standard in the industry), its giving back to the community, and the positive attitude of employees. Strong goodwill provides the company a certain clemency, in that when events outside of the company's control occur (e.g., weather delays, technology glitches) customers have a higher tolerance. This is aided by good communication with customers during the occurrence and the fact that customers can see employees are working to solve the presenting problem.

ASDIM's core values were severely tested during one critical event in the airline industry: the 9/11 terrorist attacks. The repercussions wrought by this horrific event included some airlines going out of business or declaring bankruptcy. ASDIM, however, did not lay off a single employee. A high level of trust on the part of both employees and customers resulted from how the company handled the event and its aftermath. ASDIM was the first airline back in the air. The company said, "Trust us," and people did. During the immediate aftermath of the attacks, ASDIM planes were grounded, sometimes in markets the airline did not serve and, in at least one case, at an airport not equipped to handle jet service. In these cases, crews put their customers first. Although the crews were just as fearful as customers, they bought them food and got them blankets, and staff around the country worked to get displaced customers home or to their destination. Crews were also displaced; with *all* planes grounded, it was difficult to get them home as well. When airlines were able to resume operations, three to four days later, crews had to be repositioned and their fears allayed. Company leadership repeatedly said, "We will get through this together." ASDIM passed the test posed by this critical event with flying colors.

Social Sustainability (Internal)

Best practice: Measuring employee satisfaction.

ASDIM cites the work it does in the community and the positive impact this has on employee morale as evidence of the internal social component of its TBL. Additionally, many company employees participate by donating their time to these company-supported enterprises. The company measures these practices via output measurements (e.g., how many tickets are given away, how many volunteer hours employees log, etc.). ASDIM's internal social TBL sustainability is evident by high marks received on employee satisfaction surveys, which are administered regularly.

TBL best practices are part of how ASDIM does business. The company does not have to incorporate specific TBL language into everyday practices because the employees see it as the way business is done. Public libraries can learn from how this airline has incorporated the TBL into its DNA.[2]

Rankings

Rank numbering	Domains	How subject ranks best practices in terms of importance
1	Economic	Put people (employees) first/strong labor practices.
2	Environmental	Reduce carbon footprint/fossil fuels; practice offsetting (e.g., managing fuel properly).
3	Social—external	Promoting goodwill in the community.
4	Social—internal	Measuring employee satisfaction.

International Computer/Communication Component Manufacturer (ICCM)

Company History
Founded in the Mid-20th Century

This international computer/communication component manufacturer (ICCM) started in the semiconductor manufacturing business. Since its inception, the company has expanded into microprocessors, personal computers (PCs), tablets, smartphones, wearable components, and data-center products. It now has an intellectual property division and an computer and cloud security division, and recently it reported being on the cusp of providing products to supply the burgeoning "Internet of Things" market segment.

Present Situation
Revenue (2014): $55.9 billion[3]
Income (2014): $11.7 billion[3]
Number of employees: 106,000[3]
Adopted TBL practices formally in: 2010
Sustainability function reports to the CFO

Interview
Subject: Sustainability practitioner, Master of science in environmental engineering, 20 years with company.

Future Forward: Sustainably
Summary: This international computer/communication component manufacturer (ICCM) embarked on its ever-evolving sustainability journey in the mid-1980s when it

faced its first critical event. It began to experience negative publicity centered on possible pollution of the soil and groundwater resulting from the company's manufacturing process. This prompted ICCM to hire its first environmental engineer to help navigate the situation. As the company expanded in the 1990s, it realized that Environmental Protection Agency (EPA) regulations would one day inhibit its growth. This is when the company decided to voluntarily reduce emissions (i.e., GhG), going so far as to sign an agreement with the EPA to reduce GhG well before the signing of the Kyoto Protocol. By the mid-2000s, the company had begun to make significant changes to its manufacturing process to help reduce its carbon footprint. Today ICCM is seen as an industry leader in sustainability. The company envisions a future in which it can play a major role in the sustainability systems of homes, office buildings, transportation networks, and the energy grid at large, thus helping the entire planet to be more sustainable.

Economic Sustainability

Best practice: Expand product portfolio/customer offerings.

ICCM divides its business into three main units: the client-computing group, the data center group, and the "Internet of Things" (IoT) group. Although the PC market may wane, ICCM's future looks bright, because it manufactures for the entire technology industry and places ever-growing reliance on all things connected. In fact, the fastest growing group in the company is the IoT group. Though not the largest, its growth has been exponential. The IoT promises to connect more than 200 billion items to the Internet by 2020.[4] Moreover, ICCM experienced a second critical event when it realized that the future is silicon and chips, which will be embedded in all aspects of every person's life.

The company believes the expansion of products and services offered from its three business units is the key to its financial success and thus its economic sustainability. ICCM measures the success of this aspect of the TBL via the revenue performance of each individual business unit.

Environmental Sustainability

Best practice: Reduce carbon footprint/fossil fuel use; practice offsetting.

ICCM's technology and manufacturing group is responsible for all the manufacturing sites around the world, and this group has taken a number of actions to reduce ICCM's carbon footprint globally. The company is the largest purchaser of renewable energy in the United States: Last year it purchased enough renewable energy to power all its U.S. operations. At the same time, it invested $30 million in energy conservation initiatives to help the company become more efficient. However, ICCM's efforts do not stop at the manufacturing process. It is also employing measures to reduce the energy consumption of its products. The company looks at its semiconductor chips, generation over generation, and quantifies how much energy they will use over their lifetime. ICCM then strives to make them as energy efficient as possible.

The company's third critical event, again in the environmental area, when the European Union (EU) adopted a directive regarding postconsumer waste (e.g., lead contained in discarded computer products). The company saw this, combined with the GhG emissions guidelines it had predicted would come into force earlier, as something that could hinder growth. Thus, ICCM has been both reactive and proactive to these occurrences, and of late favors being more proactive. Today, the company falls under the Environmental Protection Agency's Tailoring Rule relating to GhG emissions. However, given the company's decades-long work in this area, it was well prepared to work within these regulations. ICCM has been creating environmental reports since 1994, and the company now not only measures its carbon footprint, but also publishes the results on a publicly available website, in a very transparent fashion via a site-specific, easy-to-read dashboard. In October 2015, to further prove its environmental commitment, ICCM published a 2015 Climate Pledge that included strict targets to further reduce its carbon footprint over the next five years.

Social Sustainability (External)

Best practice: Supply chain monitoring/fair and equitable labor practices.

In each of the facilities ICCM operates, it deploys a public affairs group that works with the local community and also works with a community advisory group. ICCM characterizes its efforts to protect workers' rights in its supply chain as an external social sustainability best practice. The company is a member of the Electronic Industry Citizenship Coalition (EICC), a nonprofit membership group made up of electronics companies that have pledged to support the rights and well-being of workers and communities affected by the electronics supply chain globally. ICCM strictly adheres to the EICC code of conduct. This activity was driven by the problems that plagued Nike and Apple when news of supply-chain abuses were aired in the media. ICCM tracks this activity via regular audits of suppliers.

Social Sustainability (Internal)

Best practice: Nonhierarchical environment/open-door policies that attract and retain.

ICCM has an advantage, when it comes to recruitment and retention, due to its nonhierarchical environment and open-door policy. No one in the company has a door on his or her office, because no one has an office, including the company's chief executive officer (CEO). Many free- to low-cost conveniences have also been incorporated into its workplaces. These include fitness centers, banks, health clinics, and spas. The company also offers employees sabbaticals (4 weeks paid each 4 years or 8 weeks paid each 7 years), as well as free fitness classes. ICCM measures its workplace practices via regular surveys and receives feedback on which conveniences employees value and/or would like to see put in place in the future.

For a company that is approaching its 50-year anniversary, ICCM, for all intents and purposes, appears to be managing itself, via the TBL, toward a sustainable future that is likely to exhibit exponential growth in demand for its products. Public libraries could improve their TBL by adopting ICCM's practice of monitoring its supply chain to ensure that fair and equitable labor practices are upheld.[5]

Rankings

Rank numbering	Domains	How subject ranks best practices in terms of importance
1	Economic	Expand product portfolio/customer offerings.
2	Social—internal	Nonhierarchical environment/open-door policies that attract and retain.
3	Environmental	Reduce carbon footprint/fossil fuel use; practice offsetting (e.g., via manufacturing and products).
4	Social—external	Supply chain monitoring/fair and equitable labor practices.

International Hotel Operator (IHO)

Company History
Founded: Early 20th Century
This international hotel operator (IHO) started humbly as an urban East Coast root beer stand. Today it is one of the largest hotel operators in the world. It owns and supports numerous hotel brands, which it has either begun on its own or has acquired. Although it does operate company-owned properties, its hotels are usually operated by licensees who are held to very strict guidelines and procedures.

Present Situation
Revenue (2014): $13.8 billion[6]
Income (2014): $753 million[6]
Number of employees: 123,500[6]
Adopted TBL practices formally: 2007
Sustainability function reports to the CFO

Interview
Subject: sustainability practitioner, master's degree in public communications/international public relations, 9 years with company.

Here to SERVE[7]: Sustainably
Summary: This international hotel operator (IHO) has supported communities and conserved resources since its founding. However, it formalized these practices via its energy program in the mid-1980s and its Spirit to SERVE Our Communities program in the late 1990s. The current CEO modernized many of the company's sustainability practices when he was IHO's chief financial officer (CFO). This historical and top-down devotion to TBL sustainability practices bodes well for the company today and into the future.

Economic Sustainability

Best practice: Put people (employees) first and use strong labor practices.

The company has many practices to support its economic bottom line, including the recent acquisition of a major competitor. It holds up its labor practices and "decent work" (defined as providing jobs coupled with excellent training and opportunities) as its top economic TBL best practice. The company is proud of the fact that it hires a large number of women, many of them immigrants, as well as those on the lower end of the earning scale, often giving them their first jobs. This, together with its excellent training program, has catapulted many of these workers into productive careers that allow them to provide a better life for their families. The company has lobbied the U.S. government to relax immigration and visa restrictions, not only to promote tourism, but also to help fill its workforce pipeline and provide even more opportunities to hardworking immigrants. There is not a single critical event associated with this practice, though the company is quick to point out that each hotel opening is a major event for both the company and the community where the hotel opens. With each new hotel opening, IHO is provided an opportunity to engage in this practice. The company uses a robust human resources system to measure its success and an employee engagement survey that is administered annually to a broad cross-section of associates.

Environmental Sustainability

Best practice: Efficient operations, LEED-certified buildings
(e.g., operating more efficient and environmentally friendly hotels).

IHO has instituted many environmental sustainability practices, including targeting specific reductions in energy and water consumption and "greening" its supply chain, as well as other goals centered on reducing waste, educating guests and associates on conservation practices, and building LEED-certified hotels. This extends to development of software applications for meeting planners to control the meeting room environment; LED lighting in all guest rooms; responsible sourcing of hotel furniture, linens, uniforms, and other items; rainforest conservation and management in South America; and water conservation efforts in China, in addition to serving sustainable foods (including fish, and an outright ban on serving dishes prepared with shark fin) in all properties. The company has a Global Green Council made up of internal executives from every business discipline to help identify and provide oversight of these projects.

Inclusive of many of these practices, IHO holds up the building and operating of hotels that are more efficient as its chief best practice when it comes to environmental sustainability. That efficiency has been a part of its business since its founding. Approximately 30 years ago, however, IHO formalized this best practice under its "environmentally-conscious hospitality operations (ECHO)" program. This program evolved into long-term environmental goals that the company adopted in 2007 and then further into the environmental sustainability program it follows today. Given the length of time the company has been operating with this practice, no one critical event is necessarily associated with it. Today the company measures these practices through management reports, including a climate scorecard, that are publicly available on IHO's website.

IHO has even gone so far as to introduce gamification[8] into its sustainability efforts by developing and introducing an application (app) that allows property engineers to increase operating efficiency by competing with one another in real time on controlling property HVAC systems.

Social Sustainability (External)

Best practice: Providing jobs to those on the lower end of the economic scale.

IHO has a tradition of community engagement. As mentioned earlier, this is encapsulated in its Spirit to SERVE Our Communities program. The company has a human rights task force and at least one disaster relief fund (e.g., during a recent tragic typhoon in Southeast Asia, not only did IHO donate disaster relief funds, but many of its properties also provided critical supplies). For more than 25 years, the company has also sponsored a program that helps developmentally disabled people bridge the gap between school and work. More than 20,000 students have been served to date. IHO has even joined several other leading companies in an initiative to economically empower women globally. To this end, it has a special job/education program for young African women. The company focuses on addressing housing and hunger needs, aiding sick and impoverished children, and embracing diversity and inclusion globally.

Nonetheless, IHO says its primary best practice when it comes to external social sustainability is providing jobs: specifically, readying individuals for careers in the hotel industry (workforce readiness) via education and training. The company supports leadership training for recent college graduates and an affiliated foundation funds hospitality education efforts in China. Once employed, these newly hired recruits have multiple avenues through which they can receive additional training, including the company's leadership program. Again, no critical event is associated with this practice; however, it can be noted that many companies struggle with recruitment and retention (Hancock, Allen, Bosco, McDaniel, & Pierce, 2013), thus it makes sense for IHO to put particular emphasis on this area. As mentioned previously, the company measures progress on this front via its human resources tracking system.

Social Sustainability (Internal)

Best practice: Workforce training and leadership development.

When it comes to internal social sustainability (i.e., the workforce), IHO again demonstrates many solid practices. The company founder is reported to have once said, "You've got to make your employees happy. If the employees are happy, they are going to make the customers happy." One way the company tries to make its prospective recruits happy is by making use of social media during the hiring phase. Citing the growing number of individuals using smartphones, it has developed a jobs application to aid in recruiting. It allows a user to manage her or his entire job search with the company online. IHO has also made strides in hiring veterans. Nevertheless, IHO must maintain investment in a strong leadership pipeline to assure that associates are ready to assume advanced leadership roles. Thus, it considers its efforts in workforce training and leadership development to be its foremost best practice when it comes to its internal social sustainability. IHO trains all employees in human rights, ethics, supply chain policies, and anticorruption laws. This extends to all associates as appropriate and involves in-person training for managers worldwide. The company also executes an ethical conduct survey across a broad cross-section of associates. The company facilitates more than 10,000 training classes each year, 4,500 of which are formal learning programs. The practice of providing training opportunities to employees has been part of the company's heritage since its founding. Again, the company uses a robust human resources system to track its performance in this area.

IHO is already a leading company. As it grows and expands, it intends to introduce its TBL best practices into its newly acquired brands. Public libraries would be well served by adopting IHO's social media, online recruiting, and gamification practices.[9]

Rankings

Rank numbering	Domains	How subject ranks best practices in terms of importance
1	Social—internal	Workforce training and leadership development.
2	Economic	Put people (employees) first and use strong labor practices.
3	Environmental	Efficient operations, LEED-certified buildings (e.g., operating more efficient and environmentally friendly hotels).
4	Social—external	Providing jobs to those on the lower end of the economic scale.

Worldwide Beverage Company (WBC)

Company History
Founded: Late 19th Century
Adopted TBL practices formally: 2011
  This worldwide beverage company (WBC) started with one beverage that was sold as a tonic in drugstores. Forty years later, it expanded to a second beverage product. By the end of the 20th century, it had a total of eight beverages, added through product development and one acquisition. Today it features hundreds of different beverage products worldwide, promising "a beverage for every occasion."

Present Situation
Revenue (2014): $46 billion[10]
Income (2014): $7.1 billion
Number of employees: 129,200
Adopted TBL practices formally: 2011
Sustainability function reports to the chief administrative officer

Interview
  Subject: Sustainability practitioner, master's degree in civil engineering, 19 years with the company.

Me, We, and the World; Sustainably
  Summary: The Worldwide Beverage Company (WBC) looks at personal well-being (me), social well-being (we), and environmental well-being (the world) to enhance its productivity and enable its business. WBC did not experience any single critical event that caused it to suddenly embrace sustainability (though it did experience critical events, mentioned later, that may have caused some of its practices to be adopted more quickly than they might have been otherwise). It did, however, take many related sustainability

practices and put them under one corporate department. The company, vis-à-vis its sustainability department, now looks at sustainability through three lenses: risk mitigation, revenue savings (through productivity measures), and reputation. Realizing that it cannot do everything, WBC has set strategic priorities centered on its me, we, and the world philosophy.

Economic Sustainability

Best practice: Expand product portfolio/customer offerings.

When it comes to WBC's financial sustainability, it has many formal practices, such as tight specifications and close monitoring of its procurement policies, as well as the maintenance of its strong market share, among others. However, key among these practices is the extension of the product portfolio of beverages. The company had only one product for nearly 50 years, and by the 1970s had just 4. During the 1980s and 1990s, WBC doubled its portfolio through product development and one acquisition and is now in the "meets-all-needs" beverage business, offering "a beverage for every consumer preference, whatever the time of day or occasion." This is primarily due to reactions to consumer desires, tastes, and preferences. The success of the practice of extending its product portfolio of beverages is measured through sales data, but it is also measured by recording adherence to a specific company policy, which is that everywhere the company operates it mandates that a low- or no-calorie product be offered.

Environmental Sustainability

**Best practice: Returning natural resources taken from the earth
(e.g., water replenishment).**

A critical event did occur in the company's history concerning water supply. In one of the developing countries where WBC operates, the company was accused of lowering the water table by removing an inordinate amount of water to supply its manufacturing process. If true, this would have had a definite effect on subsistence farmers and general community well-being. Whether or not this was actually the case, the problem was one of perception. That is to say, the community locally, and to some extent even globally, believed it to be true. This perception, along with another critical event around labor organization in another developing country (see below), had the combined effect of spawning protests on college campuses in many English-speaking developed countries. This, along with other various water concerns, caused WBC to expand its view of water to outside the four walls of the plant and begin to look at it more holistically (e.g., watersheds, water policy, etc.). The company spent time conducting qualitative research within the communities in which it operated worldwide: listening, learning, and meeting with stakeholders to discuss water. This was followed by quantitative risk assessment for each of these communities. Much like library branches that are situated in their individual neighborhoods, WBC operates locally; products are manufactured and distributed in the community where they are sold. Thus, the company is a local corporate citizen. Because of this tie, the company works to restore water it has taken from the environment in many ways, such as helping communities in the developing world get access to clean drinking water, treating wastewater, mitigating its plants' use of water, restoring wetlands, and so forth. WBC's nomenclature for this practice is "water replenishment." Success in this area is measured by quantifying the volumetric benefit and tying it back to sales volume; as sales grow, the company steps up its water replenishment efforts to keep pace.

Social Sustainability (External)

Best practice: Put in place programs that empower women (globally, economically, and by the millions).

Regarding external social sustainability, WBC touts its flagship global women's empowerment program, which has a goal of empowering 5 million women economically by 2020. This program was launched in 2010 at the highest level in the company. The rationale was simple: Traditionally, and still to this day, millions of women are often not empowered economically. The program the company launched to address this problem operates within its own value chain (where WBC has the greatest control). This is being accomplished through several initiatives; chief among these initiatives are growing raw materials used in the products (i.e., farming), vending and distributing via microloans and small distribution centers into rural and remote areas, and reuse of packaging material to upcycle[11] these materials (e.g., selling artisan crafts made from recycled WBC waste products). By providing women, primarily in the developing world, with an income stream, WBC believes it is economically empowering women. The company also feels it is achieving its goal of aiding 5 million women by 2020 as it continuously monitors its progress toward this numeric and time-bound goal.

Social Sustainability (Internal)

Best practice: Supply chain monitoring/fair and equitable labor practices.

Internal social sustainability was severely tested with the aforementioned labor organization issue in another developing country and an additional issue closer to home. The first took place when a local labor organizer was murdered while he was working to organize WBC affiliated workers at local licensees' operations in that country. This event was laid squarely at the feet of WBC by critics in-country and by media in the United States and other developed nations. The second event concerned allegations of discrimination by the media against WBC, though this time in the United States. These two events contributed to WBC's creation of a workplace rights policy that also extended into the supply chain. What followed was the development of specific requirements, training, and audits to make sure workers' rights were upheld. Because of the adoption of this best practice, relationships with some suppliers were discontinued and there are some locales where the company no longer conducts business.

In summary, WBC has weathered many crises and has adopted several TBL practices to help guide it into the future. However, it is not resting on its past successes; instead, it is focused on continuous improvement. Public libraries would benefit if they adopted WBC's practice of viewing sustainability through three lenses—risk mitigation, revenue savings (through productivity measures), and reputation—when setting their strategic priorities.[12]

Rankings

Rank numbering	Domains	How subject ranks best practices in terms of importance
1	Economic	Expand product portfolio/customer offerings.
2	Environmental	Returning natural resources taken from the earth (e.g., water replenishment).
3	Social—internal	Supply chain monitoring/fair and equitable labor practices.
4	Social—external	Put in place programs that empower women (globally, economically, and by the millions).

THE LIBRARY CASE STUDIES

East North Central Library System (ENCLS)

Library History
Founded: 1873

This East North Central[13] library system (ENCLS) is well established and purported to be one of the busiest independent library districts[14] in the country. Its Central Library is currently undergoing renovation; first built in 1907, it is located just blocks from the state capitol. ENCLS reports more than 80,000 children receiving assistance at its Homework Help Centers and 40,000 job seekers registering for job help. The system hosts one of the largest summer reading clubs in the country, with 89,000 participants.

Present Situation
Population served: 870,000[15]
Library cardholders: 508,397
Number of libraries: 23; additionally, it operates a local history and genealogy center.
Employees: 794 full-time equivalents (FTEs).

Annual Statistics
Circulation: 16.5 million
Visitors: 9.0 million

Interview
Subject: Library director: 14 years with the library system, all as the system's director.

It's All About the Library Customer Experience

Summary: The director of ENCLS stated that his library was not practicing triple bottom line sustainability per se; it is actually a new concept for him. However, the interview revealed that, based on current operations, ENCLS would certainly be a solid candidate for the GRI.

Economic Sustainability

TBL Sustainable Company Best Practices	Adherence
Expand product portfolio/customer offerings.	Yes
Put people (employees) first/strong labor practices.	Yes

ENCLS offers new products regularly in order to stay relevant to its customers and give them more value for their tax dollars. The library has also expanded the space available to customers, either by building new libraries to replace old ones or reconfiguring existing space to free up more for customers and new offerings. In terms of best practices in the area of economic sustainability, the library director spoke of finance. Specifically, he mentioned the fact that his library, he, and his colleagues always treat budget dollars as their own (i.e., if it does not save taxpayer funds or return more in value than the dollars invested, this library doesn't do it). ENCLS also tries to have an entrepreneurial spirit. Its guiding question is: "How can the library continuously grow its funding or be smart about its funding in order to serve customers better?" During the 2009 economic recession, the state—and thus the library's funding from that source—was hard hit. Whereas 25 years ago 70 percent of the library's funding came from the state, this dropped to 30 percent, leaving the system's operating tax levies to make up the difference. ENCLS cites its status as an independent library district as a best practice for economic sustainability. It also uses flexible operating levy funds to fund building projects, rather than more limited capital bonds. As a result, once any of its building projects are completed, the portion of annual funds that was used for said building can once again be used to fund operations. ENCLS uses this practice rather than opting for capital bonds, where the funds expire once the project is complete. ENCLS also has a 501(c)(3)[16] library foundation with a $6 million endowment. This sister organization helps raise funds on behalf of the library. Lastly, ENCLS emphasizes the importance of the library maintaining its integrity and its status as a trusted entity. When talking with community groups about financial investment in the library system, the director always emphasizes the "ongoing value" of the library system.

Environmental Sustainability

TBL Sustainable Company Best Practices	Adherence
Reduce carbon footprint/fossil fuel use; practice offsetting.	Partial
Efficient operations, LEED-certified buildings.	Partial
Returning natural resources taken from the earth and/or recycling.	Yes

ENCLS does not practice carbon offsetting[17]; however, it has modernized its fleet of vehicles, which has had the effect of improving fuel efficiency and thereby reducing consumption. The library also tracks mileage and delivery vehicle routing. The library did seek and was granted LEED certification for two recent building projects; however, future building projects, although they will include sustainable features, will not be LEED certified, reportedly because of the cost of certification. An additional way ENCLS has improved its environmental sustainability is by converting to a single-stream recycling[18] vendor. Last year alone, the library diverted 720,000 pounds of recyclable material from landfills, returning the waste to the environment for other uses. Other practices related to environmental sustainability include an automated control system for heating and cooling across all branches that is monitored and can be adjusted centrally. This system also allows the ENCLS facility team to diagnose problems remotely. The library has also incorporated many of the latest technologies in environmental building management and even has an employee-staffed "green committee."

Social Sustainability (External)

TBL Sustainable Company Best Practices	Adherence
Programs that promote healthy living.	No
Promoting goodwill.	Yes
Providing jobs on the lower end of the economic scale.	Yes
Put in place programs that empower women.	Partial

ENCLS delivers programs that support external social sustainability on a daily basis. Although ENCLS does not offer specific programs that promote healthy living, its facilities are recipients of much community goodwill. The library's governing board is currently discussing a minimum wage hike for the lowest paid workers that will go well beyond federal and state requirements. The fact that ENCLS is discussing the need to do this illustrates that the library definitely provides jobs on the lower end of the earning scale. As evidence that it empowers women, the director cited incentives offered to minority and women-owned businesses for fulfillment of contracts to provide goods and services.

Other programs the library system engages in to promote external social sustainability include a unique kindergarten-readiness program that goes as far as mimicking the environment of a kindergarten classroom, so parents and children can get a sense of what they will experience once they arrive at school. Beyond kindergarten, the library is beginning to delve into more programs to help children in passing the third-grade reading test, as well as programs to help teenagers graduate from high school. To this end, ENCLS works with partner organizations and has set outcome targets.[19] The library system has also organized all traditional public services under a chief customer experience officer. The long-serving executive in this post is not a librarian; rather, she comes from a marketing background. She appears to completely grasp the core aim of delivering value to taxpayers for their investment.

Social Sustainability (Internal)

TBL Sustainable Company Best Practices	Adherence
Supply chain monitoring/fair and equitable labor practices.	Partial
Measuring employee satisfaction.	Yes
Workforce training and leadership development.	Yes
Nonhierarchical environment/open-door policies that attract and retain employees.	Partial

Although ENCLS does not monitor the supply chain regarding the materials it circulates or other items it might distribute, the library does point out its procurement practice of tracking awards of women-owned and minority-owned business contracts as one way in which it monitors the supply chain. The library has also conducted three organizational employee satisfaction surveys over the last decade. ENCLS is currently in the midst of a major workforce training and leadership development program for 140 managers, conducted via an outside consultant.

ENCLS touts its circular organizational chart as evidence of its nonhierarchical environment (during new employee training, the library illustrates to new hires that the customer is at the center of the chart). The library director states that although he does not work from a cubicle, he advises employees that he has an open-door policy—he suggested that the investigator ask employees if they agree! ENCLS believes all these practices help to attract and retain talent. Additionally, the library cites its diversity committee, the fact that the employee turnover rate is regularly monitored, and its healthy living program for employees and their families as best practices when it comes to internal social sustainability.

ENCLS is a library system that has organized its deliverables around its customers. It is ensuring its sustainability via established practices normally found within the TBL framework. This leading library system has a great deal of experience to share with other library systems, especially when it comes to tracking its recyclables and the way in which it puts customers first.

ENCLS Sustainable Best Practices

Economic
Expand product portfolio/customer offerings.
Put people (employees) first/strong labor practices.
Independent library district status.
Library foundation/501(c)(3).
Using operating funds (levy) to build library buildings vs. capital bonds. Offers more flexibility.
Environmental
Partial: Reduce carbon footprint/fossil fuel use; practice offsetting. (Although no offsetting, fuel management program is in place.)
Partial: Efficient operations, some LEED-certified (or equivalent) buildings.
Returning natural resources taken from the earth and/or recycling (e.g., using single-stream recycling to divert 360 tons).
Utilizing environmental systems to manage HVAC and diagnose problems.
Employee-staffed Green Committee.
Social—External
Promoting goodwill.
Providing jobs on the lower end of the economic scale (e.g., discussing minimum wage hike).

Continued

Social—External

Kindergarten readiness program that mimics the environment of a kindergarten classroom.

Jobs program.

Widely utilized summer reading program.

Deploying a chief customer experience officer to whom all branches report.

Outreach vehicles delivering library services and books outside the four walls of the library.

Beginning to measure outcomes, has conducted market segmentation study, and is using customer surveys.

Social—Internal

Partial: Supply chain monitoring/fair and equitable labor practices.

Measuring employee satisfaction (e.g., organizational climate surveys, three in past decade).

Workforce training and leadership development (e.g., 140 managers currently going through intensive).

Nonhierarchical environment/open-door policies that attract and retain employees.

Special consideration for local, women-/minority-owned businesses when awarding contracts.

Numerous committees serve additionally as leadership development opportunities for staff.

Diversity committee.

Turnover rate regularly monitored.

Healthy living program for employees and their families.

Mountain Library System (MLS)

Library History
Founded: 1886

This Mountain[20] library system (MLS) was established when its home state was still a territory. It claims to be the oldest continually operating county library system in the United States. The first library was located on the third floor of an office building downtown. It later moved to the basement of a school. Andrew Carnegie pledged significant funding toward a 10,000-square-foot building in 1899 and three years later it opened for business. This was followed by a new 38,000-square-foot building in 1969 and then by a newer (three-story, 100,000+-square-foot) LEED Gold[21] "destination library" in 2007; this was the first LEED-certified public building in the state. The system also operates two small branch libraries in neighboring rural communities in its county.

Present Situation
Population served: 95,809[22]
Library cardholders: 78,216
Number of libraries: 3
Employees: 57.4 full-time equivalents (FTEs).

Annual Statistics
Circulation: 746,422
Visitors: 492,969

Interview
   Subject: Library director: 25 years with the library system as chief deputy; system's
director less than 6 months at time of interview.

More Than Just a Library: A Destination
Summary: The director of the Mountain Library System (MLS) assumed her current
role in August 2015; however, she has been with the library system for more than 25 years.
During this time she served as deputy county librarian. In that role, among her other
duties, she served primarily as the chief of the human resources department. Thus, she
feels, "people matters" are always at the core of what she does.

Economic Sustainability

TBL Sustainable Company Best Practices	Adherence
Expand product portfolio/customer offerings.	Yes
Put people (employees) first/strong labor practices.	Yes

   In the economic sustainability domain, MLS regularly offers new products in order
to continuously meet the ever-expanding needs of its customers. MLS also reflects the
practices of the two interviewed companies that tend to put people first. For instance,
MLS recently administered an employee satisfaction survey, they make leadership training available to staff, and they offer tuition remission—all practices many of the inter-
viewee companies conduct.
   When asked if there were other economic sustainability practices the library engaged
in, the library director brought up funding as the most important facet of economic
sustainability. She said it is important for her library to understand where its funding
comes from and where libraries are placed in the political landscape. As a department of the larger county, the library receives a dedicated portion of the county property tax revenue. While the library gets many benefits from being a part of the county,
the director feels those library systems that are lucky enough to be part of an independent library district have an advantage. Additionally, there is a major industry present
in the community, and as the proverb has it, all ships rise or fall based on its performance "tide." MLS monitors the price of the commodity this industry produces, as
well as broader economic indicators, all of which have an impact on MLS's future. The
library also monitors state legislative activity and how MLS fits within what is going on
at the state level. Nonetheless, MLS feels it needs to do a better job of selling its own
story.
   Two recent challenges have been the low unemployment rate, which makes it difficult to attract good talent; and the recent market exit of the county's health insurer. The
latter left the county scrambling to find and fund a replacement. Because the library had
been paying attention to this health insurance matter, it was prepared to absorb and react
to the inevitable. MLS advocates for keeping its eye on the long-term view.

Environmental Sustainability

TBL Sustainable Company Best Practices	Adherence
Reduce carbon footprint/fossil fuel use; practice offsetting.	No
Efficient operations, LEED-certified buildings.	Yes
Returning natural resources taken from the earth and/or recycling.	Partial

MLS states that it could be doing a better job in the areas of carbon offsetting and fuel conservation. However, it does work to consolidate delivery vehicle trips to cut down on inefficiency; this also results in less fuel consumption. When it opened in 2007, the MLS central library was the first LEED-certified public building in the state. The building has efficient environmental operations and, at the time of its opening, had one of the best heating, ventilation, and air-conditioning (HVAC) systems available. A year after the building opened, an energy audit was conducted to ensure that the system was operating optimally, and it was found to be compliant.

MLS recycles paper via a nonprofit partner program that picks up its paper to be recycled. The revenue realized is used to support developmentally disabled clients. Neither the nonprofit nor MLS tracks the amount of recycled material. Unfortunately, the city no longer picks up plastic recyclables, and the library administration could not justify using vital employee resources to identify a recycling drop-off point or spend time finding a place that recycles plastic. The library does point out that system computers shut down automatically to conserve energy, but MLS does not track the associated savings.

Social Sustainability (External)

TBL Sustainable Company Best Practices	Adherence
Programs that promote healthy living.	Partial
Promoting goodwill.	Yes
Providing jobs on the lower end of the economic scale.	Yes
Put in place programs that empower women.	Yes

MLS clearly puts its customers at the core of its mission and points to a few programs that promote healthy living as one of its best practices on their behalf. These include a program centered on positive aging, and partnerships with nutrition organizations on programs that primarily target the economically disadvantaged. The library also promotes goodwill through a multitude of other partnerships that it maintains. MLS offers employment to those on the lower end of the economic scale, though two requirements must be met: a high school diploma and customer service experience. The library states that it hires many entry-level people and that they often go on to build careers with the library.

MLS also focuses on programming that empowers women, including programs that promote careers in science to young girls. It also recently hosted a series of lectures on global women's issues, as well as highlighting local domestic violence concerns. The library notes that it has had women in positions of leadership since 1979, and that

37 employees (primarily women) have gone on to get masters' degrees in library science, while countless others have received bachelor's degrees in other subjects.

The library system is also engaged in a partnership with the National Issues Forums organization,[23] which uses a trained facilitator to address controversial topics (e.g., immigration) during community discussions around the identified issue.

Social Sustainability (Internal)

TBL Sustainable Company Best Practices	Adherence
Supply chain monitoring/fair and equitable labor practices.	Partial
Measuring employee satisfaction.	Yes
Workforce training and leadership development.	Yes
Nonhierarchical environment/open-door policies that attract and retain employees.	Partial

MLS does not monitor the supply chain when it comes to the materials it circulates or other items it might distribute. The library does, however, point out that during the construction of the central library, as much building material as possible was sourced locally. In addition, the library only gives summer reading prizes provided by local businesses.

MLS recently completed a self-designed and administered employee satisfaction survey. One example of interesting data the survey provided was a disconnect revealed between managers and staff on the feeling that staff were overwhelmed. Survey results indicated that a vast majority of staff were not feeling overwhelmed, despite the sense from managers that staff were.

The library conducts workforce and leadership training both internally and under the auspices of the county. MLS has a formalized training process that begins with the interview and continues through orientation and on-the-job training. During the interview process, the hiring manager makes a point of emphasizing the fast pace of the work, in order to dispel any notion that any of its available positions are relaxing. MLS also has a strong continuing education initiative. This is due in part to a grant from a local foundation that allows employees to be reimbursed for pursuing formal education (e.g., bachelor's or other college degree, computer certification, etc.).

The library director feels that she and other organizational leaders maintain an open environment, including an open-door policy; however, she differs from the other interviewees when it comes to maintaining a nonhierarchical environment. MLS does have a hierarchy. The director declares that employees prefer it, as it lets them know what their limits are and when to "push something up the chain." She also believes it helps employees know to whom they report so that expectations can be agreed upon. The director added that MLS has a strong record of employees bringing customer or employee concerns to management's attention for redress. However, management expects employees to bring potential solutions along with those concerns. Employees are tapped for their expertise, and the library involves as many people with relevant experience as possible in solving particular problems. There is a general expectation that employees will participate in the library's continuous improvement initiative. An example of this is a practice of identifying procedures that customers cite as "stupid," and reevaluating and changing the procedures as appropriate.

MLS also feels it has very dedicated employees who display great ownership of their jobs and take great pride in the work they do and the aid they render to their community. Employees treat their positions as vocations, not merely as jobs. The director noted that although this can render people more resistant to change, management does not see this as insurmountable; rather, it is viewed as employees taking a personal stake in what they do. MLS feels that employees see the organization as taxpayer-owned rather than employee-owned.

MLS is smaller than other libraries profiled in this study. However, its economic, environmental, and social practices are strongly aligned with those of the five libraries interviewed. Other library systems, regardless of size, can learn from MLS's best practices in the areas of employee onboarding and in the way it monitors local, state, and federal economic indicators to aid its strategic planning efforts.

MLS Sustainable Best Practices

Economic
Expand product portfolio/customer offerings.
Put people (employees) first/strong labor practices.
Clarity of expectations in the employee interview process.
Knowledge of funding streams and library's placement in the political landscape.
Dedicated portion of property tax.
Partial: Keeping an eye on the "horizon" (e.g., economic indicators, potential local economic impacts, and goings-on at the state legislature). Reports it needs to do a better job in telling the "library story."

Environmental
Consolidates trips that delivery vehicles make.
Efficient operations, LEED-certified (main) building.
Partial: Returning natural resources taken from the earth (e.g., recycling paper via a partnership).
Utilizes high-efficiency HVAC; has conducted an audit on systems.

Social—External
Partial: Healthy living program (e.g., positive aging, nutrition program for economically disadvantaged).
Promoting goodwill (e.g., through partnerships).
Providing jobs on the lower end of the economic scale (only requirements for employees are a high school degree and customer service experience. Many go on to build careers with the library).
Put in place programs that empower women (e.g., "Science for Girls," lectures on global women's issues such as domestic violence, etc.); 37 employees (primarily women) have gone on to get an MLS or MLIS degree.
National Issues Forums programs: trained facilitator+controversial issue=difficult but important discussion.

Continued

Social—Internal
Partial: Supply chain monitoring/fair and equitable labor practices (building supplies, local summer reading prizes).
Measuring employee satisfaction (e.g., recently conducted employee satisfaction survey).
Workforce training and leadership development (e.g., reimburse for formal education opportunities).
Partial: Nonhierarchical environment/open-door policies that attract and retain employees. (Workplace technically hierarchical, but works for this organization.)
Employees encouraged to bring problems to management; however, expected to come with a potential solution.
Working with customers to identify "stupid" policies, re-evaluating and changing these policies.
Nurturing (or not stifling) employee's sense of dedication, i.e., work as a vocation.

Pacific Library System (PLS)

Library History
Founded: 1913

Library services in the Pacific[24] library system (PLS) started with 9 libraries, 1 small school collection, and 500 books. By the 1930s, the system had more than 150 libraries spread across the quickly growing county. After World War II, many of the buildings were expanded or replaced, whereas others were consolidated, aided by improved transportation systems. A statewide tax measure, with negative results for the library system, passed in the late 1970s, and forced curtailment of planned renovations, expansions, and new branches. Hours were cut by up to 50 percent and many staff were laid off. Some branch plans developed in the 1970s were delayed and not put into place until the 1990s. Today the system operates 33 branch libraries, but has no central library.

Present Situation
Population served: 1,081,074[25]
Library cardholders: 920,561
Locations: 33
Employees: 268.5 full-time equivalents (FTEs).

Annual Statistics
Circulation: 11 million
Visitors: 5.7 million

Interview
Subject: Library's deputy director; 14 years with library system.

The "Busy Is as Busy Does" Library

Summary: Although the PLS system suffered severely during the economic downturn that began in 2008, library management is proud that no employees lost their jobs. The library system is also proud of the fact that it is one of the busiest systems in the

United States, offering more than 31,000 programs annually, with more than 710,800 people attending.[26]

Economic Sustainability

TBL Sustainable Company Best Practices	Adherence
Expand product portfolio/customer offerings.	Yes
Put people (employees) first/strong labor practices.	Yes

PLS both continuously expands its customer offerings and states that it puts its employees first. Despite the economic downturn and pressure from its parent jurisdiction, PLS attributes the fact that it did not experience any forced reduction of its workforce during the 2008 financial crisis to its strong labor practices including excellent union relations. Additionally, it treats employees much like family, as discussed in further detail under "Social Sustainability (Internal)" in this section. All employees, including customer service staff, do programming tailored to customer needs. For example, without all staff participating, PLS feels it would be unable to offer programs as specific as computer classes taught in Arabic.

The library feels lucky to have funds earmarked for it through a dedicated portion of the county property taxes. PLS estimates that 99 percent of its funding comes from this revenue source. The library cited a city library system located in another part of its home state that was nearly decimated by the 2008 financial crisis, because that system had no dedicated funding. As PLS's area has experienced various "booms and busts," PLS is keenly aware of what havoc the bigger economic picture can wreak upon the library system. During the previously mentioned economic downturn and crisis, for example, its area experienced many foreclosures and reductions in property values which severely lessened the library system's operating budget. This did bring about a reduction in the workforce through retirements, attrition, and a hiring freeze. Fortunately, the library had project funds set aside which helped it weather the downturn. Although it was unable to work on any remodeling projects during this period, it did take this opportunity to streamline operations: it implemented one service desk versus two, an RFID[27] inventory system, customer self-checkout, and other efficiencies in order to lessen the burden on remaining staff. In its own words, PLS parlayed the economic downturn into "getting staff out of the book checking in and out business and into the programming business." For its part, the parent county jurisdiction allowed the library to implement necessary budget cuts over one year's time rather than taking the money away upfront. This allowed the library to ease into the cuts instead of having to take sudden drastic measures. PLS used its three-year strategic plan to identify what was important and what service offerings could be eliminated. Today the library system's budget has been restored to nearly pre-recession levels.

Environmental Sustainability

TBL Sustainable Company Best Practices	Adherence
Reduce carbon footprint/fossil fuel use; practice offsetting.	Partial
Efficient operations, LEED-certified buildings.	Partial
Returning natural resources taken from the earth.	Yes

PLS has implemented a fleet of hybrid vehicles for staff to use when visiting its far-flung branches, which are located across a very large geographic area. Like some of the other companies interviewed, however, PLS has not identified charging its individual work units for carbon offsets as a way forward (another common best practice). The library has implemented a floating collection policy (Van der Noordaa, 2011), which allows books to be maintained at the library where the items are returned by customers rather than having them relocated to a home library location. This policy has cut down on deliveries, thus saving fuel.

Thermostats in buildings across the PLS system are set at 78 degrees Fahrenheit in summer and 68 degrees in winter to conserve energy. The county now also requires all new buildings to be designed to achieve a minimum of LEED Silver certification. PLS is also working with the county to build a net-zero emissions branch in one of its outlying communities. Although the library is excited by this prospect and embraces it wholeheartedly, it will not allow customer service to be sacrificed in the name of net-zero achievements (e.g., needing to find a compromise to maintain sight lines in the building, even if environmental equipment that blocks sight lines is necessary.) Thus, PLS is working hand-in-hand with the county's construction department to ensure that the building meets both the needs of customers and the environment. Because the county, not the library, is responsible for the PLS buildings, most of the building-related initiatives are driven by the county. Nevertheless, the library is the beneficiary of the energy savings.

The library practices single-stream recycling but is not aware that any measurements related to positive impact on landfills are collected. The system also makes use of a company that recycles its discarded books, either by selling them or dispersing them through aid organizations in third-world countries where demand for English books exists. The library also has a battery-recycling program through the county, so that expended customer and library batteries can be recycled, avoiding landfills.

Social Sustainability (External)

TBL Sustainable Company Best Practices	Adherence
Programs that promote healthy living.	Yes
Promoting goodwill.	Yes
Providing jobs on the lower end of the economic scale.	Yes
Put in place programs that empower women.	Partial

Like other libraries in this study, PLS excels when it comes to external social sustainability. PLS says the key to all its programs that help the community are its many partnerships. This includes an extensive partnership with the local county health department, which brings a multitude of health programs into libraries—but not just any programs. The health department targets programs based on problematic health conditions in the zip codes where branch libraries are located. Additionally, the library gets children outdoors and exercising via its "recess in a box" program. PLS also provides food to children during summer, when schools are closed, via its snack program. The library deploys county public health nurses via its bookmobiles when they visit impoverished communities.

PLS cites its outreach to the many immigrant communities and its participation in a statewide initiative called First-Five, which works on pre-literacy skills for the under-five set, as just two of the important ways it promotes goodwill. Through library and county programs, those on the lower end of the economic spectrum are helped through employment working for the library. These programs include students who need to do service work for school, who often get their first work experience at the library (many of whom go on to get part-time paid work at the library); a substitute worker program, which serves as an employee feeder pipeline; a unique county program that provides jobs for former foster children who are no longer eligible for benefits; and the county's senior worker program for senior citizens.

The library also provides some programming specifically targeted to women. In PLS's case, the program is targeted toward Spanish-speaking women. These programs provide assistance to these women in acquiring third-party micro-loans to start businesses, as well as assistance in learning the necessary skills for running a business.

Social Sustainability (Internal)

TBL Sustainable Company Best Practices	Adherence
Supply chain monitoring/fair and equitable labor practices.	No
Measuring employee satisfaction.	No
Workforce training and leadership development.	Yes
Nonhierarchical environment/open-door policies that attract and retain employees.	Yes

Like other libraries in this study, PLS does not monitor its supply chain per se, but also like others, it does purchase new building construction materials locally. This is due, in part or in whole, to the county's requirement that new buildings be LEED-certified. In the past the library experienced a problem with summer reading premiums that purportedly contained a hazardous substance and had to be recalled, so it is extremely cautious when it comes to procurement of these types of giveaways.

The library does not participate in a formalized workplace cultural survey to measure employee satisfaction. It does, however, believe it listens to employee concerns by having library leadership constantly out in the branches talking with employees. PLS offers no anonymous feedback procedure for staff, as it feels this is unproductive. If employees have a grievance, there is a mechanism for them to pursue it via their union representatives.

Upon arrival in 2005, the current library director immediately set about "making friends with labor." PLS is a union environment. Like nearly all library systems, staffing is its biggest expense. When the 2008 economic downturn occurred, staff appreciated the importance of a director who put their concerns first. While other county departments were experiencing layoffs, there were none in the library. In fact, during the downturn, customer usage went up and many rather than fewer well-trained employees were necessary. PLS management knew they needed to capitalize on this upward trend, not turn customers away with fewer hours and less staff to help.

Both the county and the library offer staff leadership training as well as other training opportunities. The library also allows employees to try out new positions on a temporary basis. This allows the employee and the library a chance to evaluate whether an individual is a good match for a position. This includes positions at a higher pay grade than the one in which the employee is currently working. This sometimes allows the library to see if the person has management potential. This type of recognition carries through to the many employee awards the library gives at quarterly staff training events. The number of awards given reflects the fact that every employee is cross-trained. Anyone can make a library card, check out a library book, or conduct a program, provided in the latter case that they have the expertise to do so.

When it comes to a nonhierarchical organization and open-door policy, any employee is free to make an appointment with the director. Management believes it is very approachable and that it runs a very lean organization. It also feels that it offers great benefits, including a pension plan available through the county, which it cites as an increasingly rare benefit, even among government agencies. PLS management also believes the library is extremely humanistic in how it treats its employees. The director regularly sends cards to staffers and in one case, when an employee had a severe family crisis, the library allowed the employee to work extra available shifts so the individual could better assist her family. Employees are also allowed to make mistakes: that is, they are often given a second and sometimes third chance when a mistake that is rectifiable occurs. The management team always wishes for employees to know that they are making decisions with staff in mind.

PLS is a busy library that markets itself as the "library that never closes," citing its abundance of electronic resources available 24/7. It also likes to think of itself as proactive rather than reactive when it comes to customer and community service. It views each of its locations as one of 33 village libraries. It states that it very much honors the communities in which it is located and the individual communities respect PLS staff. The library is a good model for other libraries in how to be engaged with one's community, as well as how to present the library as a valuable community resource.

PLS Sustainable Best Practices

Economic
Expand product portfolio/customer offerings.
Put people (employees) first/strong labor practices.
Dedicated property tax.
Awareness of the bigger economic picture; plan accordingly.
(Emergency) funds set aside for projects or "rainy day."
Streamline operations (e.g., one service desk, RFID, self-check, automated materials handling) so staff can focus on proffering other services.
Has a strategic plan and makes use of it.
Environment
Partial: Reducing carbon footprint/fossil fuel use (e.g., hybrid vehicles, floating collections).
Partial: Efficient operations, LEED-certified buildings (one net-zero building in the planning stages).
Partial: Returning natural resources taken from the earth (recycling, but not yet tracking amount). Also using recycling vendors for book and battery discards.

Continued

Social—External

Programs that promote healthy living (in conjunction with County Health Department): "Recess in a box" program to help children stay active.

Promoting goodwill.

Providing jobs on the lower end of the economic scale (e.g., youth service work, substitute workers, former foster children, and seniors programs).

Partial: Put in place programs that empower women (e.g., offering small business skills training and help in identifying financial assistance for their burgeoning businesses to Spanish-speaking women).

All employees, including customer service staff, do tailored-to-customer-needs programming.

Extensive use of partnerships, especially in programming provision.

Provide snacks to impoverished children during summer. Provides age 0-5 pre-literacy skills.

Social—Internal

Partial: Supply chain monitoring/fair and equitable labor practices.

Workforce training and leadership development.

Nonhierarchical environment/open-door policies that attract and retain employees (e.g., any employee can make an appointment with the director).

Good union relations (aided by lack of layoffs during economic downturn).

Director and leadership team visit all locations often, talk with employees while there.

Employees can temporarily try out different positions, including those at a higher pay grade (based on need/availability).

All employees are cross-trained, especially in basic functions.

Quarterly recognition awards given; director sends cards to staff often.

Employees are allowed to make rectifiable mistakes.

South Atlantic Library System (SALS)

Library History
Founded: 1940

Library service in this South Atlantic[28] library system (SALS) started in 1940. Funds were raised for the first library, located in a portable building, beginning two years prior to the opening, by a local women's civic club. Located in the county seat, the library moved to rented quarters above a meat store a few years later. A civic leader encouraged county commissioners to add two pennies to the tax rate to help fund a permanent library. Unfortunately, once open this library was destroyed by a flood. Finally, in 1962, two individuals donated property and funds for a building. Today the library has grown into six locations throughout the county, each with a specialized center of learning, but all focused overall on education.

Present Situation
Population served: 309,284[29]

Library cardholders: 278,355
Locations: 6
Employees: 234 full-time equivalents (FTEs)

Annual Statistics
Circulation: 7.2 million
Visitors: 2.9 million

Interview
Subject: Library's director; 15 years with library system.

Education Is the Name of This Library's Game

Summary: SALS has positioned itself as a hub of education alongside public schools and the local community college. All library messaging is about the library as educator; specifically, "high quality public education is for everyone." Many staff are referred to as "instructors" and programs as "classes." When seeking funding from local municipalities and/or the state and federal governments, the library cites education as these bodies' highest priority. Generally speaking, the director believes that all libraries would be well served by positioning themselves as part of the educational system.

Economic Sustainability

TBL Sustainable Company Best Practices	Adherence
Expand product portfolio/customer offerings.	Yes
Put people (employees) first/strong labor practices.	Yes

With respect to economic sustainability, the SALS library does not have a dedicated property tax; rather, all county departments vie for the same dollars. Each year the library has to make its case for the dollars it needs to operate. By positioning itself as an educational provider, the library gains the county's support for funding. This helps to ensure its long-term viability. The library budget does not break out workforce, books, and administrative costs as individual line items, as is typically done. Instead, it reinforces the theme of education as its priority by assigning these expenses to categories labeled "instruction," "research assistance," "self-directed learning," and "customer service." In fact, 50 percent of the budget is dedicated to instruction. Recently, when a children's instructor position was advertised, more than 300 applicants responded. The library is always adding new offerings to these categories, whether it is new technology to aid customer service or classes such as robotics, tai chi, or how to hang drywall. It feels that its employees, whether they teach classes or not, are its biggest asset.

Library branches serve as centers of "different learnings" (e.g., teen center, children's center, art library, historical center, etc.). The "coolest center of learning," in the director's opinion, is the STEM learning center located in the county's most disadvantaged neighborhood. These offerings, in the library's opinion, are all part of its portfolio of products.

Environmental Sustainability

TBL Sustainable Company Best Practices	Adherence
Reduce carbon footprint/fossil fuel use; practice offsetting.	No
Efficient operations, LEED-certified buildings.	Partial
Returning natural resources taken from the earth.	Partial

SALS does not track carbon offsets, nor has it implemented any fuel saving policies. Two of the six branches are LEED-certified buildings and the library system has installed LED lighting throughout its buildings to help reduce energy use. SALS does recycle used books, like other libraries in this study, through a vendor who specializes in finding new homes for discarded books. The library publicizes these environmentally friendly activities through educational placards in its LEED-certified branches, focusing on how the buildings help the environment (e.g., how bioswales[30] help the watershed). SALS also offers classes on gardening and has several raised-bed specialty gardens at one of its branches.

Social Sustainability (External)

TBL Sustainable Company Best Practices	Adherence
Programs that promote healthy living.	Yes
Promoting goodwill.	Yes
Providing jobs on the lower end of the economic scale.	Yes
Put in place programs that empower women.	Partial

SALS excels when it comes to external social sustainability. The library credits its model of education provision as the key to its success. In its communication both internally and externally, it uses the phrase "instruction first." Through one of its 25 partnerships, which include its "Well and Wise" partnership with a local hospital, SALS offers classes that promote healthy living. In addition, as noted earlier, it offers many gardening courses via its demonstration gardens. The library promotes goodwill through these service offerings and many others, which include classes in animation and Adobe Illustrator®, for example. Approximately 15 percent of the customer service and back-office staff may come from the lower end of the economic scale and are in positions that have lower educational requirements.

SALS policies regarding gender preference are neutral. All classes are available to all customers regardless of gender or age. However, when the library wished to promote STEM careers to young women, it ran into a problem: The young women on the teen advisory council wanted the library to offer classes on fashion. Wishing to give customers what they wanted but also to achieve its goal of promoting STEM careers to adolescent women, the library compromised and built a fashion program around the technology of the fashion industry, including computer-aided design. SALS points out that it empowers local women economically by providing contracting incentives for female-owned businesses, as well as other minority-represented constituents.

The library also engages its public in strategic planning. In addition to other questions noted earlier, the library asks its customers, "What do you like best about the library now and what do you think you will like best in 25 years?" The stakeholders who attend the planning community meetings are divided into three groups, each focused on one of the library's strategic pillars: self-directed education, research assistance and instruction, and instructive and enlightening experiences.

Social Sustainability (Internal)

TBL Sustainable Company Best Practices	Adherence
Supply chain monitoring/fair and equitable labor practices.	No
Measuring employee satisfaction.	No
Workforce training and leadership development.	Yes
Nonhierarchical environment/open-door policies that attract and retain employees.	Yes

Like other libraries in this study, SALS does not monitor its supply chain, though, as required by LEED certification requirements, it does purchase locally as many new building construction materials as is possible.

When it comes to employees, the library regularly asks, "Do the employees feel appreciated?" This said, it does not conduct employee satisfaction surveys, but the director and other leadership team members are regularly out in the branches, the director at least once quarterly. The director has monthly meetings with employees (including snacks) and she shares with staff what is going on in the system and the community. There is no mechanism for anonymous input from staff. Rather, SALS cites its use of appreciative inquiry for daily operations as well as strategic planning.[31] The library believes that if you ask staff what is wrong, you are "feeding staff negativity." Instead, staff are asked what they like, or "what we are doing well?," "what can we do even better?," and "how can technology improve this?"

The library has a robust staff-training program that aligns with its educational focus for customers. This training starts when new employees join the organization, to help them acclimate to the culture. SALS also believes it has a nonhierarchical environment and an open-door policy that helps it to attract and retain talent. Even the library's customer service philosophies (one for external stakeholders and one for internal stakeholders) were written by staff.

Employees at SALS get their birthdays off; they are involved in team projects; and the director regularly sends staff thank-you notes, especially after some of the extremely large annual events the library hosts that require all staff to participate. The library has also moved staff into new positions, rather than dismissing them, "when things don't work out." One employee was demoted, but was allowed to keep her same salary. The individual received no subsequent raises for many years until the salary earned equaled that of her new position.

SALS is a busy library that markets itself as the library that is all about education. It also has the class offerings and workforce structure to back up this claim. The library proves its merit each year, as reflected in the funding from its county board of supervisors. Based on its practices, it takes care of its employees and in turn its employees, per the director, take care of the customers. Libraries across the United States could learn much from this award-winning, education-focused library.

SALS Sustainable Best Practices

Economic

Expand product portfolio/customer offerings.

Put people (employees) first/strong labor practices.

Education focus; helps to assure continuous funding.

Aligning budget programmatically, not traditionally; more outcome focused.

Has a strategic plan and makes use of it.

Environmental

Efficient operations, LEED-certified buildings (two).

Partial: Returning natural resources taken from the earth (e.g., using recycling vendor for book discards).

Using LED lighting throughout system.

Offering educational programming focused on the environment and sustainability.

Social—External

Programs that promote healthy living ("Well and Wise" program in conjunction with local hospital; gardening programs).

Promoting goodwill.

Providing jobs on the lower end of the economic scale.

Partial: Put in place programs that empower women (offers programs that promote STEM careers to young women; contractual preference for female-owned businesses).

Offers specialized centers of learning.

Extensive use of partnerships, especially in programming provision.

Offers a wide variety of programs, including a great number that are STEM-focused.

Written external customer service philosophy created by staff.

Engages in public strategic planning.

Social—Internal

Partial: Supply chain monitoring/fair and equitable labor practices.

Workforce training and leadership development (e.g., monthly meetings with staff).

Nonhierarchical environment/open-door policies that attract and retain employees.

Director and leadership team visit all locations often.

Director sends cards to staff often.

Using appreciative Inquiry, focusing on positivism. No mechanism for anonymous input.

Written internal customer service philosophy created by staff.

Staff get birthdays off.

Give staff opportunity to succeed in other position, if existing one is not successful.

NOTES

1. Per ASDIM's SEC 10K filing for the fiscal year ending December 31, 2014.

2. Other practices mentioned: Setting core values, banked financial reserves to weather unforeseen difficulties, performance measures, high-performance expectations, a sought-after internship program, and high résumé submission due to strong reputation.

3. Per ICCM's SEC 10K filing for the fiscal year ending December 27, 2014.

4. Per ICCM's 2014 annual report.

5. Other practices mentioned were an online manager dashboard tool which provides resources that help managers run the "people" side of their business; the company's ICCM She Will Connect program, which aims to connect millions of women to new opportunities; employee and executive compensation partially linked to TBL metrics; the company's code of conduct; a corporate responsibility matrix that compares stakeholder interests (high to low) with the impact each measure has on the business; programs to improve the digital divide for children; programs specifically for girls (inspiring them to become creators of technology); a high employee participation rate in ICCM's organizational culture survey (77%), the company's status as a UN Global Compact signatory; and its multi-year commitment to aid development of world health care workers via access to technology.

6. Per IHO's SEC 10K filing for the fiscal year ending December 31, 2014.

7. IHO's "Spirit to SERVE our Communities" program uses the acronym SERVE to mean: Shelter and food, Environment, Readiness for hotel careers, Vitality of children, and Embracing diversity and people with disabilities.

8. "Gamification" refers to a software system that has been designed to have use, design, elements, and characteristics similar to those of video games (reward and reputation systems with points, badges, levels, leader boards, etc.), but is applied in a nongame context (Deterding, Sicart, Nacke, O'Hara, & Dixon, 2011).

9. Other practices and items mentioned were: devotion to continuous improvement, internal cultural surveys, the company's committee for excellence (senior leadership), its Human Rights Taskforce (executive level), employee volunteerism and socially beneficial activities (e.g., charitable 10K walks), 10 stakeholder groups (e.g., associates (employees), communities, government, etc.), and goal/target setting.

10. Per WBC's SEC 10K Filing for the fiscal year ending December 31, 2014.

11. Torstensson (2011) describes *upcycling* as a process whereby waste or useless products are converted into new materials or products of equal or better quality or a higher environmental value (as opposed to merely recycling).

12. Other practices and items mentioned during the interview were: measurement/setting of targets, UN Global Compact participation, stakeholder engagement, workplace safety training, and a pilot project: an in-community social enterprise that provides solar power, other much-needed services, and sales of WBC and other products in small, remote communities via a kiosk). Additionally, the practitioner mentioned his local public library, which is U.S.-based and housed in a hub containing a public library; a theater group; and a community arts center that offers classes, summer camps, storytelling, book exchanges, recycling center, and a polling place. The practitioner viewed this as the community's attempt to keep its public library relevant.

13. One of nine official U.S. Census regions (U.S. Bureau of the Census, 2015).

14. Libraries are funded in many ways in different jurisdictions. An *independent library district* (Robey, O'Brien, Julien, & Winograd, 2012) is a separate taxing entity, usually limited by geographical bounds, for which voters have approved an annual (usually perpetual) tax to fund the library.

15. Per 2015 Public Library Association Public Library Data Service Statistical Report. Data are from 2014.

16. U.S. Internal Revenue Service (2015) designation for a nonprofit founded as a charitable organization. See https://www.irs.gov/charities-non-profits/charitable-organizations/exemption -requirements-section-501c3-organizations

17. A *carbon offset* is a unit of carbon dioxide-equivalent (CO2e) that is reduced, avoided, or sequestered to compensate for emissions occurring elsewhere (Goodward & Kelly, 2010).

18. *Single-stream recycling* (Wang, 2006) refers to a system in which all standard recyclables are mixed in a collection container, instead of being sorted by the depositor into separate containers. They are later sorted by a recycling vendor.

19. *Outcome targets* or *outcome measurement* is the systematic, empirical observation of the effects of social programs on the achievement of objectives having to do with improvement (Morino, 2011).

20. One of nine official U.S. Census regions (U.S. Bureau of the Census, 2015).

21. Per the U.S. Green Building Council (2015), the current Leadership in Energy & Environmental Design (LEED) levels are: Certified, Silver, Gold, and Platinum. See www.usgbc.org/leed

22. Per 2015 Public Library Association Public Library Data Service Statistical Report. Data are from 2014.

23. Based in Dayton, Ohio, the National Issues Forums Institute (NIFI, 2015), is a nonprofit, nonpartisan organization that serves to promote public deliberation and coordinate activities. Its activities include publishing the issue guides and other materials used by local forum groups, encouraging collaboration among forum sponsors, and sharing information about current activities in the network.

24. One of nine official U.S. Census regions (U.S. Bureau of the Census, 2015).

25. Per Public Library Association Public Library Data Service Statistical Report (2015). Data are from 2014.

26. Per the PLS 2014 annual report.

27. Radio frequency identification (RFID) is a method of controlling inventory, offering customer self-checkout, and using automated materials handling in libraries. An RFID tag is small and can be affixed within the jacket of a book. It can be programmed to hold unique information about the book in order to distinguish it from another. The tag communicates its information to the computer inventory system (American Library Association, n.d.).

28. One of nine official U.S. Census regions (U.S. Bureau of the Census, 2015).

29. Per the library system. Annual statistics are from the most recent fiscal year (2015) close.

30. *Bioswales* (Winston, Luell, & Hunt, 2012) are stormwater runoff conveyance systems that provide an alternative to storm sewers.

31. *Appreciative inquiry* (Cooperrider & Srivastva, 1987) is a change model which uses valuing "the best of what is," envisioning what might be, engaging in dialogue about what should be, and innovating what will be, rather than problem-solving.

REFERENCES

American Library Association. (n.d.). RFID: Radio frequency identification technology/RFID discussion list. Retrieved from http://www.ala.org/Template.cfm?Section=ifissues&Template =/ContentManagement/ContentDisplay.cfm&ContentID=77689

Boles, S. (n.d.) What are the differences between scope 1, 2 and 3 greenhouse gas emissions? Retrieved from http://www.icomplisustainability.com/index.php/ask-the-expert/ghg -management/item/63-what-are-the-differences-between-scope-1-2-and-3-greenhouse-gas -emissions/63-what-are-the-differences-between-scope-1-2-and-3-greenhouse-gas-emissions

Cooperrider, D. L., & Srivastva, S. (1987). Appreciative inquiry in organizational life. *Research in Organizational Change and Development, 1*(1), 129–169.

Deterding, S., Sicart, M., Nacke, L., O'Hara, K., & Dixon, D. (2011). Gamification: Using game-design elements in non-gaming contexts. In CHI'11, *Extended abstracts on human factors in computing systems* (pp. 2425–2428). New York: ACM.

Goodward, J., & Kelly, A. (2010, August). *Bottom line on offsets*. Washington, DC: World Resources Institute.

Hancock, J., Allen, D., Bosco, F., McDaniel, K., & Pierce, C. (2013). Meta-analytic review of employee turnover as a predictor of firm performance. *Journal of Management, 39*(3).

Morino, M. (2011). *Leap of reason: Managing to outcomes in an era of scarcity*. Washington, DC: Venture Philanthropy Partners.

National Issues Forums Institute. (2015). About. Retrieved from https://www.nifi.org/en/about

Public Library Association. (2015). Public library data service statistical report. Retrieved from

Robey, C., O'Brien, K., Julien, K., & Winograd, S. (2012). Fiscal Review of the Cleveland Public Library and scan of state and national trends in library funding. *Urban Publications.* Paper 463.

Torstensson, R. (2011). *A new player in the accelerating textile industry – upcycled textile products*. Borås, Sweden: University of Borås/Swedish School of Textiles.

U.S. Green Building Council. (2015). Achieve better buildings with LEED. Retrieved from www.usgbc.org/leed

Van der Noordaa, N. (2011). *Will Dutch library collections float?* (Master's thesis). Delft University of Technology.

Wang, J. (2006). *All in one: Do single-stream curbside recycling programs increase recycling rates?* Retrieved from https://nature.berkeley.edu/classes/es196/projects/2006final/wang.pdf Van der Noordaa,. (2011).

Winston, R. J., Luell, S. K., & Hunt, W. F. (2010). *Retrofitting with bioretention and bioswale to treat bridge deck stormwater runoff*. In Green Streets and Highways 2010 interactive conference on the state of the art and how to achieve sustainable outcomes. American Society of Civil Engineers.

Appendix 2: The Leadership in Environmental and Energy Design (LEED) Framework

 LEED v4 for BD+C: New Construction and Major Renovation

Project Checklist

Project Name:

Date:

Y	?	N			
			Credit	Integrative Process	**1**

Y	?	N			
0	**0**	**0**	**Location and Transportation**		**16**
			Credit	LEED for Neighborhood Development Location	16
			Credit	Sensitive Land Protection	1
			Credit	High Priority Site	2
			Credit	Surrounding Density and Diverse Uses	5
			Credit	Access to Quality Transit	5
			Credit	Bicycle Facilities	1
			Credit	Reduced Parking Footprint	1
			Credit	Green Vehicles	1

0	0	0	**Sustainable Sites**		**10**
Y			Prereq	Construction Activity Pollution Prevention	Required
			Credit	Site Assessment	1
			Credit	Site Development—Protect or Restore Habitat	2
			Credit	Open Space	1
			Credit	Rainwater Management	3
			Credit	Heat Island Reduction	2
			Credit	Light Pollution Reduction	1

0	0	0	**Water Efficiency**		**11**
Y			Prereq	Outdoor Water Use Reduction	Required
Y			Prereq	Indoor Water Use Reduction	Required
Y			Prereq	Building-Level Water Metering	Required
			Credit	Outdoor Water Use Reduction	2
			Credit	Indoor Water Use Reduction	6
			Credit	Cooling Tower Water Use	2
			Credit	Water Metering	1

0	0	0	**Energy and Atmosphere**		**33**
Y			Prereq	Fundamental Commissioning and Verification	Required
Y			Prereq	Minimum Energy Performance	Required
Y			Prereq	Building-Level Energy Metering	Required
Y			Prereq	Fundamental Refrigerant Management	Required
			Credit	Enhanced Commissioning	6
			Credit	Optimize Energy Performance	18
			Credit	Advanced Energy Metering	1
			Credit	Demand Response	2
			Credit	Renewable Energy Production	3
			Credit	Enhanced Refrigerant Management	1
			Credit	Green Power and Carbon Offsets	2

0	0	0	**Materials and Resources**		**13**
Y			Prereq	Storage and Collection of Recyclables	Required
Y			Prereq	Construction and Demolition Waste Management Planning	Required

			Credit	Building Life-Cycle Impact Reduction	5
			Credit	Building Product Disclosure and Optimization—Environmental Product Declarations	2
			Credit	Building Product Disclosure and Optimization—Sourcing of Raw Materials	2
			Credit	Building Product Disclosure and Optimization—Material Ingredients	2
			Credit	Construction and Demolition Waste Management	2

0	**0**	**0**	**Indoor Environmental Quality**		**16**
Y			Prereq	Minimum Indoor Air Quality Performance	Required
Y			Prereq	Environmental Tobacco Smoke Control	Required
			Credit	Enhanced Indoor Air Quality Strategies	2
			Credit	Low-Emitting Materials	3
			Credit	Construction Indoor Air Quality Management Plan	1
			Credit	Indoor Air Quality Assessment	2
			Credit	Thermal Comfort	1
			Credit	Interior Lighting	2
			Credit	Daylight	3
			Credit	Quality Views	1
			Credit	Acoustic Performance	1

0	**0**	**0**	**Innovation**		**6**
			Credit	Innovation	5
			Credit	LEED Accredited Professional	1

0	**0**	**0**	**Regional Priority**		**4**
			Credit	Regional Priority: Specific Credit	1
			Credit	Regional Priority: Specific Credit	1
			Credit	Regional Priority: Specific Credit	1
			Credit	Regional Priority: Specific Credit	1

0	**0**	**0**	**TOTALS**	Possible Points:	**110**

Certified: 40 to 49 points, **Silver:** 50 to 59 points, **Gold:** 60 to 79 points, **Platinum:** 80 to 110

LEED v4 for Operations & Maintenance: Existing Buildings

Project Checklist   Project Name:

Date:

Y	?	N			
0	**0**	**0**	**Location and Transportation**		**15**
			Credit	Alternative Transportation	15

Y	?	N			
0	**0**	**0**	**Sustainable Sites**		**10**
Y			Prereq	Site Management Policy	Required
			Credit	Site Development—Protect or Restore Habitat	2
			Credit	Rainwater Management	3
			Credit	Heat Island Reduction	2
			Credit	Light Pollution Reduction	1
			Credit	Site Management	1
			Credit	Site Improvement Plan	1

Y	?	N			
0	**0**	**0**	**Water Efficiency**		**12**
Y			Prereq	Indoor Water Use Reduction	Required
Y			Prereq	Building-Level Water Metering	Required
			Credit	Outdoor Water Use Reduction	2
			Credit	Indoor Water Use Reduction	5
			Credit	Cooling Tower Water Use	3
			Credit	Water Metering	2

Y	?	N			
0	**0**	**0**	**Energy and Atmosphere**		**38**
Y			Prereq	Energy Efficiency Best Management Practices	Required
Y			Prereq	Minimum Energy Performance	Required
Y			Prereq	Building-Level Energy Metering	Required
Y			Prereq	Fundamental Refrigerant Management	Required
			Credit	Existing Building Commissioning—Analysis	2
			Credit	Existing Building Commissioning—Implementation	2
			Credit	Ongoing Commissioning	3
			Credit	Optimize Energy Performance	20

			Credit	Advanced Energy Metering	2
			Credit	Demand Response	3
			Credit	Renewable Energy and Carbon Offsets	5
			Credit	Enhanced Refrigerant Management	1

0	0	0	**Materials and Resources**		8
Y			Prereq	Ongoing Purchasing and Waste Policy	Required
Y			Prereq	Facility Maintenance and Renovations Policy	Required
			Credit	Purchasing—Ongoing	1
			Credit	Purchasing—Lamps	1
			Credit	Purchasing—Facility Management and Renovation	2
			Credit	Solid Waste Management—Ongoing	2
			Credit	Solid Waste Management—Facility Management and Renovation	2

0	0	0	**Materials and Resources**		13
Y			Prereq	Storage and Collection of Recyclables	Required
Y			Prereq	Construction and Demolition Waste Management Planning	Required
				Building Life-Cycle Impact Reduction	5
			Credit	Building Product Disclosure and Optimization—Environmental Product Declarations	2
			Credit	Building Product Disclosure and Optimization—Sourcing of Raw Materials	2
			Credit	Building Product Disclosure and Optimization—Material Ingredients	2
			Credit	Construction and Demolition Waste Management	2

0	0	0	**Indoor Environmental Quality**		16
Y			Prereq	Minimum Indoor Air Quality Performance	Required
Y			Prereq	Environmental Tobacco Smoke Control	Required
			Credit	Enhanced Indoor Air Quality Strategies	2
			Credit	Low-Emitting Materials	3
			Credit	Construction Indoor Air Quality Management Plan	1
			Credit	Indoor Air Quality Assessment	2
			Credit	Thermal Comfort	1

			Credit	Interior Lighting	2
			Credit	Daylight	3
			Credit	Quality Views	1
			Credit	Acoustic Performance	1

0	0	0	**Innovation**		**6**
			Credit	Innovation	5
			Credit	LEED Accredited Professional	1

0	0	0	**Regional Priority**		**4**
			Credit	Regional Priority: Specific Credit	1
			Credit	Regional Priority: Specific Credit	1
			Credit	Regional Priority: Specific Credit	1
			Credit	Regional Priority: Specific Credit	1

0	0	0	**TOTALS**	Possible Points:	**110**

Certified: 40 to 49 points, **Silver:** 50 to 59 points, **Gold:** 60 to 79 points, **Platinum:** 80 to 110

Appendix 3: Fair Labor Association (FLA) Workplace Code of Conduct

FLA's Workplace Code of Conduct is reprinted with permission. Available at www .fairlabor.org/our-work/code-of-conduct

PREAMBLE

The FLA Workplace Code of Conduct defines labor standards that aim to achieve decent and humane working conditions. The Code's standards are based on [the United Nations'] International Labor Organization standards and internationally accepted good labor practices.

Companies affiliated with the FLA are expected to comply with all relevant and applicable laws and regulations of the country in which workers are employed and to implement the Workplace Code in their applicable facilities. When differences or conflicts in standards arise, affiliated companies are expected to apply the highest standard.

The FLA monitors compliance with the Workplace Code by carefully examining adherence to the Compliance Benchmarks and the Principles of Monitoring. The Compliance Benchmarks identify specific requirements for meeting each Code standard, while the Principles of Monitoring guide the assessment of compliance. The FLA expects affiliated companies to make improvements when Code standards are not met and to develop sustainable mechanisms to ensure ongoing compliance.

The FLA provides a model of collaboration, accountability, and transparency and serves as a catalyst for positive change in workplace conditions. As an organization that promotes continuous improvement, the FLA strives to be a global leader in establishing best practices for respectful and ethical treatment of workers, and in promoting sustainable conditions through which workers earn fair wages in safe and healthy workplaces.

EMPLOYMENT RELATIONSHIP

Employers shall adopt and adhere to rules and conditions of employment that respect workers and, at a minimum, safeguard their rights under national and international labor and social security laws and regulations.

NONDISCRIMINATION

No person shall be subject to any discrimination in employment, including hiring, compensation, advancement, discipline, termination or retirement, on the basis of gender, race, religion, age, disability, sexual orientation, nationality, political opinion, social group or ethnic origin.

HARASSMENT OR ABUSE

Every employee shall be treated with respect and dignity. No employee shall be subject to any physical, sexual, psychological or verbal harassment or abuse.

FORCED LABOR

There shall be no use of forced labor, including prison labor, indentured labor, bonded labor or other forms of forced labor.

CHILD LABOR

No person shall be employed under the age of 15 or under the age for completion of compulsory education, whichever is higher.

FREEDOM OF ASSOCIATION AND COLLECTIVE BARGAINING

Employers shall recognize and respect the right of employees to freedom of association and collective bargaining.

HEALTH, SAFETY AND ENVIRONMENT

Employers shall provide a safe and healthy workplace setting to prevent accidents and injury to health arising out of, linked with, or occurring in the course of work or as a result of the operation of employers' facilities. Employers shall adopt responsible measures to mitigate negative impacts that the workplace has on the environment.

HOURS OF WORK

Employers shall not require workers to work more than the regular and overtime hours allowed by the law of the country where the workers are employed. The regular work week shall not exceed 48 hours. Employers shall allow workers at least 24 consecutive hours of rest in every seven-day period. All overtime work shall be consensual. Employers shall not request overtime on a regular basis and shall compensate all overtime work at a premium rate. Other than in exceptional circumstances, the sum of regular and overtime hours in a week shall not exceed 60 hours.

COMPENSATION

Every worker has a right to compensation for a regular work week that is sufficient to meet the worker's basic needs and provide some discretionary income. Employers shall pay at least the minimum wage or the appropriate prevailing wage, whichever is higher, comply with all legal requirements on wages, and provide any fringe benefits required by law or contract. Where compensation does not meet workers' basic needs and provide some discretionary income, each employer shall work with the FLA to take appropriate actions that seek to progressively realize a level of compensation that does.

Appendix 4: The Global Reporting Initiative© (GRI) Framework

GRI™ is an international independent organization that has pioneered corporate sustainability reporting since 1997. GRI helps businesses, governments and other organizations understand and communicate the impact of business on critical sustainability issues such as climate change, human rights, corruption and many others. With thousands of reporters in over 100 countries, GRI provides the world's most trusted and widely used standards on sustainability reporting, enabling organizations and their stakeholders to make better decisions based on information that matters. Currently, 45 countries and regions reference GRI in their policies. GRI is built upon a unique multi-stakeholder principle, which ensures the participation and expertise of diverse stakeholders in the development of its standards. GRI's mission is to empower decision-makers everywhere, through its standards and multi-stakeholder network, to take action towards a more sustainable economy and world.

The GRI Standards are free to use and are available at globalreporting.org/standards. The GRI Standards also include guidance and contextual information which is not reprinted here.

GRI SUSTAINABILITY REPORTING STANDARDS 2016

GRI 101: Foundation

1. Reporting Principles

Stakeholder Inclusiveness

1.1 The reporting organization shall identify its stakeholders, and explain how it has responded to their reasonable expectations and interests.

Sustainability Context

1.2 The report shall present the reporting organization's performance in the wider context of sustainability.

Materiality

1.3 The report shall cover topics that:
   1.3.1 reflect the reporting organization's significant economic, environmental, and social impacts; or
   1.3.2 substantively influence the assessments and decisions of stakeholders.

Completeness

1.4 The report shall include coverage of material topics and their boundaries, sufficient to reflect significant economic, environmental, and social impacts, and to enable stakeholders to assess the reporting organization's performance in the reporting period.

Principles for defining report quality

Accuracy

1.5 The reported information shall be sufficiently accurate and detailed for stakeholders to assess the reporting organization's performance.

Balance

1.6 The reported information shall reflect positive and negative aspects of the reporting organization's performance to enable a reasoned assessment of overall performance.

Clarity

1.7 The reporting organization shall make information available in a manner that is understandable and accessible to stakeholders using the information.

Comparability

1.8 The reporting organization shall select, compile, and report information consistently. The reported information shall be presented in a manner that enables stakeholders to analyze changes in the organization's performance over time, and that could support analysis relative to other organizations.

Reliability

1.9 The reporting organization shall gather, record, compile, analyze, and report information and processes used in the preparation of the report in a way that they can be subject to examination, and that establishes the quality and materiality of the information.

Timeliness

1.10 The reporting organization shall report on a regular schedule so that information is available in time for stakeholders to make informed decisions.

2. Using the GRI Standards for sustainability reporting

Applying the reporting principles

2.1 The reporting organization shall apply all Reporting Principles from Section 1 to define report content and quality.

Reporting general disclosures
2.2 The reporting organization shall report the required disclosures from GRI 102: General Disclosures.

Identifying material topics and their boundaries
2.3 The reporting organization shall identify its material topics using the Reporting Principles for defining report content.
    2.3.1 The reporting organization should consult the GRI Sector Disclosures that relate to its sector, if available, to assist with identifying its material topics.
2.4 The reporting organization shall identify the Boundary for each material topic.

Reporting on material topics
2.5 For each material topic, the reporting organization:
    2.5.1 shall report the management approach disclosures for that topic, using GRI 103: Management Approach; and either:
    2.5.2 shall report the topic-specific disclosures in the corresponding GRI Standard, if the material topic is covered by an existing GRI Standard (series 200, 300, and 400); or
    2.5.3 should report other appropriate disclosures, if the material topic is not covered by an existing GRI Standard.

Presenting information

Reporting required disclosures using references
2.6 If the reporting organization reports a required disclosure using a reference to another source where the information is located, the organization shall ensure:
    2.6.1 the reference includes the specific location of the required disclosure; and
    2.6.2 the referenced information is publicly available and readily accessible.

Compiling and presenting information in the report
2.7 When preparing a sustainability report, the reporting organization should:
    2.7.1 present information for the current reporting period and at least two previous periods, as well as future short and medium-term targets if they have been established;
    2.7.2 compile and report information using generally accepted international metrics (such as kilograms or liters) and standard conversion factors, and explain the basis of measurement/calculation where not otherwise apparent;
    2.7.3 provide absolute data and explanatory notes when using ratios or normalized data; and
    2.7.4 define a consistent reporting period for issuing a report.

3. Making claims related to the use of the GRI Standards

Claims that a report has been prepared in accordance with the GRI Standards
3.1 To claim that a sustainability report has been prepared in accordance with the GRI Standards, the reporting organization shall meet all criteria for the respective option (Core or Comprehensive) from Table 1 (on page 23): https://www.globalreporting.org/standards/gri-standards-download-center/

Reasons for omission

3.2 If, in exceptional cases, an organization preparing a sustainability report in accordance with the GRI Standards cannot report a required disclosure, the organization shall provide in the report a reason for omission that:

3.2.1 describes the specific information that has been omitted; and

3.2.2 specifies one of the following reasons for omission from Table 2, including the required explanation for that reason.

Using selected Standards with a GRI-referenced claim

3.3 If the reporting organization uses selected GRI Standards, or parts of their content, to report specific information, but has not met the criteria to prepare a report in accordance with the GRI Standards (as per clause 3.1), the organization:

3.3.1 shall include in any published material with disclosures based on the GRI Standards a statement that:

3.3.1.1 contains the following text: 'This material references [title and publication year of the Standard]', for each Standard used;

3.3.1.2 indicates which specific content from the Standard has been applied, if the Standard has not been used in full;

3.3.2 shall comply with all reporting requirements that correspond to the disclosures reported;

3.3.3 shall notify GRI of the use of the Standards, as per clause 3.4;

3.3.4 should apply the Reporting Principles for defining report quality from Section 1 (on page 10) [see https://www.globalreporting.org/standards/gri-standards-download -center/]; and

3.3.5 should report its management approach by applying GRI 103: Management Approach together with any topic-specific Standard (series 200, 300, or 400) used.

Notifying GRI of the use of the Standards

3.4 The reporting organization shall notify GRI of its use of the GRI Standards, and the claim it has made in the report or published material, by either:

3.4.1 sending a copy to GRI at standards@globalreporting.org; or

3.4.2 registering the report or published material at www.globalreporting.org /standards.

GRI 102: General Disclosures

1. Organizational profile

102-1 Name of the organization
  a. Name of the organization.

102-2 Activities, brands, products, and services
  a. A description of the organization's activities.
  b. Primary brands, products, and services, including an explanation of any products or services that are banned in certain markets.

102-3 Location of headquarters
  a. Location of the organization's headquarters.

102-4 Location of operations
  a. Number of countries where the organization operates, and the names of countries where it has significant operations and/or that are relevant to the topics covered in the report.

102-5 Ownership and legal form

a. Nature of ownership and legal form.

102-6 Markets served

a. Markets served, including:
     i. geographic locations where products and services are offered;
    ii. sectors served;
   iii. types of customers and beneficiaries.

102-7 Scale of the organization

a. Scale of the organization, including:
     i. total number of employees;
    ii. total number of operations;
   iii. net sales (for private sector organizations) or net revenues (for public sector organizations);
    iv. total capitalization (for private sector organizations) broken down in terms of debt and equity;
     v. quantity of products or services provided.

102-8 Information on employees and other workers

a. Total number of employees by employment contract (permanent and temporary), by gender.
b. Total number of employees by employment contract (permanent and temporary), by region.
c. Total number of employees by employment type (full-time and part-time), by gender.
d. Whether a significant portion of the organization's activities are performed by workers who are not employees. If applicable, a description of the nature and scale of work performed by workers who are not employees.
e. Any significant variations in the numbers reported in Disclosures 102-8-a, 102-8-b, and 102-8-c (such as seasonal variations in the tourism or agricultural industries).
f. An explanation of how the data have been compiled, including any assumptions made.

102-9 Supply chain

a. A description of the organization's supply chain, including its main elements as they relate to the organization's activities, primary brands, products, and services.

102-10 Significant changes to the organization and its supply chain

a. Significant changes to the organization's size, structure, ownership, or supply chain, including:
     i. Changes in the location of, or changes in, operations, including facility openings, closings, and expansions;
    ii. Changes in the share capital structure and other capital formation, maintenance, and alteration operations (for private sector organizations);
   iii. Changes in the location of suppliers, the structure of the supply chain, or relationships with suppliers, including selection and termination.

102-11 Precautionary Principle or approach

a. Whether and how the organization applies the Precautionary Principle or approach.

102-12 External initiatives

a. A list of externally-developed economic, environmental and social charters, principles, or other initiatives to which the organization subscribes, or which it endorses.

102-13 Membership of associations
  a. A list of the main memberships of industry or other associations, and national or international advocacy organizations.

2. Strategy

102-14 Statement from senior decision-maker
  a. A statement from the most senior decision-maker of the organization (such as CEO, chair, or equivalent senior position) about the relevance of sustainability to the organization and its strategy for addressing sustainability.
102-15 Key impacts, risks, and opportunities
  a. A description of key impacts, risks, and opportunities.

3. Ethics and integrity

102-16 Values, principles, standards, and norms of behavior
  a. A description of the organization's values, principles, standards, and norms of behavior.
102-17 Mechanisms for advice and concerns about ethics
  a. A description of internal and external mechanisms for:
    i. seeking advice about ethical and lawful behavior, and organizational integrity;
    ii. reporting concerns about unethical or unlawful behavior, and organizational integrity.

4. Governance

102-18 Governance structure
  a. Governance structure of the organization, including committees of the highest governance body.
  b. Committees responsible for decision-making on economic, environmental, and social topics.
102-19 Delegating authority
  a. Process for delegating authority for economic, environmental, and social topics from the highest governance body to senior executives and other employees.
102-20 Executive-level responsibility for economic, environmental, and social topics
  a. Whether the organization has appointed an executive-level position or positions with responsibility for economic, environmental, and social topics.
  b. Whether post holders report directly to the highest governance body.
102-21 Consulting stakeholders on economic, environmental, and social topics
  a. Processes for consultation between stakeholders and the highest governance body on economic, environmental, and social topics.
  b. If consultation is delegated, describe to whom it is delegated and how the resulting feedback is provided to the highest governance body.
102-22 Composition of the highest governance body and its committees
  a. Composition of the highest governance body and its committees by:
    i. executive or non-executive;
    ii. independence;

        iii. tenure on the governance body;

        iv. number of each individual's other significant positions and commitments, and the nature of the commitments;

        v. gender;

        vi. membership of under-represented social groups;

        vii. competencies relating to economic, environmental, and social topics;

        viii. stakeholder representation

102-23 Chair of the highest governance body

    a. Whether the chair of the highest governance body is also an executive officer in the organization.

    b. If the chair is also an executive officer, describe his or her function within the organization's management and the reasons for this arrangement.

102-24 Nominating and selecting the highest governance body

    a. Nomination and selection processes for the highest governance body and its committees.

    b. Criteria used for nominating and selecting highest governance body members, including whether and how:

        i. stakeholders (including shareholders) are involved;

        ii. diversity is considered;

        iii. independence is considered;

        iv. expertise and experience relating to economic, environmental, and social topics are considered

102-25 Conflicts of interest

    a. Processes for the highest governance body to ensure conflicts of interest are avoided and managed.

    b. Whether conflicts of interest are disclosed to stakeholders, including, as a minimum:

        i. Cross-board membership;

        ii. Cross-shareholding with suppliers and other stakeholders;

        iii. Existence of controlling shareholder;

        iv. Related party disclosures.

102-26 Role of highest governance body in setting purpose, values, and strategy

    a. Highest governance body's and senior executives' roles in the development, approval, and updating of the organization's purpose, value or mission statements, strategies, policies, and goals related to economic, environmental, and social topics.

102-27 Collective knowledge of highest governance body

    a. Measures taken to develop and enhance the highest governance body's collective knowledge of economic, environmental, and social topics.

102-28 Evaluating the highest governance body's performance

    a. Processes for evaluating the highest governance body's performance with respect to governance of economic, environmental, and social topics.

    b. Whether such evaluation is independent or not, and its frequency.

    c. Whether such evaluation is a self-assessment.

    d. Actions taken in response to evaluation of the highest governance body's performance with respect to governance of economic, environmental, and social topics, including, as a minimum, changes in membership and organizational practice.

102-29 Identifying and managing economic, environmental, and social impacts

   a. Highest governance body's role in identifying and managing economic, environmental, and social topics and their impacts, risks, and opportunities—including its role in the implementation of due diligence processes.

   b. Whether stakeholder consultation is used to support the highest governance body's identification and management of economic, environmental, and social topics and their impacts, risks, and opportunities.

102-30 Effectiveness of risk management processes

   a. Highest governance body's role in reviewing the effectiveness of the organization's risk management processes for economic, environmental, and social topics.

Disclosure 102-31 Review of economic, environmental, and social topics

   a. Frequency of the highest governance body's review of economic, environmental, and social topics and their impacts, risks, and opportunities.

Disclosure 102-32 Highest governance body's role in sustainability reporting

   a. The highest committee or position that formally reviews and approves the organization's sustainability report and ensures that all material topics are covered.

Disclosure 102-33 Communicating critical concerns

   a. Process for communicating critical concerns to the highest governance body.

Disclosure 102-34 Nature and total number of critical concerns

   a. Total number and nature of critical concerns that were communicated to the highest governance body.

   b. Mechanism(s) used to address and resolve critical concerns.

Disclosure 102-35 Remuneration policies

   a. Remuneration policies for the highest governance body and senior executives for the following types of remuneration:

      i. Fixed pay and variable pay, including performance-based pay, equity-based pay, bonuses, and deferred or vested shares;

      ii. Sign-on bonuses or recruitment incentive payments;

      iii. Termination payments;

      iv. Clawbacks;

      v. Retirement benefits, including the difference between benefit schemes and contribution rates for the highest governance body, senior executives, and all other employees.

   b. How performance criteria in the remuneration policies relate to the highest governance body's and senior executives' objectives for economic, environmental, and social topics.

Disclosure 102-36 Process for determining remuneration

   a. Process for determining remuneration.

   b. Whether remuneration consultants are involved in determining remuneration and whether they are independent of management.

   c. Any other relationships that the remuneration consultants have with the organization.

Disclosure 102-37 Stakeholders' involvement in remuneration

   a. How stakeholders' views are sought and taken into account regarding remuneration.

   b. If applicable, the results of votes on remuneration policies and proposals.

Disclosure 102-38 Annual total compensation ratio

   a. Ratio of the annual total compensation for the organization's highest-paid individual in each country of significant operations to the median annual total compensation for all employees (excluding the highest-paid individual) in the same country.

Disclosure 102-39 Percentage increase in annual total compensation ratio

   a. Ratio of the percentage increase in annual total compensation for the organization's highest-paid individual in each country of significant operations to the median percentage increase in annual total compensation for all employees (excluding the highest-paid individual) in the same country.

5. Stakeholder engagement

Disclosure 102-40 List of stakeholder groups

   a. A list of stakeholder groups engaged by the organization.

Disclosure 102-41 Collective bargaining agreements

   a. Percentage of total employees covered by collective bargaining agreements.

Disclosure 102-42 Identifying and selecting stakeholders

   a. The basis for identifying and selecting stakeholders with whom to engage.

Disclosure 102-43 Approach to stakeholder engagement

   a. The organization's approach to stakeholder engagement, including frequency of engagement by type and by stakeholder group, and an indication of whether any of the engagement was undertaken specifically as part of the report preparation process.

Disclosure 102-44 Key topics and concerns raised

   a. Key topics and concerns that have been raised through stakeholder engagement, including:

      i. how the organization has responded to those key topics and concerns, including through its reporting;

      ii. the stakeholder groups that raised each of the key topics and concerns.

6. Reporting practice

Disclosure 102-45 Entities included in the consolidated financial statements

   a. A list of all entities included in the organization's consolidated financial statements or equivalent documents.

   b. Whether any entity included in the organization's consolidated financial statements or equivalent documents is not covered by the report.

Disclosure 102-46 Defining report content and topic boundaries

   a. An explanation of the process for defining the report content and the topic boundaries.

   b. An explanation of how the organization has implemented the Reporting Principles for defining report content.

Disclosure 102-47 List of material topics

   a. A list of the material topics identified in the process for defining report content.

Disclosure 102-48 Restatements of information

   a. The effect of any restatements of information given in previous reports, and the reasons for such restatements.

Disclosure 102-49 Changes in reporting
  a. Significant changes from previous reporting periods in the list of material topics
     and topic boundaries.
Disclosure 102-50 Reporting period
  a. Reporting period for the information provided.
Disclosure 102-51 Date of most recent report
  a. If applicable, the date of the most recent previous report.
Disclosure 102-52 Reporting cycle
  a. Reporting cycle.
Disclosure 102-53 Contact point for questions regarding the report
  a. The contact point for questions regarding the report or its contents.
Disclosure 102-54 Claims of reporting in accordance with the GRI Standards
  a. The claim made by the organization, if it has prepared a report in accordance with
     the GRI Standards, either:
       i. 'This report has been prepared in accordance with the GRI Standards: Core
          option';
      ii. 'This report has been prepared in accordance with the GRI Standards: Com-
          prehensive option'.
Disclosure 102-55 GRI content index
  a. The GRI content index, which specifies each of the GRI Standards used and lists
     all disclosures included in the report.
  b. For each disclosure, the content index shall include:
       i. the number of the disclosure (for disclosures covered by the GRI
          Standards);
      ii. the page number(s) or URL(s) where the information can be found, either
          within the report or in other published materials;
     iii. if applicable, and where permitted, the reason(s) for omission when a required
          disclosure cannot be made.
Disclosure 102-56 External assurance
  a. A description of the organization's policy and current practice with regard to seek-
     ing external assurance for the report.
  b. If the report has been externally assured:
       i. A reference to the external assurance report, statements, or opinions. If not
          included in the assurance report accompanying the sustainability report, a
          description of what has and what has not been assured and on what basis,
          including the assurance standards used, the level of assurance obtained, and
          any limitations of the assurance process;
      ii. The relationship between the organization and the assurance provider;
     iii. Whether and how the highest governance body or senior executives are
          involved in seeking external assurance for the organization's sustainability
          report.

GRI 103: MANAGEMENT APPROACH 2016

General requirements for reporting the management approach
Reporting requirements
1.1 If management approach disclosures are combined for a group of material topics,
    the reporting organization shall state which topics are covered by each disclosure.

1.2 If there is no management approach for a material topic, the reporting organization shall describe:

    1.2.1 any plans to implement a management approach; or

    1.2.2 the reasons for not having a management approach.

Disclosure 103-1 Explanation of the material topic and its boundary

For each material topic, the reporting organization shall report the following information:

    a. An explanation of why the topic is material.

    b. The boundary for the material topic, which includes a description of:

        i. where the impacts occur;

        ii. the organization's involvement with the impacts. For example, whether the organization has caused or contributed to the impacts, or is directly linked to the impacts through its business relationships.

    c. Any specific limitation regarding the topic boundary.

Disclosure 103-2 The management approach and its components

    a. An explanation of how the organization manages the topic.

    b. A statement of the purpose of the management approach.

    c. A description of the following, if the management approach includes that component:

        i. Policies

        ii. Commitments

        iii. Goals and targets

        iv. Responsibilities

        v. Resources

        vi. Grievance mechanisms

        vii. Specific actions, such as processes, projects, programs and initiatives

Disclosure 103-3 Evaluation of the management approach

    a. An explanation of how the organization evaluates the management approach, including:

        i. the mechanisms for evaluating the effectiveness of the management approach;

        ii. the results of the evaluation of the management approach;

        iii. any related adjustments to the management approach.

GRI 201: ECONOMIC PERFORMANCE 2016

Disclosure 201-1 Direct economic value generated and distributed

The reporting organization shall report the following information:

    a. Direct economic value generated and distributed (EVG&D) on an accruals basis, including the basic components for the organization's global operations as listed below. If data are presented on a cash basis, report the justification for this decision in addition to reporting the following basic components:

        i. Direct economic value generated (EVG): revenues;

        ii. Economic value distributed (D): operating costs, employee wages and benefits, payments to providers of capital, payments to government by country, and community investments;

        iii. Economic value retained: 'direct economic value generated' less 'economic value distributed'.

    b. Where significant, report EVG&D separately at country, regional, or market levels, and the criteria used for defining significance.

Disclosure 201-2 Financial implications and other risks and opportunities due to climate change

    a. Risks and opportunities posed by climate change that have the potential to generate substantive changes in operations, revenue, or expenditure, including:

        i. a description of the risk or opportunity and its classification as either physical, regulatory, or other;

        ii. a description of the impact associated with the risk or opportunity;

        iii. the financial implications of the risk or opportunity before action is taken;

        iv. the methods used to manage the risk or opportunity;

        v. the costs of actions taken to manage the risk or opportunity.

Disclosure 201-3 Defined benefit plan obligations and other retirement plans

    a. If the plan's liabilities are met by the organization's general resources, the estimated value of those liabilities.

    b. If a separate fund exists to pay the plan's pension liabilities:

        i. the extent to which the scheme's liabilities are estimated to be covered by the assets that have been set aside to meet them;

        ii. the basis on which that estimate has been arrived at;

        iii. when that estimate was made.

    c. If a fund set up to pay the plan's pension liabilities is not fully covered, explain the strategy, if any, adopted by the employer to work towards full coverage, and the timescale, if any, by which the employer hopes to achieve full coverage.

    d. Percentage of salary contributed by employee or employer.

    e. Level of participation in retirement plans, such as participation in mandatory or voluntary schemes, regional, or country-based schemes, or those with financial impact.

Disclosure 201-4 Financial assistance received from government

    a. Total monetary value of financial assistance received by the organization from any government during the reporting period, including:

        i. tax relief and tax credits;

        ii. subsidies;

        iii. investment grants, research and development grants, and other relevant types of grant;

        iv. awards;

        v. royalty holidays;

        vi. financial assistance from Export Credit Agencies (ECAs);

        vii. financial incentives;

        viii. other financial benefits received or receivable from any government for any operation.

    b. The information in 201-4-a by country.

    c. Whether, and the extent to which, any government is present in the shareholding structure.

GRI 202: MARKET PRESENCE 2016

Disclosure 202-1 Ratios of standard entry-level wage by gender compared to local minimum wage

    a. When a significant proportion of employees are compensated based on wages subject to minimum wage rules, report the relevant ratio of the entry level wage by gender at significant locations of operation to the minimum wage.

b. When a significant proportion of other workers (excluding employees) performing the organization's activities are compensated based on wages subject to minimum wage rules, describe the actions taken to determine whether these workers are paid above the minimum wage.

c. Whether a local minimum wage is absent or variable at significant locations of operation, by gender. In circumstances in which different minimums can be used as a reference, report which minimum wage is being used.

d. The definition used for 'significant locations of operation'.

Disclosure 202-2 Proportion of senior management hired from the local community

a. Percentage of senior management at significant locations of operation that are hired from the local community.

b. The definition used for 'senior management'.

c. The organization's geographical definition of 'local'.

d. The definition used for 'significant locations of operation'.

GRI 203: INDIRECT ECONOMIC IMPACTS 2016

Disclosure 203-1 Infrastructure investments and services supported

a. Extent of development of significant infrastructure investments and services supported.

b. Current or expected impacts on communities and local economies, including positive and negative impacts where relevant.

c. Whether these investments and services are commercial, in-kind, or pro bono engagements.

Disclosure 203-2 Significant indirect economic impacts

a. Examples of significant identified indirect economic impacts of the organization, including positive and negative impacts.

b. Significance of the indirect economic impacts in the context of external benchmarks and stakeholder priorities, such as national and international standards, protocols, and policy agendas.

GRI 204: PROCUREMENT PRACTICES 2016

Disclosure 204-1 Proportion of spending on local suppliers

a. Percentage of the procurement budget used for significant locations of operation that is spent on suppliers local to that operation (such as percentage of products and services purchased locally).

b. The organization's geographical definition of 'local'.

c. The definition used for 'significant locations of operation'.

GRI 205: ANTI-CORRUPTION 2016

Disclosure 205-1 Operations assessed for risks related to corruption

a. Total number and percentage of operations assessed for risks related to corruption.

b. Significant risks related to corruption identified through the risk assessment.

Disclosure 205-2 Communication and training about anti-corruption policies and procedures

a. Total number and percentage of governance body members that the organization's anti-corruption policies and procedures have been communicated to, broken down by region.

b. Total number and percentage of employees that the organization's anti-corruption policies and procedures have been communicated to, broken down by employee category and region.

c. Total number and percentage of business partners that the organization's anti-corruption policies and procedures have been communicated to, broken down by type of business partner and region. Describe if the organization's anti-corruption policies and procedures have been communicated to any other persons or organizations.

d. Total number and percentage of governance body members that have received training on anti-corruption, broken down by region.

e. Total number and percentage of employees that have received training on anti-corruption, broken down by employee category and region.

Disclosure 205-3 Confirmed incidents of corruption and actions taken

a. Total number and nature of confirmed incidents of corruption.

b. Total number of confirmed incidents in which employees were dismissed or disciplined for corruption.

c. Total number of confirmed incidents when contracts with business partners were terminated or not renewed due to violations related to corruption.

d. Public legal cases regarding corruption brought against the organization or its employees during the reporting period and the outcomes of such cases.

GRI 206: ANTI-COMPETITIVE BEHAVIOR 2016

Disclosure 206-1 Legal actions for anti-competitive behavior, anti-trust, and monopoly practices

a. Number of legal actions pending or completed during the reporting period regarding anti-competitive behavior and violations of anti-trust and monopoly legislation in which the organization has been identified as a participant.

b. Main outcomes of completed legal actions, including any decisions or judgments.

GRI 301: MATERIALS 2016

Disclosure 301-1 Materials used by weight or volume

a. Total weight or volume of materials that are used to produce and package the organization's primary products and services during the reporting period, by:
    i. non-renewable materials used;
    ii. renewable materials used.

Disclosure 301-2 Recycled input materials used

a. Percentage of recycled input materials used to manufacture the organization's primary products and services.

Disclosure 301-3 Reclaimed products and their packaging materials

a. Percentage of reclaimed products and their packaging materials for each product category.

b. How the data for this disclosure have been collected.

GRI 302: ENERGY 2016

Disclosure 302-1 Energy consumption within the organization

a. Total fuel consumption within the organization from non-renewable sources, in joules or multiples, and including fuel types used.

b. Total fuel consumption within the organization from renewable sources, in joules or multiples, and including fuel types used.

c. In joules, watt-hours or multiples, the total:
   i. electricity consumption
   ii. heating consumption
   iii. cooling consumption
   iv. steam consumption

d. In joules, watt-hours or multiples, the total:
   i. electricity sold
   ii. heating sold
   iii. cooling sold
   iv. steam sold

e. Total energy consumption within the organization, in joules or multiples.

f. Standards, methodologies, assumptions, and/or calculation tools used.

g. Source of the conversion factors used.

Disclosure 302-2 Energy consumption outside of the organization

a. Energy consumption outside of the organization, in joules or multiples.

b. Standards, methodologies, assumptions, and/or calculation tools used.

c. Source of the conversion factors used.

Disclosure 302-3 Energy intensity

a. Energy intensity ratio for the organization.

b. Organization-specific metric (the denominator) chosen to calculate the ratio.

c. Types of energy included in the intensity ratio; whether fuel, electricity, heating, cooling, steam, or all.

d. Whether the ratio uses energy consumption within the organization, outside of it, or both.

Disclosure 302-4 Reduction of energy consumption

a. Amount of reductions in energy consumption achieved as a direct result of conservation and efficiency initiatives, in joules or multiples.

b. Types of energy included in the reductions; whether fuel, electricity, heating, cooling, steam, or all.

c. Basis for calculating reductions in energy consumption, such as base year or baseline, including the rationale for choosing it.

d. Standards, methodologies, assumptions, and/or calculation tools used.

Disclosure 302-5 Reductions in energy requirements of products and services

a. Reductions in energy requirements of sold products and services achieved during the reporting period, in joules or multiples.

b. Basis for calculating reductions in energy consumption, such as base year or baseline, including the rationale for choosing it.

c. Standards, methodologies, assumptions, and/or calculation tools used.

GRI 303: WATER 2016

Disclosure 303-1 Water withdrawal by source

a. Total volume of water withdrawn, with a breakdown by the following sources:
   i. Surface water, including water from wetlands, rivers, lakes, and oceans;
   ii. Ground water;
   iii. Rainwater collected directly and stored by the organization;

   iv. Waste water from another organization;

   v. Municipal water supplies or other public or private water utilities.

  b. Standards, methodologies, and assumptions used.

Disclosure 303-2 Water sources significantly affected by withdrawal of water

  a. Total number of water sources significantly affected by withdrawal by type:

   i. Size of the water source;

   ii. Whether the source is designated as a nationally or internationally protected area;

   iii. Biodiversity value (such as species diversity and endemism, and total number of protected species);

   iv. Value or importance of the water source to local communities and indigenous peoples.

  b. Standards, methodologies, and assumptions used.

Disclosure 303-3 Water recycled and reused

  a. Total volume of water recycled and reused by the organization.

  b. Total volume of water recycled and reused as a percentage of the total water withdrawal as specified in Disclosure 303-1.

  c. Standards, methodologies, and assumptions used.

GRI 304: BIODIVERSITY 2016

Disclosure 304-1 Operational sites owned, leased, managed in, or adjacent to, protected areas and areas of high biodiversity value outside protected areas

  a. For each operational site owned, leased, managed in, or adjacent to, protected areas and areas of high biodiversity value outside protected areas, the following information:

   i. Geographic location;

   ii. Subsurface and underground land that may be owned, leased, or managed by the organization;

   iii. Position in relation to the protected area (in the area, adjacent to, or containing portions of the protected area) or the high biodiversity value area outside protected areas;

   iv. Type of operation (office, manufacturing or production, or extractive);

   v. Size of operational site in km2 (or another unit, if appropriate);

   vi. Biodiversity value characterized by the attribute of the protected area or area of high biodiversity value outside the protected area (terrestrial, freshwater, or maritime ecosystem);

   vii. Biodiversity value characterized by listing of protected status (such as International Union for Conservation of Nature (IUCN), Protected Area Management Categories, Ramsar Convention, national legislation).

Disclosure 304-2 Significant impacts of activities, products, and services on biodiversity

  a. Nature of significant direct and indirect impacts on biodiversity with reference to one or more of the following:

   i. Construction or use of manufacturing plants, mines, and transport infrastructure;

   ii. Pollution (introduction of substances that do not naturally occur in the habitat from point and non-point sources);

     iii. Introduction of invasive species, pests, and pathogens;
     iv. Reduction of species;
     v. Habitat conversion;
     vi. Changes in ecological processes outside the natural range of variation (such as salinity or changes in groundwater level).
  b. Significant direct and indirect positive and negative impacts with reference to the following:
     i. Species affected;
     ii. Extent of areas impacted;
     iii. Duration of impacts;
     iv. Reversibility or irreversibility of the impacts.

Disclosure 304-3 Habitats protected or restored
  a. Size and location of all habitat areas protected or restored, and whether the success of the restoration measure was or is approved by independent external professionals.
  b. Whether partnerships exist with third parties to protect or restore habitat areas distinct from where the organization has overseen and implemented restoration or protection measures.
  c. Status of each area based on its condition at the close of the reporting period.
  d. Standards, methodologies, and assumptions used.

Disclosure 304-4 IUCN Red List species and national conservation list species with habitats in areas affected by operations
  a. Total number of IUCN Red List species and national conservation list species with habitats in areas affected by the operations of the organization, by level of extinction risk:
     i. Critically endangered
     ii. Endangered
     iii. Vulnerable
     iv. Near threatened
     v. Least concern

GRI 305: EMISSIONS 2016

Disclosure 305-1 Direct (Scope 1[1]) GhG emissions
  a. Gross direct (Scope 1) GhG emissions in metric tons of CO_2 equivalent.
  b. Gases included in the calculation; whether CO_2, CH_4, N_2O, HFCs, PFCs, SF_6, NF_3, or all.
  c. Biogenic CO_2 emissions in metric tons of CO_2 equivalent.
  d. Base year for the calculation, if applicable, including:
     i. the rationale for choosing it;
     ii. emissions in the base year;
     iii. the context for any significant changes in emissions that triggered recalculations of base year emissions.
  e. Source of the emission factors and the global warming potential (GWP) rates used, or a reference to the GWP source.
  f. Consolidation approach for emissions; whether equity share, financial control, or operational control.
  g. Standards, methodologies, assumptions, and/or calculation tools used.

Disclosure 305-2 Energy indirect (Scope 2[2]) GhG emissions

    a. Gross location-based energy indirect (Scope 2) GhG emissions in metric tons of CO2 equivalent.

    b. If applicable, gross market-based energy indirect (Scope 2) GhG emissions in metric tons of CO2 equivalent.

    c. If available, the gases included in the calculation; whether CO2, CH4, N2O, HFCs, PFCs, SF6, NF3, or all.

    d. Base year for the calculation, if applicable, including:

        i. the rationale for choosing it;

        ii. emissions in the base year;

        iii. the context for any significant changes in emissions that triggered recalculations of base year emissions.

    e. Source of the emission factors and the global warming potential (GWP) rates used, or a reference to the GWP source.

    f. Consolidation approach for emissions; whether equity share, financial control, or operational control.

    g. Standards, methodologies, assumptions, and/or calculation tools used.

Disclosure 305-3 Other indirect (Scope 3[3]) GhG emissions

    a. Gross other indirect (Scope 3) GhG emissions in metric tons of CO2 equivalent.

    b. If available, the gases included in the calculation; whether CO2, CH4, N2O, HFCs, PFCs, SF6, NF3, or all.

    c. Biogenic CO2 emissions in metric tons of CO2 equivalent.

    d. Other indirect (Scope 3) GhG emissions categories and activities included in the calculation.

    e. Base year for the calculation, if applicable, including:

        i. the rationale for choosing it;

        ii. emissions in the base year;

        iii. the context for any significant changes in emissions that triggered recalculations of base year emissions.

    f. Source of the emission factors and the global warming potential (GWP) rates used, or a reference to the GWP source.

    g. Standards, methodologies, assumptions, and/or calculation tools used.

Disclosure 305-4 GhG emissions intensity

    a. GhG emissions intensity ratio for the organization.

    b. Organization-specific metric (the denominator) chosen to calculate the ratio.

    c. Types of GhG emissions included in the intensity ratio; whether direct (Scope 1), energy indirect (Scope 2), and/or other indirect (Scope 3).

    d. Gases included in the calculation; whether CO2, CH4, N2O, HFCs, PFCs, SF6, NF3, or all.

Disclosure 305-5 Reduction of GhG emissions

    a. GhG emissions reduced as a direct result of reduction initiatives, in metric tons of CO2 equivalent.

    b. Gases included in the calculation; whether CO2, CH4, N2O, HFCs, PFCs, SF6, NF3, or all.

    c. Base year or baseline, including the rationale for choosing it.

    d. Scopes in which reductions took place; whether direct (Scope 1), energy indirect (Scope 2), and/or other indirect (Scope 3).

    e. Standards, methodologies, assumptions, and/or calculation tools used.

Disclosure 305-6 Emissions of ozone-depleting substances (ODS)

    a. Production, imports, and exports of ODS in metric tons of CFC-11 (trichlorofluo-romethane) equivalent.

    b. Substances included in the calculation.

    c. Source of the emission factors used.

    d. Standards, methodologies, assumptions, and/or calculation tools used.

Disclosure 305-7 Nitrogen oxides (NOX), sulfur oxides (SOX), and other significant air emissions

    a. Significant air emissions, in kilograms or multiples, for each of the following:

        i. NOX

        ii. SOX

        iii. Persistent organic pollutants (POP)

        iv. Volatile organic compounds (VOC)

        v. Hazardous air pollutants (HAP)

        vi. Particulate matter (PM)

        vii. Other standard categories of air emissions identified in relevant regulations

    b. Source of the emission factors used.

    c. Standards, methodologies, assumptions, and/or calculation tools used.

GRI 306: EFFLUENTS AND WASTE 2016

Disclosure 306-1 Water discharge by quality and destination

    a. Total volume of planned and unplanned water discharges by:

        i. destination;

        ii. quality of the water, including treatment method;

        iii. whether the water was reused by another organization.

    b. Standards, methodologies, and assumptions used.

Disclosure 306-2 Waste by type and disposal method

    a. Total weight of hazardous waste, with a breakdown by the following disposal methods where applicable:

        i. Reuse

        ii. Recycling

        iii. Composting

        iv. Recovery, including energy recovery

        v. Incineration (mass burn)

        vi. Deep well injection

        vii. Landfill

        viii. On-site storage

        ix. Other (to be specified by the organization)

    b. Total weight of non-hazardous waste, with a breakdown by the following disposal methods where applicable:

        i. Reuse

        ii. Recycling

        iii. Composting

        iv. Recovery, including energy recovery

        v. Incineration (mass burn)

        vi. Deep well injection

        vii. Landfill

    viii. On-site storage

    ix. Other (to be specified by the organization)

  c. How the waste disposal method has been determined:

    i. Disposed of directly by the organization, or otherwise directly confirmed

    ii. Information provided by the waste disposal contractor

    iii. Organizational defaults of the waste disposal contractor

Disclosure 306-3 Significant spills

  a. Total number and total volume of recorded significant spills.

  b. The following additional information for each spill that was reported in the organization's financial statements:

    i. Location of spill;

    ii. Volume of spill;

    iii. Material of spill, categorized by: oil spills (soil or water surfaces), fuel spills (soil or water surfaces), spills of wastes (soil or water surfaces), spills of chemicals (mostly soil or water surfaces), and other (to be specified by the organization).

  c. Impacts of significant spills.

Disclosure 306-4 Transport of hazardous waste

  a. Total weight for each of the following:

    i. Hazardous waste transported

    ii. Hazardous waste imported

    iii. Hazardous waste exported

    iv. Hazardous waste treated

  b. Percentage of hazardous waste shipped internationally.

  c. Standards, methodologies, and assumptions used.

Disclosure 306-5 Water bodies affected by water discharges and/or runoff

  a. Water bodies and related habitats that are significantly affected by water discharges and/or runoff, including information on:

    i. the size of the water body and related habitat;

    ii. whether the water body and related habitat is designated as a nationally or internationally protected area;

    iii. the biodiversity value, such as total number of protected species.

GRI 307: ENVIRONMENTAL COMPLIANCE 2016

Disclosure 307-1 Non-compliance with environmental laws and regulations

  a. Significant fines and non-monetary sanctions for non-compliance with environmental laws and/or regulations in terms of:

    i. total monetary value of significant fines;

    ii. total number of non-monetary sanctions;

    iii. cases brought through dispute resolution mechanisms.

  b. If the organization has not identified any non-compliance with environmental laws and/or regulations, a brief statement of this fact is sufficient.

GRI 308: SUPPLIER ENVIRONMENTAL ASSESSMENT 2016

Disclosure 308-1 New suppliers that were screened using environmental criteria

  a. Percentage of new suppliers that were screened using environmental criteria.

Disclosure 308-2 Negative environmental impacts in the supply chain and actions taken

a. Number of suppliers assessed for environmental impacts.
b. Number of suppliers identified as having significant actual and potential negative environmental impacts.
c. Significant actual and potential negative environmental impacts identified in the supply chain.
d. Percentage of suppliers identified as having significant actual and potential negative environmental impacts with which improvements were agreed upon as a result of assessment.
e. Percentage of suppliers identified as having significant actual and potential negative environmental impacts with which relationships were terminated as a result of assessment, and why.

GRI 401: EMPLOYMENT 2016

Disclosure 401-1 New employee hires and employee turnover
a. Total number and rate of new employee hires during the reporting period, by age group, gender and region.
b. Total number and rate of employee turnover during the reporting period, by age group, gender and region.

Disclosure 401-2 Benefits provided to full-time employees that are not provided to temporary or part-time employees
a. Benefits which are standard for full-time employees of the organization but are not provided to temporary or part-time employees, by significant locations of operation. These include, as a minimum:
   i. life insurance;
   ii. health care;
   iii. disability and invalidity coverage;
   iv. parental leave;
   v. retirement provision;
   vi. stock ownership;
   vii. others.
b. The definition used for 'significant locations of operation'.

Disclosure 401-3 Parental leave
a. Total number of employees that were entitled to parental leave, by gender.
b. Total number of employees that took parental leave, by gender.
c. Total number of employees that returned to work in the reporting period after parental leave ended, by gender.
d. Total number of employees that returned to work after parental leave ended that were still employed 12 months after their return to work, by gender.
e. Return to work and retention rates of employees that took parental leave, by gender.

GRI 402: LABOR/MANAGEMENT RELATIONS 2016

Disclosure 402-1 Minimum notice periods regarding operational changes
a. Minimum number of weeks' notice typically provided to employees and their representatives prior to the implementation of significant operational changes that could substantially affect them.
b. For organizations with collective bargaining agreements, report whether the notice period and provisions for consultation and negotiation are specified in collective agreements.

GRI 403: OCCUPATIONAL HEALTH AND SAFETY 2016

Disclosure 403-1 Workers representation in formal joint management–worker health and safety committees
    a. The level at which each formal joint management-worker health and safety committee typically operates within the organization.
    b. Percentage of workers whose work, or workplace, is controlled by the organization, that are represented by formal joint management-worker health and safety committees.

Disclosure 403-2 Types of injury and rates of injury, occupational diseases, lost days, and absenteeism, and number of work-related fatalities
    a. Types of injury, injury rate (IR), occupational disease rate (ODR), lost day rate (LDR), absentee rate (AR), and work-related fatalities, for all employees, with a breakdown by:
        i. region;
        ii. gender.
    b. Types of injury, injury rate (IR), and work-related fatalities, for all workers (excluding employees) whose work, or workplace, is controlled by the organization, with a breakdown by:
        i. region;
        ii. gender.
    c. The system of rules applied in recording and reporting accident statistics.

Disclosure 403-3 Workers with high incidence or high risk of diseases related to their occupation
    a. Whether there are workers whose work, or workplace, is controlled by the organization, involved in occupational activities who have a high incidence or high risk of specific diseases.

Disclosure 403-4 Health and safety topics covered in formal agreements with trade unions
    a. Whether formal agreements (either local or global) with trade unions cover health and safety.
    b. If so, the extent, as a percentage, to which various health and safety topics are covered by these agreements.

GRI 404: TRAINING AND EDUCATION 2016

Disclosure 404-1 Average hours of training per year per employee
    a. Average hours of training that the organization's employees have undertaken during the reporting period, by:
        i. gender;
        ii. employee category.

Disclosure 404-2 Programs for upgrading employee skills and transition assistance programs
    a. Type and scope of programs implemented and assistance provided to upgrade employee skills.
    b. Transition assistance programs provided to facilitate continued employability and the management of career endings resulting from retirement or termination of employment.

Disclosure 404-3 Percentage of employees receiving regular performance and career development reviews

a. Percentage of total employees by gender and by employee category who received a regular performance and career development review during the reporting period.

GRI 405: DIVERSITY AND EQUAL OPPORTUNITY 2016

Disclosure 405-1 Diversity of governance bodies and employees

a. Percentage of individuals within the organization's governance bodies in each of the following diversity categories:
    i. Gender;
    ii. Age group: under 30 years old, 30–50 years old, over 50 years old;
    iii. Other indicators of diversity where relevant (such as minority or vulnerable groups).
b. Percentage of employees per employee category in each of the following diversity categories:
    i. Gender;
    ii. Age group: under 30 years old, 30–50 years old, over 50 years old;
    iii. Other indicators of diversity where relevant (such as minority or vulnerable groups).

Disclosure 405-2 Ratio of basic salary and remuneration of women to men

a. Ratio of the basic salary and remuneration of women to men for each employee category, by significant locations of operation.
b. The definition used for 'significant locations of operation'.

GRI 406: NON-DISCRIMINATION 2016

Disclosure 406-1 Incidents of discrimination and corrective actions taken

a. Total number of incidents of discrimination during the reporting period.
b. Status of the incidents and actions taken with reference to the following:
    i. Incident reviewed by the organization;
    ii. Remediation plans being implemented;
    iii. Remediation plans that have been implemented, with results reviewed through routine internal management review processes;
    iv. Incident no longer subject to action.

GRI 407: FREEDOM OF ASSOCIATION AND COLLECTIVE BARGAINING 2016

Disclosure 407-1 Operations and suppliers in which the right to freedom of association and collective bargaining may be at risk

a. Operations and suppliers in which workers' rights to exercise freedom of association or collective bargaining may be violated or at significant risk either in terms of:
    i. type of operation (such as manufacturing plant) and supplier;
    ii. countries or geographic areas with operations and suppliers considered at risk.
b. Measures taken by the organization in the reporting period intended to support rights to exercise freedom of association and collective bargaining.

GRI 408: CHILD LABOR 2016

Disclosure 408-1 Operations and suppliers at significant risk for incidents of child labor
  a. Operations and suppliers considered to have significant risk for incidents of:
    i. child labor;
    ii. young workers exposed to hazardous work.
  b. Operations and suppliers considered to have significant risk for incidents of child labor either in terms of:
    i. type of operation (such as manufacturing plant) and supplier;
    ii. countries or geographic areas with operations and suppliers considered at risk.
  c. Measures taken by the organization in the reporting period intended to contribute to the effective abolition of child labor.

GRI 409: FORCED OR COMPULSORY LABOR

Disclosure 409-1 Operations and suppliers at significant risk for incidents of forced or compulsory labor
  a. Operations and suppliers considered to have significant risk for incidents of forced or compulsory labor either in terms of:
    i. type of operation (such as manufacturing plant) and supplier;
    ii. countries or geographic areas with operations and suppliers considered at risk.
  b. Measures taken by the organization in the reporting period intended to contribute to the elimination of all forms of forced or compulsory labor.

GRI 410: SECURITY PRACTICES

Disclosure 410-1 Security personnel trained in human rights policies or procedures
  a. Percentage of security personnel who have received formal training in the organization's human rights policies or specific procedures and their application to security.
  b. Whether training requirements also apply to third-party organizations providing security personnel.

GRI 411: RIGHTS OF INDIGENOUS PEOPLES

Disclosure 411-1 Incidents of violations involving rights of indigenous peoples
  a. Total number of identified incidents of violations involving the rights of indigenous peoples during the reporting period.
  b. Status of the incidents and actions taken with reference to the following:
    i. Incident reviewed by the organization;
    ii. Remediation plans being implemented;
    iii. Remediation plans that have been implemented, with results reviewed through routine internal management review processes;
    iv. Incident no longer subject to action.

GRI 412: HUMAN RIGHTS ASSESSMENT

Disclosure 412-1 Operations that have been subject to human rights reviews or impact assessments
  a. Total number and percentage of operations that have been subject to human rights reviews or human rights impact assessments, by country.

Disclosure 412-2 Employee training on human rights policies or procedures

a. Total number of hours in the reporting period devoted to training on human rights policies or procedures concerning aspects of human rights that are relevant to operations.

b. Percentage of employees trained during the reporting period in human rights policies or procedures concerning aspects of human rights that are relevant to operations.

Disclosure 412-3 Significant investment agreements and contracts that include human rights clauses or that underwent human rights screening

a. Total number and percentage of significant investment agreements and contracts that include human rights clauses or that underwent human rights screening.

b. The definition used for 'significant investment agreements'.

GRI 413: LOCAL COMMUNITIES

Disclosure 413-1 Operations with local community engagement, impact assessments, and development programs

a. Percentage of operations with implemented local community engagement, impact assessments, and/or development programs, including the use of:
    i. social impact assessments, including gender impact assessments, based on participatory processes;
    ii. environmental impact assessments and ongoing monitoring;
    iii. public disclosure of results of environmental and social impact assessments;
    iv. local community development programs based on local communities' needs;
    v. stakeholder engagement plans based on stakeholder mapping;
    vi. broad based local community consultation committees and processes that include vulnerable groups;
    vii. works councils, occupational health and safety committees and other worker representation bodies to deal with impacts;
    viii. formal local community grievance processes.

Disclosure 413-2 Operations with significant actual and potential negative impacts on local communities

a. Operations with significant actual and potential negative impacts on local communities, including:
    i. the location of the operations;
    ii. the significant actual and potential negative impacts of operations.

GRI 414: SUPPLIER SOCIAL ASSESSMENT

Disclosure 414-1 New suppliers that were screened using social criteria

a. Percentage of new suppliers that were screened using social criteria.

Disclosure 414-2 Negative social impacts in the supply chain and actions taken

a. Number of suppliers assessed for social impacts.

b. Number of suppliers identified as having significant actual and potential negative social impacts.

c. Significant actual and potential negative social impacts identified in the supply chain.

d. Percentage of suppliers identified as having significant actual and potential negative social impacts with which improvements were agreed upon as a result of assessment.

e. Percentage of suppliers identified as having significant actual and potential negative social impacts with which relationships were terminated as a result of assessment, and why.

GRI 415: PUBLIC POLICY

Disclosure 415-1 Political contributions
  a. Total monetary value of financial and in-kind political contributions made directly and indirectly by the organization by country and recipient/beneficiary.
  b. If applicable, how the monetary value of in-kind contributions was estimated.

GRI 416: CUSTOMER HEALTH AND SAFETY

Disclosure 416-1 Assessment of the health and safety impacts of product and service categories
  a. Percentage of significant product and service categories for which health and safety impacts are assessed for improvement.

Disclosure 416-2 Incidents of non-compliance concerning the health and safety impacts of products and services
  a. Total number of incidents of non-compliance with regulations and/or voluntary codes concerning the health and safety impacts of products and services within the reporting period, by:
      i. incidents of non-compliance with regulations resulting in a fine or penalty;
      ii. incidents of non-compliance with regulations resulting in a warning;
      iii. incidents of non-compliance with voluntary codes.
  b. If the organization has not identified any non-compliance with regulations and/or voluntary codes, a brief statement of this fact is sufficient.

GRI 417: MARKETING AND LABELING

Disclosure 417-1 Requirements for product and service information and labeling
  a. Whether each of the following types of information is required by the organization's procedures for product and service information and labeling:
      i. The sourcing of components of the product or service;
      ii. Content, particularly with regard to substances that might produce an environmental or social impact;
      iii. Safe use of the product or service;
      iv. Disposal of the product and environmental or social impacts;
      v. Other (explain).
  b. Percentage of significant product or service categories covered by and assessed for compliance with such procedures.

Disclosure 417-2 Incidents of non-compliance concerning product and service information and labeling
  a. Total number of incidents of non-compliance with regulations and/or voluntary codes concerning product and service information and labeling, by:
      i. incidents of non-compliance with regulations resulting in a fine or penalty;

        ii. incidents of non-compliance with regulations resulting in a warning;

        iii. incidents of non-compliance with voluntary codes.

  b. If the organization has not identified any non-compliance with regulations and/or voluntary codes, a brief statement of this fact is sufficient.

Disclosure 417-3 Incidents of non-compliance concerning marketing communications

  a. Total number of incidents of non-compliance with regulations and/or voluntary codes concerning marketing communications, including advertising, promotion, and sponsorship, by:

        i. incidents of non-compliance with regulations resulting in a fine or penalty;

        ii. incidents of non-compliance with regulations resulting in a warning;

        iii. incidents of non-compliance with voluntary codes.

  b. If the organization has not identified any non-compliance with regulations and/or voluntary codes, a brief statement of this fact is sufficient.

GRI 418: CUSTOMER PRIVACY

Disclosure 418-1 Substantiated complaints concerning breaches of customer privacy and losses of customer data

  a. Total number of substantiated complaints received concerning breaches of customer privacy, categorized by:

        i. complaints received from outside parties and substantiated by the organization;

        ii. complaints from regulatory bodies.

  b. Total number of identified leaks, thefts, or losses of customer data.

  c. If the organization has not identified any substantiated complaints, a brief statement of this fact is sufficient.

GRI 419: SOCIOECONOMIC COMPLIANCE

Disclosure 419-1 Non-compliance with laws and regulations in the social and economic area

  a. Significant fines and non-monetary sanctions for non-compliance with laws and/or regulations in the social and economic area in terms of:

        i. total monetary value of significant fines;

        ii. total number of non-monetary sanctions;

        iii. cases brought through dispute resolution mechanisms.

  b. If the organization has not identified any non-compliance with laws and/or regulations, a brief statement of this fact is sufficient.

  c. The context against which significant fines and non-monetary sanctions were incurred.

GRI™ is an international independent organization that has pioneered corporate sustainability reporting since 1997. GRI helps businesses, governments and other organizations understand and communicate the impact of business on critical sustainability issues such as climate change, human rights, corruption and many others. With thousands of reporters in over 100 countries, GRI provides the world's most trusted and widely used standards on sustainability reporting, enabling organizations and their stakeholders to make better decisions based on information that matters. Currently, 45 countries and regions reference GRI in their policies. GRI is built upon a unique multi-stakeholder principle, which ensures the participation and expertise of diverse stakeholders in the development of its standards. GRI's mission is to empower decision-makers everywhere, through its standards and multi-stakeholder network, to take action towards a more sustainable economy and world.

The GRI Standards are free to use and are available at globalreporting.org/standards. The GRI Standards also include guidance and contextual information which is not reprinted here.

© 2016, Global Reporting Initiative. Reprinted here with permission.

NOTES

1. Scope 1 are also referred to as Direct GhG, and are defined as 'emissions from sources that are owned or controlled by an organization (S. Boles, n.d.).

2. Scope 2 are also referred to as Energy Indirect GhG, and are defined as 'emissions from the consumption of purchased electricity, steam, or other sources of energy (e.g. chilled water) generated upstream from the organization' (S. Boles, n.d.).

3. Scope 3 are also referred to as Other Indirect GhG, and are defined as 'emissions that are a consequence of the operations of an organization, but are not directly owned or controlled by the organization'. Scope 3 includes a number of different sources of GhG (e.g. employee commuting, business travel, third-party distribution and logistics, etc.). Per Boles (n.d.) Scope 3 are the largest component of most organizations' carbon footprint.

Appendix 5: The U.S. Department of Commerce National Institute of Standards and Technology Malcolm Baldrige Award Excellence Framework

The Malcolm Baldrige Award Excellence Framework is free to use and is available at https://www .nist.gov/sites/default/files/documents/2017/02/09/2017-2018-baldrige-excellence-builder.pdf

The U.S. Department of Commerce's National Institute of Standards and Technology (NIST) Malcolm Baldrige Award Excellence Framework and website also include guidance and contextual information that is not reprinted here (NIST, 2017).

MALCOLM BALDRIGE AWARD EXCELLENCE FRAMEWORK

Organizational Profile

P.1 Organizational Description:
What are your key organizational characteristics?
a. Organizational Environment
1. Product Offerings
2. Mission, Vision, and Values
3. Workforce Profile
4. Assets
5. Regulatory Requirements

b. Organizational Relationships
1. Organizational Structure
2. Customers and Stakeholders
3. Suppliers and Partners

P.2 Organizational Situation:
a. Competitive Environment
  1. Competitive Position
  2. Competitiveness Changes
  3. Comparative Data

b. Strategic Context
c. Performance Improvement System

1 Leadership

1.1 Senior Leadership:
How do your senior leaders lead the organization?
  1. How do senior leaders set your organization's vision and values?
  2. How do senior leaders' actions demonstrate their commitment to legal and ethical behavior?
  3. How do senior leaders communicate with and engage the entire workforce and key customers?
  4. How do senior leaders' actions create an environment for success now and in the future?
  5. How do senior leaders create a focus on action that will achieve the organization's mission?

1.2 Governance and Societal Responsibilities:
How do you govern your organization and fulfill your societal responsibilities?
  1. How does your organization ensure responsible governance?
  2. How do you evaluate the performance of your senior leaders and your governance board?
  3. How do you address and anticipate legal, regulatory, and community concerns with your products and operations?
  4. How do you promote and ensure ethical behavior in all interactions?
  5. How do you consider societal well-being and benefit as part of your strategy and daily operations?
  6. How do you actively support and strengthen your key communities?

2 Strategy

2.1 Strategy Development:
How do you develop your strategy?
  1. How do you conduct your strategic planning?
  2. How does your strategy development process stimulate and incorporate innovation?
  3. How do you collect and analyze relevant data and develop information for your strategic planning process?
  4. How do you decide which key processes will be accomplished by your workforce and which by external suppliers and partners?
  5. What are your organization's key strategic objectives and timetable for achieving them?
  6. How do your strategic objectives achieve appropriate balance among varying and potentially competing organizational needs?

2.2 Strategy Implementation:

How do you implement your strategy?

1. What are your key short- and longer-term action plans?
2. How do you deploy your action plans?
3. How do you ensure that financial and other resources are available to support the achievement of your action plans while you meet current obligations?
4. What are your key workforce plans to support your short- and longer-term strategic objectives and action plans?
5. What key performance measures or indicators do you use to track the achievement and effectiveness of your action plans?
6. For these key performance measures or indicators, what are your performance projections for your short- and longer-term planning horizons?
7. How do you establish and implement modified action plans if circumstances require a shift in plans and rapid execution of new plans?

3 Customers

3.1 Voice of the Customer:

How do you obtain information from your customers?

1. How do you listen to, interact with, and observe customers to obtain actionable information?
2. How do you listen to potential customers to obtain actionable information?
3. How do you determine customer satisfaction, dissatisfaction, and engagement?
4. How do you obtain information on customers' satisfaction with your organization relative to other organizations?

3.2 Customer Engagement:

How do you engage customers by serving their needs and building relationships?

1. How do you determine product offerings?
2. How do you enable customers to seek information and support?
3. How do you determine your customer groups and market segments?
4. How do you build and manage customer relationships?
5. How do you manage customer complaints?

4 Measurement, Analysis, and Knowledge Management

4.1 Measurement, Analysis, and Improvement of Organizational Performance:

How do you measure, analyze, and then improve organizational performance?

1. How do you track data and information on daily operations and overall organizational performance?
2. How do you select comparative data and information to support fact-based decision making?
3. How do you select voice-of-the-customer and market data and information?
4. How do you ensure that your performance measurement system can respond to rapid or unexpected organizational or external changes?
5. How do you review your organization's performance and capabilities?
6. How do you project your organization's future performance?
7. How do you use findings from performance reviews (addressed in question 5) to develop priorities for continuous improvement and opportunities for innovation?

4.2 Information and Knowledge Management:
How do you manage your information and your organizational knowledge assets?
1. How do you verify and ensure the quality of organizational data and information?
2. How do you ensure the availability of organizational data and information?
3. How do you build and manage organizational knowledge?
4. How do you share best practices in your organization?
5. How do you use your knowledge and resources to embed learning in the way your organization operates?

5 Workforce

5.1 Workforce Environment:
How do you build an effective and supportive workforce environment?
1. How do you assess your workforce capability and capacity needs?
2. How do you recruit, hire, place, and retain new workforce members?
3. How do you prepare your workforce for changing capability and capacity needs?
4. How do you organize and manage your workforce?
5. How do you ensure workplace health, security, and accessibility for the workforce?
6. How do you support your workforce via services, benefits, and policies?

5.2 Workforce Engagement:
How do you engage your workforce to achieve a high-performance work environment?
1. How do you foster an organizational culture that is characterized by open communication, high-performance, and an engaged workforce?
2. How do you determine the key drivers of workforce engagement?
3. How do you assess workforce engagement?
4. How does your workforce performance management system support high-performance and workforce engagement?
5. How does your learning and development system support the organization's needs and the personal development of your workforce members, managers, and leaders?
6. How do you evaluate the effectiveness and efficiency of your learning and development system?
7. How do you manage career progression for your workforce and your future leaders?

6 Operations

6.1 Work Processes:
How do you design, manage, and improve your key products and work processes?
1. How do you determine key product and work process requirements?
2. What are your organization's key work processes?
3. How do you design your products and work processes to meet requirements?
4. How does your day-to-day operation of work processes ensure that they meet key process requirements?
5. How do you determine your key support processes?
6. How do you improve your work processes to improve products and performance, enhance your core competencies, and reduce variability?
7. How do you manage your supply chain?
8. How do you pursue your opportunities for innovation?

6.2 Operational Effectiveness:

How do you ensure effective management of your operations?

1. How do you control the overall costs of your operations?
2. How do you ensure the reliability of your information systems?
3. How do you ensure the security and cybersecurity of sensitive or privileged data and information?
4. How do you provide a safe operating environment?
5. How do you ensure that your organization is prepared for disasters or emergencies?

7 Results

7.1 Product and Process Results:

What are your product performance and process effectiveness results?

1. What are your results for your products and your customer service processes?
2. What are your process effectiveness and efficiency results?
3. What are your safety and emergency preparedness results?
4. What are your supply-chain management results?

7.2 Customer-Focused Results:

What are your customer-focused performance results?

1. What are your customer satisfaction and dissatisfaction results?
2. What are your customer engagement results?

7.3 Workforce-Focused Results:

What are your workforce-focused performance results?

1. What are your workforce capability and capacity results?
2. What are your workforce climate results?
3. What are your workforce engagement results?
4. What are your workforce and leader development results?

7.4 Leadership and Governance Results:

What are your senior leadership and governance results?

1. What are your results for senior leaders' communication and engagement with the workforce and customers?
2. What are your results for governance accountability?
3. What are your legal and regulatory results?
4. What are your results for ethical behavior?
5. What are your results for societal responsibilities and support of your key communities?
6. What are your results for the achievement of your organizational strategy and action plans?

7.5 Financial and Market Results:

What are your results for financial viability?

1. What are your financial performance results?
2. What are your marketplace performance results?

REFERENCE

National Institute of Standards and Technology. (2017). *Baldrige excellence builder: Key questions for improving your organization's performance.* Gaithersburg, MD: Author.

Index

About the Author

GARY SHAFFER, PhD, serves as the head of the Library and Information Management programs at the Marshall School of Business and as an Assistant Dean of USC Libraries. In these capacities he oversees an American Library Association-accredited Master of Management in Library and Information Science (MMLIS) program and a post-master's Graduate Certificate in Library and Information Management program as well. He also directs the Center for Library Leadership and Management at USC Libraries.

He is the former CEO of the Tulsa City-County Library (TCCL), a 24-location public library system, with more than 405 employees located in northeastern Oklahoma. In 2014 TCCL was awarded an Oklahoma Quality Award from Governor Mary Falin for its sustainability-based application. Additionally, the Central Library Project, a $55 million renovation project that Shaffer shepherded, won a Henry Bellmon (former governor) Environmental Stewardship Sustainability Award from Sustainable Tulsa.

Dr. Shaffer started his library career as a trainee at the Brooklyn Public Library. He then worked for the Los Angeles County and Sacramento public libraries before relocating to Tulsa. As a library trainee, he was named a *Library Journal* Mover & Shaker for his library marketing and partnership work. In 2014 he was awarded an Oklahoma Library Association Special Project Award for his fundraising work to help rebuild two school libraries destroyed by a tornado.

In addition to his PhD in Managerial Leadership in the Information Professions from Simmons College, Shaffer holds a Master's in Library and Information Science from the Pratt Institute, a Master's of Professional Writing from USC, and a Master of Laws in Intellectual Property Law from the University of Turin School of Law in Italy.

Shaffer is active in several professional organizations, including the American Library Association (ALA), the Association of Library and Information Science Educators (ALISE), the International Federation of Library Associations and Institutions (IFLA), the Library Leadership and Management Association (LLAMA), the Public Library Association (PLA), the Special Library Association (SLA), and the ALA Sustainability Roundtable (SRT). He has served on numerous committees and task forces for ALA and PLA. He currently serves on the ALA Development (fundraising) Task Force. Shaffer speaks nationally and internationally on sustainability, emotionally intelligent library leaders, and the creation of 21st century-responsive libraries. He is a tireless advocate for libraries and archives at the state capitol; in Washington, D.C.; and at the international conference table. This advocacy includes serving within state advocacy organizations, on the PLA U.S. Capitol Library Advocacy Day Task Force, and as an IFLA delegate to the United Nations' World Intellectual Property Organization's Standing Committee on Copyright and Related Rights.

He is a past member of the PLA Board, a past ALA Councilor at Large, and a former member of the Digital Public Library of America Audience and Participation Workstream.

Prior to working in libraries, Shaffer supervised Fortune 500 accounts for various advertising agencies. He has authored scholarly articles and a book chapter in addition to this book.